PORTRAIT OF BRISTOL

Portrait of BRISTOL

KEITH BRACE

ROBERT HALE · LONDON

First published in Great Britain 1971
New edition 1976

ISBN 0 7091 5435 6

Robert Hale & Company
Clerkenwell House
Clerkenwell Green
London EC1R 0HT

To my
Mother and Father
who told me about Bristol

Printed and bound in Great Britain by
REDWOOD BURN LIMITED
Trowbridge & Esher

CONTENTS

ILLUSTRATIONS

Picture Credits

The two photographs facing page 17 are by courtesy of British Aircraft Corporation, Filton; the photograph facing page 193 by courtesy of Brian Middleton; the remainder by courtesy of W. E. Hall.

MAPS

ACKNOWLEDGMENTS

I OWE a special debt for help and advice to Bryan Little, historian of Bristol, distinguished writer on architecture and topography, former Chairman of Bristol Civic Society—which has done so much to preserve the heritage of the city and to help it plan wisely for the future. I am much indebted, too, to Reece Winstone, whose collections of photographs of Bristol are a unique visual record of a city's history; and to Geoffrey Woodruff, whose eye for Bristol character and ear for Bristol speech are impeccable. Captain C. B. Short of Failand has been a source of valuable information about the life and work of the City Docks. J. Lavery Crook, Bristol's City Public Relations Officer, and his staff, have been most helpful, as has John Corin, Information Officer to the Port of Bristol Authority. Frank Brown showed me round Clifton and Peter Floyd showed me round the model of the new Bristol at the permanent planning exhibition at Quakers Friars. Douglas Cleverdon told me about one of Bristol's Golden Ages. Ronald Avery of Averys, and Ronnie Norton and Tim Ladd of Harveys supplied me with much information about Bristol's most romantic trade. J. C. Trewin told me all about the Theatre Royal, and S. J. McWatters, former Headmaster of Clifton College, allowed me to tread the Close.

Others to whom I am indebted are: Mrs. Joyce Allen; Charles Causley; the late Bertram Davis; Michael Dineen; J. Farrell of Bristol University Library; Peter Harris of the Bristol Branch of the Historical Association; Marcus Hartnell; W. S. Haugh, City Librarian, and his staff; Michael Hill; R. J. Knecht; Marilyn Lawes, Librarian of *Punch*; Peter Midforth; Gethyn Morgan; Michael Morgan; D. H. A. Redway, Public Relations, W. D. & H. O. Wills; Norman Rich, Research Editor, *Western Daily Press*; Christopher Ricks; H. S. Thompson, Chief Education Officer; Glynne Wickham; the Reverend Malcolm Widdecombe; G. R. Williams, Bristol Commercial Rooms; Anthony Wedgwood Benn, MP., and D. L. Woodhouse, Assistant Sales Publicity Manager, B.A.C. Filton. Bristol's newspapers, the *Evening Post* and the *Western Daily Press* have been sources of essential information.

PREFACE

THIS is a very personal view of a highly idiosyncratic city. If there is a nostalgic tone to this 'Portrait' it is because I believe that Bristol is at a point of crisis in its history and that the modest-sized, relaxed, intimate city we have known is all too likely to become a disproportionately large provincial metropolis, resembling all other provincial metropolises of the future in clinical impersonality. While we can, we should remember the qualities that have made Bristol uniquely attractive among large British cities. My knowledge and impressions of the city are conditioned and possibly limited by the fact that though I was born in Bristol of Bristol parents I have not lived there, apart from a year's residence as a student. Perhaps, though, my many compulsive visits over the years have enabled me to see and feel things about Bristol that the residents take for granted. Certainly, the book does not pretend to be a detailed guide—Bristol is changing so rapidly that it would be quickly out of date. Still less is it a comprehensive history; in any case, this has already been written by Bryan Little. I have found atmosphere more compelling than architectural detail, people, character and traditions more revealing than industrial and commercial history. If there is a theme to the book it is that cities are for people—something we are in danger of forgetting.

KEITH BRACE

BIBLIOGRAPHY

The City and County of Bristol. A Study in Atlantic Civilization, by Bryan Little, Werner Laurie, 1954; S.R. Publishers, 1967.

North Somerset and Bristol, by Sir Nikolaus Pevsner, The Buildings of England, Penguin Books, 1958.

Publications of the Bristol Branch of the Historical Association, The University, Bristol.

Bristol. City, Suburbs and Countryside, by Arthur L. Salmon, Bristol Times and Mirror, 1922.

Gloucestershire, by David Verey, a Shell Guide, Faber, 1951 and 1970.

Bristol Cream, by Godfrey Harrison, Batsford, 1955.

Reece Winstone: collections of Bristol photographs, 1957–70, 13 volumes.

Portrait of Somerset, by Bryan Little, Robert Hale & Co., 1969.

The City in History, by Lewis Mumford, Secker, 1961; Pelican, 1966.

Victorian Cities, by Asa Briggs, Odhams, 1963.

Port of Bristol Official Handbooks.

Publications of the Bristol Archaeological Research Group, City Museum, Bristol.

Bristol, Sea-Port City, by Martin Ballard, Constable Young Books, 1966.

The Industrial Archaeology of the Bristol Region, by R. A. Buchanan and Neil Cossons, David & Charles, 1969.

Bristol. Industrial History in Pictures, by R. A. Buchanan and Neil Cossons, David & Charles, 1970.

Bristol and Its Adjoining Counties, British Association, 1955.

Krek Waiter's Peak Bristle, edited by Dirk Robson (Derek Robinson), Abson Press, 1970.

Bristol and Its Famous Associations, by Stanley Hutton, 1907.

John Addington Symonds, by Phyllis Grosskurth, Longmans, 1964.

Isambard Kingdom Brunel, by L. T. C. Rolt, Longmans, 1957.

Local Review of Charities for the Poor and Sick Poor in the City and County of Bristol, by G. G. N. Candy, Bristol Council of Social Service, 1968.

Bristol As It Was and Is, by George Frederick Stone, Bristol Evening News, 1909.

Eight Bristol Churches, by Patrick Brown, Bristol and Somerset Society of Architects.

The Bristol Old Vic. The First Ten Years, by Audrey Williamson and Charles Landstone, J. Garnet Miller, 1957.

Reminiscences of Coleridge and Southey, by Joseph Cottle, Lime Tree Bower Press, 1970.

The Theatre Royal. The Beginning of a Bicentenary, Bristol Building and Design Centre Journal, 1964.

A Life of Thomas Chatterton, by E. H. W. Meyerstein, 1930.

Life of Ernest Bevin, Vols. 1 and 2, by Alan Bullock, Heinemann, 1960, 1967.

Burke, by G. M. Young, From Today and Yesterday, Hart-Davis, 1948.

Shipshape and Bristol Fashion, by John C. G. Hill, The Journal of Commerce and Shipping Telegraph.

Bristol under Blitz, by T. H. J. Underdown, Lord Mayor of Bristol, 1940–41, J. W. Arrowsmith, 1942.

The People's War, by Angus Calder, Cape, 1969.

Bristol Commercial Rooms, 1811–1951, by A. G. Powell.

Voting in Cities (contains article by Roger Clements on Bristol), edited by L. Sharp, Macmillan, 1967.

Centenary Essays on Clifton College, 1962.

Edward Colston, by H. J. Wilkins, 1920.

Migration and Race Relations in an English City: A Study in Bristol, by Anthony H. Richmond, Institute of Race Relations, Oxford University Press, 1973.

The City and County of Bristol, by Bryan Little, Werner Laurie, London, 1954.

I

BRISTOL THE GOOD PLACE

ONCE in a while, when the editor of a London newspaper remembers that something of Britain exists north of St. Albans and west of London Airport, he sends a feature-writer out into the darkness to report on one or other of the major provincial cities. Duly the report comes back. Liverpool is bustling, aggressively friendly, with a witty Lancashire-Irish folk-culture. Manchester is quietly efficient, somewhat self-regarding, nostalgic about the great days of Hans Richter and C. P. Scott. Leeds is cosmopolitan and urbane, Bradford northern and inward-looking, Newcastle proud of an independent culture.

When the writer gets to Bristol, though, he finds a different and awkward set of facts. The city does not fit into London's condescending idea of what a provincial city should be. He finds a city that does not, despite its London-based observers, think of itself as the West of England equivalent of London, on the same latitude and with a similar geographical and mercantile development. Indeed, Bristol does not think much about London at all, despite the comparatively short two-hour train journey between the cities. When it has troubled to look beyond itself in the past it has been to Spain, France, Iceland, Newfoundland, the West Indies and Virginia rather than to London.

Bristolians do not see much reason for leaving their city, certainly not much beyond a 15-mile commuting range; while many people seem to want to come to Bristol. Its most articulate admirers are more often than not non-Bristolians, like Sir John Betjeman, who has said "there is no city in England with so much character", or J. B. Priestley, who in *English Journey* in 1933 called it "a city after my own heart . . . it has kept its own pride!" It has one of the most sought-after universities in Britain; in the 1970s it was getting 15–16 applications for every place. Professional jobs are much in demand, largely because of the charm of the city's residential areas and amenities; and it is one of the few large cities where it is popular to live as close to the city centre as possible. It is beautiful in a general sense rather than in particulars: in its rolling hills, open spaces, contrasts, surprises, in its unique green places like the Downs, the Blaise woods and the surrounding villages.

In the early 1970s, with many of the ravages of the blitz repaired, quietly adapting itself to science and technology as it had adapted itself to industry and commerce in the past, Bristol was still a Good Place to live, or at least, if not a Utopia then at least an 'entopia', a practical half-way stage towards Utopia, in the language of the Greek city planner, Constantinos Doxiadis in his book *Between Dystopia and Utopia* (Faber, 1968). Bristol was certainly a Good Place rather than a 'dystopia' or Bad Place. It continued, as in the past, to spread economic risk over a diversity of trades and skills; and it remained a democratic city, as far as such a place exists, in that there is no aristocratic class, no obvious 'county' set, while employment is more or less equally shared between professional and administrative occupations on one side and industrial and distributive on the other. There are differences, of course; some suburbs are all gentility and laburnums, others are new, raw and hooligan at the edges. But over the wide central areas of the city, working-class Victorian terraces, restored Georgian houses, suburbia of the 1920s and 30s, Regency alleys, post-war flats and houses, supermarkets, corner shops with loyal customers, churches, chapels, student hostels, offices, banks and warehouses, mingle or merge or shade off into each other comfortably and often almost imperceptibly.

Bristol is still a city of light and air, of dramatic views, of city waterways, Georgian squares, trees, elegant and shabby streets, terraces and courts, bookshops, theatres and churches. You could still, in the early 1970s, see ships at the ends of city streets—though fewer and fewer—and the citizens of Clifton on their lofty terraces could still hear the clangour of ship-building and repairing from the one remaining shipyard on the Floating Harbour below. It is a city of good popular eating, of sherry bars and of a dour boisterousness which breaks through the respectable surface of everyday Bristol when office staffs hold their parties in the city pubs and steak bars. It is a city of good public libraries and schools, of good labour relations and of flourishing organized charity and welfare; a city that has—with one brief exception in the 1960s—accepted its 12,000 (plus) coloured immigrants as one more phase of a long history.

Though its trades and products have changed, its diversified commercial pattern remains. Bristol no longer makes soap, glass, or china, nor does it refine sugar; but it still makes tobacco, imports wine, produces chocolate (now at Keynsham 2 miles outside the city boundary, though many of the workers live in Bristol). It is today a great importing rather than exporting port, though in the Middle Ages and the eighteenth century exports were quite as large as imports, all sorts of goods being shipped to the plantation colonies. Today, the aircraft and 'aerospace' industry—again, strictly outside the city boundary, at Filton—employs some 25,000 workers, while food, drink and tobacco employ 20,000, printing, paper and publishing 16,000, and mechanical and electrical engineering 14,000. But the biggest employers are the service trades, with the financial and professional services employing 40,000, the distributive trades over 30,000, and transport and communications nearly 20,000.

For all its sense of economic and social balance, Bristol is a city of subtle contrasts, so subtle that the casual visitor (or London feature-writer) may find them elusive and confusing. It is possible, for example, to feel disagreeably claustrophobic in the narrow city streets. Sometimes, too, on winter evenings at the rush hour, when the traffic plays sinister dodgem car games around the roaring wastes of the Centre, the built-up heights around the Royal Infirmary and the university loom a little too threateningly. By contrast, the open spaces of the Downs, the sudden switches in street level in Clifton, or the dizzying walks along the edges of the Gorge near Sion Hill or the Sea Walls, can produce another sort of unnerving effect. The demographic history of Bristol has been of successive escapes from the huddled medieval city to the healthier and higher outlying suburbs. Today Bristol is one of the few large cities whose population has declined rather than increased as residents have moved outside the city boundary; the population was 442,994 in 1951, 437,048 in 1961, 427,230 in June 1969, 421,800 in 1974.

The contrasts begin in the setting of the city: a low, central, flood-prone basin around the rivers Avon and Frome, with slopes rising, sometimes gradually, sometimes sharply, to the considerable heights of the Downs on one side and Dundry ridge, with the well-known landmark of its church tower, on the other. But this is not a simple amphitheatre; a number of low but strikingly visible ridges, like stranded whales, rise in some of the suburbs. Purdown, just under 300 feet high and largely free of housing, falls into north-east Bristol, while the ridge that runs from Filton and Horfield ends splendidly in the sudden rise and spread of the Downs and the dramatic fissure of the Gorge. The unpredictable rise and fall of these hills, downs and ridges, sometimes tamed into civic parks, sometimes still undeveloped and even bleak and unkempt, break up what might otherwise be blanket suburbia. Mean streets suddenly end in fields or little dingles and glens of allotments, straggly bits of country left unfilled during the great building boom of the 1840s and 50s. These, together with rural survivals like Snuff Mills Park along the Frome at Stapleton, Coombe Dingle and Blaise woods at Henbury, St. Anne's Wood at Brislington, all ensure that Bristol will always have its lungs, its paths of escape. Bristol, fortunately for its future, has avoided the dangerous philosophy of the Green Belt, by which a city salves its conscience by creating an open swathe around the perimeter and then gradually nibbles into it as housing demands outweigh considerations of amenity. Bristol has Green Enclaves rather than a Green Belt, and many of them are not likely to be nibbled into because it is more practical to build houses on the outlying flat country than on their steep slopes.

The city's geology is also a series of contrasts. Few cities seem so strewn with visible geology, from the great geological fault of the Avon Gorge to the scattered limestone outcrops on the Downs, the disused quarry-workings of the Gorge, and the old quarries left around the fringes of the Downs, one of which, the Glen, has long been a place for dancing and entertainment. Although Bristol has lias, sandstone and limestone, it has had to look elsewhere for its chief building materials, which accounts for the higgledy-piggledy look of Bristol compared with the uniformity of Bath, dominated by one main building stone. In his indispensable *The City and County of Bristol*, Bryan Little points out two important effects of Bristol's geography. One is a shallowness of soil which, with frequent marshy ground, makes the area not noticeably fertile. The other is the presence of carboniferous limestone, giving Bristol a local coalfield, a unique

St. Mary Redcliffe and Redcliffe Parade from Prince Street Bridge

Concorde

advantage among southern and western cities before the Industrial Revolution. The local coal, which was still being dug within the city boundaries in this century, was a key factor in Bristol's early prosperity in the seventeenth and eighteenth centuries; it may also have played a significant part in the formation of the local character, particularly the over-confidence, complacency and lack of foresight that have marked the Bristol attitude to economic fortunes at times and have resulted in lengthy periods of stagnation. A population used to getting coal from its own doorstep may easily take things too easily for economic safety.

There has, in fact, always been an idiosyncratic and rather endearing contrast between business sense and self-indulgence in Bristol's mercantile character, a contrast which may partly account, along with obvious causes like foreign wars, for recessions like those under Elizabeth I and in the first half of the nineteenth century, when the rest of the country was pushing ahead. A surviving merchant's house, like that of the West India merchant John Pinney, now a Georgian museum in Great George Street near Brandon Hill, illustrates how easy it would have seemed to an eighteenth-century Bristol merchant to sit on his fortune in comfort. There is perhaps a comparison here between Bristol and the German Hanseatic ports: in both the merchants, against all good economic principles, sometimes used their profits to create a civilized life for themselves instead of ploughing them back into the business, and in both, as recorded by the novelist Thomas Mann of his native Lübeck, there was a risk of trade stagnating.

Bristol's successes in the national and world context are indisputable. They include a leading part, as patron, in the exploring and settling of North America and the spread of the English language. From Bristol John Wesley directed the early stages of his great movement of Christian and moral reform. It was among the first places in England to make brass and the first to make English porcelain from clay. Bristol built the first ocean-going steamship, Brunel's *Great Western*, and the first ocean-going, iron, propeller-driven steamship, the *Great Britain*, also by Brunel. McAdam's system of road-making was planned and first applied in Bristol. The Great Western Railway was almost wholly a Bristol project. Bristol's 'firsts' include the first Methodist chapel, the first savings bank, the first American consulate in Britain, and

Concorde in flight
The assembly hall at Filton

the first workhouse established by Act of Parliament. Bristol even produced the first ready-made suit. Yet the city has long had a reputation for over-caution, lack of imagination, philistinism, intolerance of or indifference to foreigners and outsiders. Outside comments on them were generally unfavourable; even John Wesley said: "I often wonder at the people of Bristol. They are so honest, yet so dull; 'tis scarce possible to strike any fire into them." Yet these same dull people financed the Cabots on their wild voyages, provided the first congregations for the rebel Wesley, encouraged the young Cornish chemist Humphrey Davy, accepted Brunel and his grandiose schemes, and carry a fine reputation for humanitarian reform and technological experiment. They were un-philistine enough to save their old Theatre Royal from demolition during the 1939–45 war, and today Bristol's name is associated with the risky Concorde airliner project.

Bristolians are fascinated by their own history. Schoolchildren are taught about the Cabots, and the survivals of ancient ceremonies, like Rush Sunday at St. Mary Redcliffe, the various Colston commemorations and services for founders of the city's old schools, all remind the citizens of their deep historical roots. They are also taught, pointedly, that Bristol became a separate county of its own in as 1373 (it is that no longer, of course). Yet they are also indifferent to their history when it is represented by old buildings that stand in the way of new roads. There is a tendency to be proud of the idea of Bristol and yet to be careless about preserving the city itself. This contrast is not inconsistent with other aspects of the Bristol character, with the mixture of commercial caution and general emotional diffidence common among sailors, merchants dependent on the sea, airline pilots and marine insurers, and therefore not unlikely to be the character of people in a city so closely connected with the sea. These attitudes have led to a certain wary empiricism in Bristol's views of itself, to an historical tendency to move on, to replace, to develop variety rather than concentrate on one particular industry or trade, to invent or produce disparate objects, machines and processes, or to support disparate causes, rather than focus on one dominant industry, trade, political or religious creed. This variety has enabled the city to survive many changes of economic fortune. It has kept it cautiously safe in times of political trouble from the Norman Conquest on. It has enabled it to be mercantile and cultured, Anglican and nonconformist, radical and reactionary, provincial and metropolitan, without tearing itself apart psychologically. But it has also prevented it from having one dominant historical character. It has tended to take its genius from outside, and, arguably, has not always fulfilled its own native potential and genius. It is almost as if the city has not been able to believe its own good luck or to act upon it. If the Bristolians had been less civilized and intelligent, and more ruthless, they might have been more consistently successful from their own resources, instead of borrowing the Cabots and Brunel to create their greatness for them. Was it the balmy climate, the 'relaxing' airs of the city that stood in the way of Bristol ambition? Have the variety and contrasts of its life and interests acted against each other rather than stimulated each other?

It is tempting for those who care to watch anxiously over the city as if over a deceptively healthy-looking invalid. Sometimes its leisurely, amiable, live-for-the-day mood is charming and seductive. But the developers and planners are in like angry viruses, and their mood is neither charming nor seductive. They could do things to Bristol that Bristol might regret when it comes round to noticing them. One cares because Bristol is still—just—a living symbol of man's ability to create a Good Place, to combine human variety in a tolerant, complex community. And one cares because Bristol is an aesthetic experience, a city so rich in historical overtones and in the ghosts of old ambitions and loves wisping around the waterways on autumn evenings that the city can sometimes seem emptied of real people, as it is in the haunting mural frieze of Bristol scenes that once adorned the buffet at Temple Meads station.

Bristol's contrasts and obsessions were always realities to me, though we left the city when I was very young and my awareness of them could hardly have been conscious. We went back often to visit relatives, an aunt near the White Tree, that durable bus stop on the Downs, an uncle in Bishopston. Bristol was a huge, sprawling mystery on the other side of the low hills we could see from Monmouthshire, a mystery that began with the flat, Dutch country around the Gloucestershire mouth of the Severn Tunnel. My Bristol cousins seemed knowing and metropolitan compared with us. They went to ancient schools and wore curious old costumes on occasion. One uncle was urban and sardonic; another was a large Somerset countryman miscast as a Bristol policeman (we used his spiked helmet in Christmas charades, but he was not happy about it). He never went back to the village pub he dreamed of owning. Through the Christmas chatter, half-heard above our heads, flowed the names of great-aunts and eccentric second cousins who had married oddly or sadly, or of friends who had not come back from the war (their War, the Great one) and wistful memories of tennis-club evenings in the 1920s before the families began, happy moments out of two decades of recovering from one war and preparing for the next. We could have been listening to Trojan parents talking about the siege and what uncle Pandarus said to the food officer. All cities have their undercurrents of gossip, scandal and their communal myths; but those of Bristol, unshared with any industrial hinterland, are particularly persistent and private.

During the 1939–45 war we saw Bristol burning behind its low hills and felt a compassionate affection that we should not otherwise have dared to feel towards so unemotional a city. "Poor old Bristol," we said. When I began to visit it again after the war, Jones's store, where we shopped and lunched, had gone, together with the Dutch House with its cut-out soldier on the balcony, and the whole of the narrow medieval shopping centre. It was not only physical damage that Bristol suffered in the blitzes of 1940–1941. Angus Calder, in his book *The People's War*, a brilliantly evocative account of the 'Home Front', records the damage to Bristol's morale caused by repeated night raids, despite the newsreels of Churchill being applauded by weary rescue workers. For the first time a city, which had always played safe with history, secretly disliking the political wars that interrupted trade with France, Spain and the American colonies, found violent history on its doorstep. This dismay was a brief recoil from attack, and Bristol, which had been reluctant to make bogey-men out of Philip II, Washington and Napoleon, knew well enough that Hitler was not just one more political enemy, but an evil principle that would, if victorious, quickly destroy the radical, independent spirit of such a city.

Despite the cost—1,299 citizens killed, 3,000 homes destroyed and 90,000 damaged (not statistics that would much impress a Dresdener who had been in his city in 1945)—Bristol quickly began to plan its rebirth. As a hopeful book of the late 1940s put it: "The problem of replanning the centre of the old city was enormously simplified. Enemy bombs had cleared the site for us, and a unique opportunity offered to rectify the mistakes of the past"—words that ought to be inscribed on the central blitz-site that was still being used as a shabby car-park a quarter of a century later!

My own attitude to the city is complex and fluctuating. By kinship I claim the right to find it ugly at times, a right I should deny to less involved observers. There are days when the rain blots out the surrounding heights, the people look sullen and suspicious, and Bristol is more depressing than it has any right to be. And there are golden autumn afternoons, when the Clifton terraces stand out in stereoscope depth, the mica-grains in the paving-stones sparkle, and the view from the heights back over the Cumberland Basin is a noble Brangwyn print, with sunlight, gleaming water, cranes and warehouses, church steeples and huddling streets and the green Somerset hills behind mingling to form the most varied and dramatic cityscape (Edinburgh possibly excepted) in Britain.

Returning to Bristol now is not only a personal search for roots and meaning, but a field-study of the whole concept of the city in European history and culture, a concept now threatened for the first time since the city arose on top of the village in pre-literate ages. It becomes possible to see Bristol as an example of such an abstract concept rather than a living, flawed city; to understand how it became what it is it is necessary to narrow and intensify our focus from vague images down to the immediate, specific instances of the city itself, and particularly, to the river-crossing—'the place of the bridge'—where the city began and from which it took its name.

II

THE PLACE OF THE BRIDGE

EVEN today, with much of the traffic that used to flood across it diverted to Redcliffe Way, Temple Way and other inner circuit routes of our century, and with the shopping centre moved from bombed Wine Street to upstart Broadmead, Bristol Bridge still looks like the beginning and centre of something. "A-leaning against old Bristol Bridge" like the character in Hardy's *The Dynasts* ("and the winter sun a-slanting over Baldwin Street as 'a used to do") one can still sense echoes of the city's ancient pulse on the Victorian superstructure that partly conceals the Georgian bridge that in 1769 replaced the medieval bridge—lined with houses, with a notable chapel built across it, and boasting the highest rents in the city—that replaced who knows what.

A feeling of centrality lingers despite the emptiness and mild squalor of much of the scene. Gulls sweep and plane over the oil-patches and sodden cigarette packets on the still water of the Floating Harbour, as this section of the Avon has been known since it was locked in the first decade of the nineteenth century. Buses grind past St. Nicholas's Church, gutted in the Blitz and recently magnificently restored, to cross the bridge in the direction of Temple Meads Station and Bath, and the smoke plumes off Courage's massive riverside brewery that used to be George's. (Courage's have attractively painted up many old city pubs, and in the waste and decaying areas particularly, the firm's red cockerel sign beacons like a fairy-tale inn at the safe end of a forest). Above the bridge the launch *Kingstonian* lay up for the winter or rested between excursions round the Harbour or up-river to Keynsham. Below the bridge a Dunkirk flotilla of boats, in various stages of river-worthiness or flotsam, jostles moodily. Further down, the *Badminton* or her sister-ship the *Camerton*, the last regular visitors to this upper reach of the Harbour, unload the sand they have brought from out in the Channel at the yard behind St. Thomas's Church in Redcliff Street.

To the north stretch the ugly twenty-five-year-old car parks and waste spaces of the bombed Wine Street area—or did until moves were made to tidy and landscape them in the early 1970s. Beyond the brewery, where the Harbour bends for its gloomy passage through St. Philip's, are towering warehouses. On both sides of the bridge, but particularly down the Welsh Back towards the Redcliffe swing bridge, there is a Hanseatic air about the warehouses and moss-covered quay-walls, the drooped chains guarding the unused lading places, the cobbles and harbour sheds. Hamburg and Bremen, Lübeck and Bergen, have this northern Venetian look, and the disappearance of the great brick façades of the warehouses—some of them not in good condition—would be as serious a loss to the look of Bristol as any covering in of the disused waterways.

On the Temple-Redcliffe end of the bridge the newish fifteen-storey building of Bristol's famous printing, packaging and paper firm, E. & S. Robinson, (now the head office of the Dickinson-Robinson group), sits heavily on an admittedly not very harmonious scene. Sir Basil Spence thought the design "of an exceptionally high standard" and that it would give a general effect of "a gleaming white structure". But a visiting journalist wrote, about five years after the building was completed in 1963, that it was "already weeping black tears" from its honeycomb of tiny windows. Local critics have complained that although it is not a bad building in itself it blocks in and dominates the city's sky-line of steeples, and looms unhappily over picturesque King Street across the river, a scheduled area in which such a building would not have been permitted.

One of the first fully air-conditioned office buildings in Britain, it is 260 feet high and cost £1 million. The see-through effect of the entrance halls, and the concrete, paved and cobbled surround, lighten its bulkiness. It was designed by the group's own architects and it has at least been thought about seriously, if not entirely successfully, unlike the drab pop-up buildings that have filled the nearby bomb-sites since the war. Beyond the Robinson building towards Temple Meads marches Victoria Street, once called, not quite fairly, "the ugliest street in Europe".

An ornamental garden with roses and urban pigeons flourishes

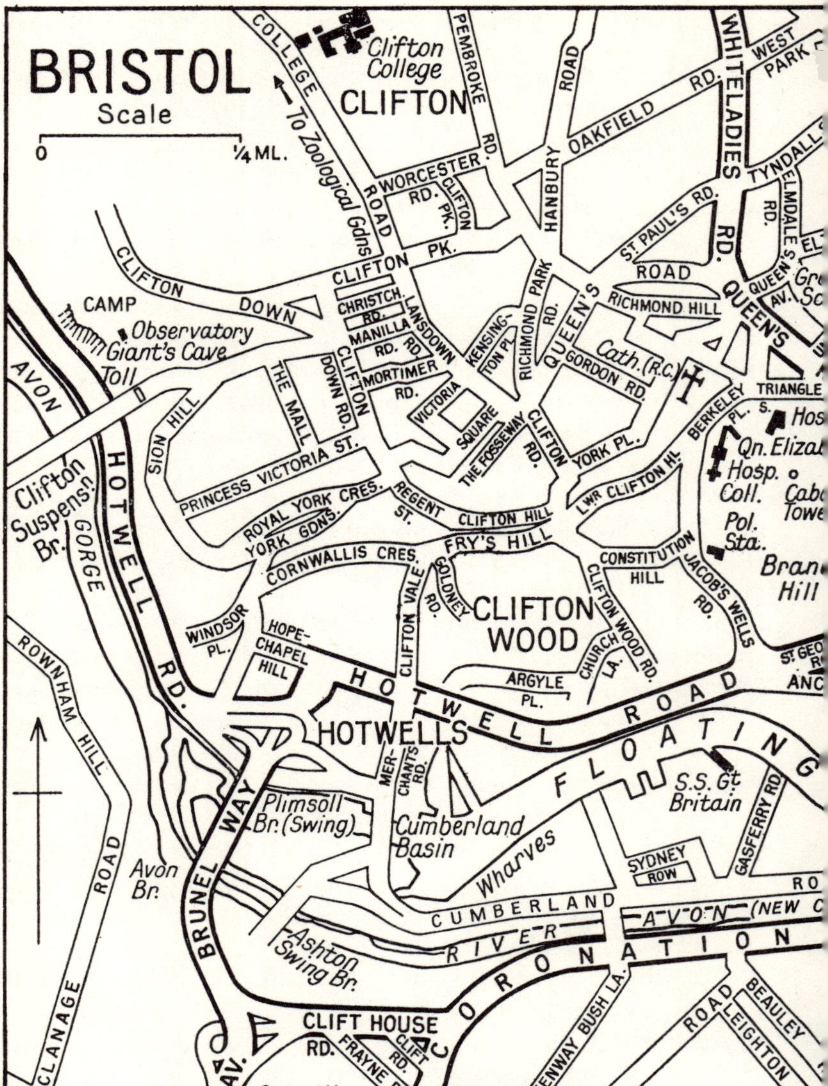

BRISTOL
Scale
0
¼ ML.
Clifton College
CLIFTON
To Zoological Gdns
COLLEGE ROAD
PEMBROKE RD.
HANBURY ROAD
OAKFIELD RD.
WEST PARK
WHITELADIES RD.
TYNDALLS
ELMDALE RD.
WORCESTER RD.
CLIFTON PK.
ST. PAUL'S RD.
ROAD
CLIFTON DOWN
CAMP
Observatory
Giant's Cave
Toll
CHRISTCH. RD.
MANILLA RD.
MORTIMER RD.
LANSDOWN RD.
CLIFTON DOWN RD.
THE MALL
SION HILL
RICHMOND PARK RD.
KENSINGTON PL.
QUEEN'S RD.
RICHMOND HILL
QUEEN'S AV.
Cath. (R.C.)
GORDON RD.
TRIANGLE
VICTORIA SQUARE
THE FOSSEWAY
CLIFTON RD.
YORK PL.
BERKELEY PL.
Qn. Elizab
Hosp.
Coll.
Cabo Towe
Pol. Sta.
Bran Hill
AVON
Clifton Suspens.n Br.
GORGE
HOTWELL RD.
PRINCESS VICTORIA ST.
ROYAL YORK CRES.
YORK GDNS.
REGENT ST.
CLIFTON HILL
LWR CLIFTON HL.
FRY'S HILL
CORNWALLIS CRES.
CONSTITUTION HILL
JACOB'S WELLS RD.
CLIFTON WOOD RD.
GOLDNEY RD.
CLIFTON VALE
CLIFTON WOOD
WINDSOR PL.
HOPE-CHAPEL HILL
CHURCH LA.
ARGYLE PL.
ST. GEO
ANC
ROWNHAM HILL
HOTWELL ROAD
HOTWELLS
FLOATING
MERCHANTS RD.
S.S. Gt Britain
GASFERRY RD.
Plimsoll Br. (Swing)
Cumberland Basin
Wharves
BRUNEL WAY
Avon Br.
ROAD
SYDNEY ROW
CUMBERLAND RO
RIVER AVON (NEW C
Ashton Swing Br.
CORONATION
CLANAGE ROAD
CLIFT HOUSE RD.
CLIFT RD.
FRAYNE RD.
GREENWAY BUSH LA.
ROAD
BEAULEY
LEIGHTON
ASHTON AV.
Greville Smyth Park
NORTH
ASHTON RD.
ASHTON GATE
RALEIGH ST.
BEDMINSTER
CLANAGE RD.

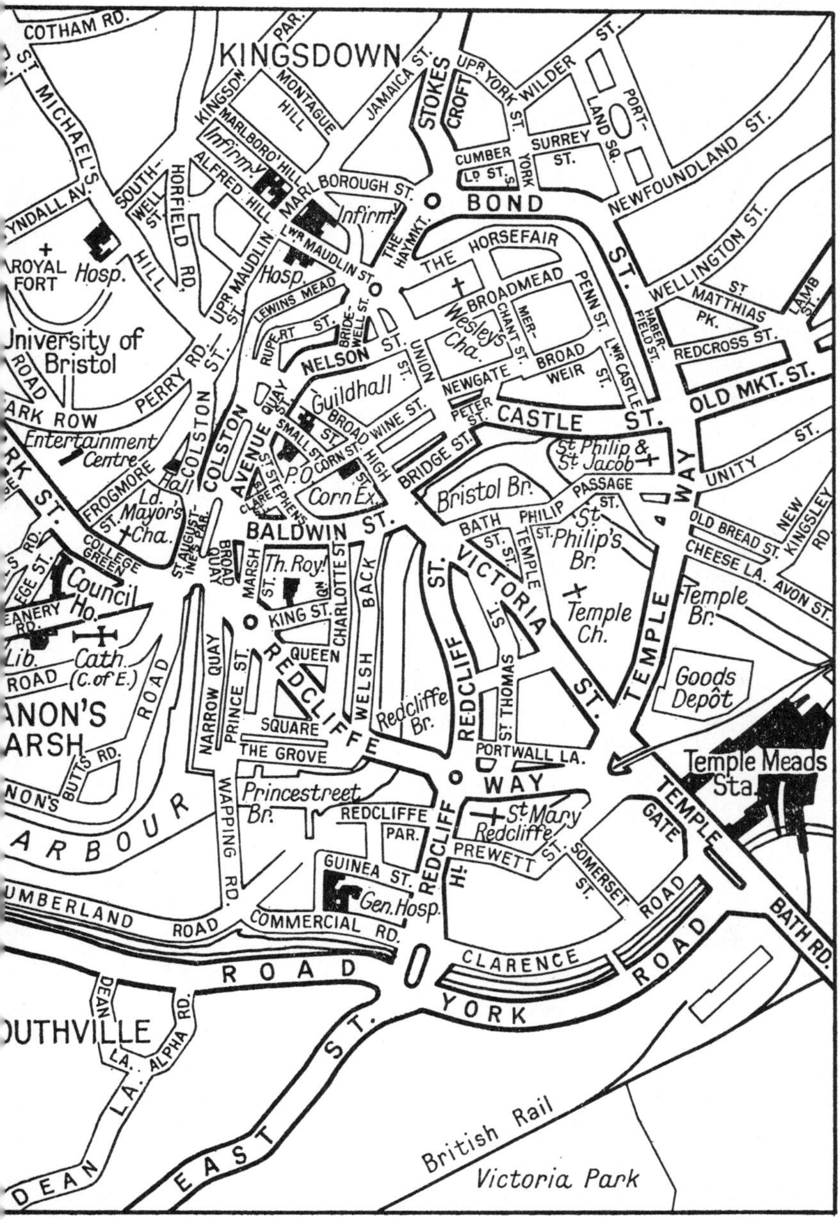
COTHAM RD.
KINGSDOWN
KINGSDN PAR.
MONTAGUE HILL
JAMAICA ST.
STOKES CROFT
UPR YORK ST.
WILDER ST.
PORTLAND SQ.
ST. MICHAEL'S HILL
MARLBORO' HILL
Infirmy
SURREY ST.
CUMBER LD. ST.
YORK ST.
NEWFOUNDLAND ST.
TYNDALL AV.
SOUTHWELL ST.
HORFIELD RD.
ALFRED HILL
MARLBOROUGH ST.
Infirmy
BOND ST.
ROYAL FORT
Hosp.
LWR MAUDLIN ST.
UPR MAUDLIN ST.
THE HAYMKT.
THE HORSEFAIR
WELLINGTON ST.
Hosp.
LEWINS MEAD
BRIDEWELL ST.
BROADMEAD
PENN ST.
HABERFIELD ST.
ST MATTHIAS PK.
LAMB ST.
University of Bristol
RUPERT ST.
Wesley's Cha.
MERCHANT ST.
REDCROSS ST.
ROAD
PERRY RD.
NELSON ST.
UNION ST.
BROAD WEIR
LWR CASTLE ST.
OLD MKT. ST.
PARK ROW
COLSTON ST.
QUAY ST.
Guildhall
NEWGATE
PETER ST.
CASTLE ST.
Entertainment Centre
BROAD ST.
WINE ST.
St. Philip & St. Jacob
ST.
PARK ST.
COLSTON AVENUE
SMALL ST.
CORN ST.
HIGH ST.
BRIDGE ST.
UNITY
COLSTON Hall
ST. STEPHENS
P.O.
Corn Ex.
Bristol Br.
PHILIP PASSAGE
WAY
FROGMORE ST.
Ld. Mayor's Cha.
CLARE ST.
ST. AUGUSTINE'S PAR.
BALDWIN ST.
BATH ST.
PHILIP ST.
ST. TEMPLE ST.
St. Philip's Br.
OLD BREAD ST.
NEW KINGSLEY RD.
COLLEGE GREEN
BROAD QUAY
MARSH ST.
Th. Roy.
QN. CHARLOTTE ST.
BACK
ST.
VICTORIA
CHEESE LA.
COLLEGE ST.
Council Ho.
KING ST.
Temple Br.
AVON ST.
DEANERY RD.
Lib.
Cath. (C. of E.)
QUEEN
ST. THOMAS
Temple Ch.
TEMPLE
REDCLIFF
ROAD
NARROW QUAY
PRINCE ST.
REDCLIFFE
WELSH
Redcliffe Br.
REDCLIFF ST.
Goods Depôt
CANON'S MARSH
SQUARE
ST THOMAS
ST.
THE GROVE
PORTWALL LA.
Temple Meads Sta.
BUTTS RD.
WAY
CANON'S
HARBOUR
WAPPING RD.
Princestreet Br.
REDCLIFFE PAR.
St. Mary Redcliffe
TEMPLE GATE
PREWETT ST.
SOMERSET ST.
REDCLIFF HL.
GUINEA ST.
Gen. Hosp.
CUMBERLAND ROAD
COMMERCIAL RD.
ROAD
BATH RD.
ROAD
CLARENCE
ROAD
YORK
DEAN LA.
ALPHA RD.
SOUTHVILLE
EAST ST.
DEAN LA.
British Rail
Victoria Park

under the shadows of the Robinson building, one of those many little patches of suburban garden and geranium-bordered civic roundabout that abound in Bristol. Sir Nikolaus Pevsner found them irritating, and they are perhaps rather fussy. But Bristol likes them and is generally proud of its flower-islands among the traffic. They are certainly more attractive than the self-consciously antique cobbles around the new Bank of England and the new Norwich Union building that front the bombed side of High Street north of the bridge. Both follow the current tendency of buildings concerned with guarding money to look like super-safes, with polished steel doors and massive door-handles like the combination controls of vaults in bank robbery films. The Norwich Union building partly encloses the isolated tower of St. Mary le Port Church, gutted in the blitz, like a businessman hoping his friends will not associate him with his angular, elderly wife. Neither building, despite the space and the trees around them, adequately makes up for the tottering medieval variety and liveliness of the old shops that lined the High Street before the bombing. On the immediate skyline beyond the blitzed area stands Southey House, one of the first and worst of the post-war buildings, monumental in its drabness and banality.

Its neighbour, the C.W.S. store, that looks disquieteningly like a scenic railway at a funfair, is not much better, and it is a relief to turn to the west and look down Baldwin Street towards the Centre. Cut through a tangle of old streets, including an earlier street of the same name, in the early 1880s, Baldwin Street is still busy, perhaps the one central street in Bristol that looks like a central street. Changing focuses of city life have neither drained it of variety, as Victoria Street beyond the bridge has been drained, nor overwhelmed it with crawling traffic and commercial gimcrackery as in Broadmead. With its rain-drenched Saturday night cinema queues, tourist offices, serve-yourself cafés, expensive restaurants, music and sports shops, banks and insurance offices, it is generically the New Street, Birmingham, or the Sauchiehall Street, Glasgow, of Bristol though mercifully shorter than either. It is right that a large commercial city should have this sort of self-confident central thoroughfare—the sort of street painted, gas-lit and gleaming with rain, by the Victorian 'moonlight' artist Atkinson Grimshaw—and right for Bristol that it should be as discreet as it is.

Incomparably the finest view from the bridge, though, is that which carries the gaze downriver, past the quays, cobbles and wharf-sheds of the Welsh Back, named for Bristol's old trade with Wales, to the Redcliffe swing bridge, which, in turn, gives a famous view back upriver (now thickened and spoilt by modern buildings) to Bristol Bridge and the many-steepled city sky-line. But the light-toned stonework of the churches—All Saints, Christ Church, St. Nicholas outstanding among them—still gleams in the sun, making the drab white office blocks look even drabber.

Here is the new Post Office building, faced with rough sandstone. Here is the Dockers' (Sports and Social) Club on the quayside, ringing with 'Rugby' songs from the showers on late Saturday afternoons and with pop music on Saturday dance-evenings. And here is Ponton and Gough's superb 'Bristol Byzantine' granary of 1869, now lit up at night by orange bulbs among the Ruskinesque false brick arches to indicate that Mr. Acker Bilk's jazz club is in action. 'Bristol Byzantine', which should perhaps really be 'Bristol Venetian', is a term apparently invented by Sir John Summerson to describe a characteristically Bristol style of nineteenth-century commercial architecture, which vaguely re-created Italian Gothic in local materials, especially the harsh red bricks from Cattybrook outside Bristol. The style can still be seen in the Colston Hall façade and in the Christopher Thomas soap works of the 1880s (now Gardiner's warehouse and showrooms) and scattered through the inner city in the ogee arches and multi-coloured brickwork of surviving nineteenth-century buildings.

The style may derive from an acquaintance between the architects of the granary and John Addington Symonds the Bristol-born historian of the Italian Renaissance, and it is certainly bizarre, though made acceptable by its bold handling and romantic setting; it did not seem inappropriate for the disused granary to be taken over for 'The Avon Cities' group or for the 'Progressive Pop and Light Shows'. The view from the bridge takes in many contrasting styles confidently and closes in the exquisite late eighteenth-century terrace of Redcliffe Parade (being converted into offices in late 1970, though with the façades preserved), that rules an elegant Georgian line across the aesthetic ledger.

Bristol began here at the river-crossing, though some local

historians have disputed the usually accepted derivation of the city's name from Bridge-stow, the Place of the Bridge, mutated by Bristol's intrusive terminal 'l' (though see the later discussion of 'Bristle' speech as to whether or not it really is an 'l') into Bristol. But the derivation is logical, evocative, appropriate, and the place is 'Brycgstow' in the Anglo-Saxon Chronicle entry for 1051. And the bridge is a good starting-place for a city whose origins are rather vague. It has its mythical founder, a 'British' king, whose sons, Brennus and Belinus, in stone and paint, look down from their niches in St. John's Church in Broad Street. The city has a few prehistoric remains and sites, like the ancient stone the children still play around on Redland Green, and the Iron Age camps on Observatory Hill, Clifton, and at Stokeleigh and Burwalls on the heights on the Somerset side of the Avon Gorge. It was not a major Roman settlement—why live there when you could enjoy the hot baths at Bath?—though coins have been found and there are fragments of a Roman port at Sea Mills near Avonmouth. It is first mentioned in a coin of Ethelred the Unready in the tenth century, when it must have been big enough to have a mint. But nothing much, historically speaking, happened until Geoffrey de Mowbray, Bishop of Coutances and Exeter, began to build a great castle on a strait of land between the natural moat-defences of the Rivers Frome and Avon.

Walls grew round it and the adjoining criss-cross of narrow streets, as the river-crossing lost its village innocence. Castle and walls on their moated island became a strategic strong-point, used notably by Robert, Earl of Gloucester, who completed the castle, to support the claim of his half-sister, Matilda (also known to history as Maud), daughter of Henry I, to the English throne claimed and seized by Stephen. Stephen himself was a prisoner of Matilda in the castle, which thus played an important part in the various struggles for the throne in the Middle Ages, including the dispute between Edward II, later barbarously murdered up-country at Berkeley Castle, and his Queen Isabella and her lover Mortimer. The Bristolians, one imagines, stood sullenly by waiting to see who would win, though they had committed themselves early on to the Normans as bringers of strong rule and secure trade.

This vanished castle—why it vanished so completely is something of a mystery—is almost more impressive in its absence than many surviving Norman castles are in their ruined presence. It had a great keep, exceeded only by those of Colchester and the Tower of London, and the place brooded over the imaginations of local historians and antiquaries long after it was destroyed by Cromwell following the siege of Bristol in the 1640s. They were always looking for bits of it, tracing the course of the moat, exploring chambers, lowering themselves on ropes into dungeons. Substantial parts survived, built into the surrounding premises, right up to the 1940 blitz, which completed its 'slighting'. Today all that survives are two thirteenth-fourteenth century vaulted chambers in Tower Lane, though evidence of a guardroom was unearthed during pipe-laying in March 1970, to be covered up again almost immediately by the urgencies of redevelopment. More letters than one would expect appear in the local Press demanding that the surviving fragments of the castle should be properly displayed in the new plans for the Wine Street–Castle Street area. Fortunately, these plans include the development of the Castle Mound as a park and recreation area, so there will still be—when they are carried out—an evocative central space to remind the city of its great castle.

The preoccupation with the castle suggests a sense of loss, an emptiness at the heart of the city, which a sensitive local historian would try to fill retrospectively by finding, he hoped, traces of the city's original focus. But Bristol remains curiously without a central point of focus. The medieval centre was the High Cross, where Wine Street, Broad Street, High Street and Corn Street met, scene of executions and proclamations. The old city tended to group itself in parish cells around local churches rather than one central church or meeting-point: Redcliffe around St. Mary's; the weavers' and artisans' quarter of the Temple around Temple Church; the commercial quarter around the city churches. The Cathedral, originally an Augustinian abbey, lay on the other side of the River Frome and never formed an integral part of the life of the old city as the cathedrals of York, Canterbury, Salisbury and Gloucester did. The Centre, or Tramways Centre, as it was once familiarly known, is a nineteenth-century creation, built over the covered-in arm of the Frome, once crowded with ships.

Bristol's shifting 'centres' trace, more accurately than those of any English city except London, the city's growth away from its starting-point. Indeed, Bristol has gone to extremes: one of the new 'centres' is the district around the university at the top of Park Street (complete with shops, restaurants, hotels, banks and schools), nearly a mile from Bristol Bridge. This curious loping stride of the city through history accounts for the visitors' feeling today that it is much larger and more spacious than its population seems to justify.

The first shift away from the castle on the north of the river was to the crossing-point of Wine, High, Broad and Corn Streets, which formed a bustling medieval warren that kept its character up to its destruction by bombs in 1940, and is now difficult to remember at all, though it was the city's main shopping centre. It looked in the 1930s as it looked to Celia Fiennes in 1698: "the buildings of the town are pretty high most of timber work, the streetes are narrow and something darkish, because the roomes on the upper storys are more jutting out. . . ."

Here stood the Dutch House, a magnificent seventeenth-century house towering above the streets, with its banks of windows like the stern galleries of a man o' war, its mock-medieval battlements and its wooden soldier (now in the City Museum) on the balcony, always to be looked for by a small boy on a day trip to the city. One of Bristol's most enduring myths is that the house was brought piece by piece from Holland: architecturally unlikely, but a pleasant thought. Here were the overhanging timber-framed houses of Mary le Port Street and the great climbing Regency terrace of Bridge Street. Here were the churches, St. Mary le Port and St. Peter's, and here especially was Bristol's loveliest old building and her greatest architectural loss in the blitz, St. Peter's Hospital.

This beautiful house, first mentioned in 1402, was rebuilt by the merchant Robert Aldworth in 1612. It was used at one time as a sugar-refining house and later as the Bristol mint. It was a hospital for the sick poor, and finally a registry office before its obliteration. Photographs of it exist, of course, but they do not capture the special charm the hospital held for local people; this can be seen better in Victorian water-colours. With the hospital went the heart and spirit of the area in the catastrophic raid of 24th November 1940, which laid waste this old intimate focus of the city's life.

Will it ever regain its heart? This question has been nagging at Bristol since 1945. An answer was attempted in 1970 with the site-levelling and first stages of the Hugh Casson plan to re-create the Wine Street–Castle mound area as a culture-play precinct. Admittedly the area presented a special planning problem after the new shopping centre had been rebuilt in neighbouring Broadmead; the Wine Street area could no longer be rebuilt as a shopping district and the business quarter the other side of the High Street was largely untouched by bombs. But there was never an excuse for not tidying it up, turning it into gardens and keeping the shabby car-parks in their place. Perhaps, though, it was as well that the area was not rebuilt when the immediate post-war building on the far side of Wine Street was done. Bristol has at least escaped that, and civic and commercial building in the city—such as the Unicorn Hotel and multi-storey car-park and the University Union in Clifton—has greatly improved in the last ten years.

Sir Hugh Casson's scheme for a "city with a village green", first suggested early in the 1960s, envisaged a large landscaped area around the old Castle mound, a new museum and art gallery in the middle, a sports centre overlooking the stretch of the Harbour by Courage's brewery, and gardens between the museum and the Norwich Union and Bank of England buildings already in existence. It was to be a traffic-free pedestrian area, with trees, kiosks, a new pub, riverside walks, possibly a moored ship as a youth centre, provisions for a marina, facilities for kicking a ball (into the Harbour?), kite-flying, flower and newspaper sellers at the foot of a carefully restored St. Peter's tower.

It was an attractive plan, though, a magnificent set-piece as well as a charming amenity, restoring life to a dead land to offset the commercial banality of Broadmead. It could have been democratic and popular in the best senses and less of a bluntly commercial enterprise than the neon-flashing entertainment centre off Park Street. The plan had taken nearly ten years to get anywhere and Bristol had argued fiercely over the details; for example, whether the tower of gutted St. Peter's should be preserved at an estimated cost of £28,000—seeing what a visual flop the preservation of St. Mary le Port tower has been—or whether the area should be traffic-free or not. Landscaping began at the Castle mound site in the late 1960s, and it seemed as if the scheme might get under way at last. But in 1970 the planners began to wonder if the area was really suitable as a site for an arts-recreation centre so far from the Park Street–University cultural quarter. The whole scheme has now been dropped, and the future of the area as a much-needed open space is still being discussed.

In strong contrast, the area to the west of the bridge, the tangle of churches and banks, markets, offices and alleys, is alive and well. Here God and Mammon received their due in the days when both meant something. The group of city churches, St. Stephen's, All Saints, Christ Church, St. John's over its gateway—through which Elizabeth I entered Bristol on a white horse in 1574—together with the gutted shell and surviving tower and crypt of St. Nicholas by the bridge, are as striking as the city churches of York and as the London City churches in their much larger area. They began to lose their congregations long before the blitz eroded the residential parts of the city centre, and have lost more of them through the departure of residents for the suburbs since the war. But they are not entirely deserted. They have their loyal supporters and their parish councils still, made up of parishioners who often live many miles away from their old parishes, and of local office workers at week-day lunch hour services.

St. Stephen's in particular has reorganized and revitalized itself in recent years as the parish church for the city area, with a coffee bar for office workers to bring their sandwiches to (to serve sandwiches as well might harm local sandwich bars, the vicar thought). Its tall, mid-fifteenth-century interior has been restored, repainted and regilded in recent years, too much so, some purist visitors may think, looking around at the red and gold angels on the capitals, the gilded roof bosses and the sumptuous tapestry behind the altar.

More than any city church St. Stephen's is an archive of Bristol history. The city's part in Atlantic exploration is recalled by a lovely wall monument, draped with painted mermaids and mermen, with verses to Martin Pring, who sailed from Bristol in 1603 to Cape Cod under licence from Sir Walter Raleigh. There is a sombre tomb monument of 1617 to a city judge, Sir George Snygge, and the tomb of Edward Blanket, M.P. for Bristol in 1362, often said in Bristol mythology to have given his name to the blanket.

The climax of St. Stephen's is its magnificent fifteenth-century 'Somerset' tower with its Gloucestershire crown of arcaded battlements, pinnacles and open-work arcading, now restored

The monument of Admiral William Penn in St. Mary Redcliffe

Thus He took Leave of the Sea his old Element, But
Continued still his other Employs till 1669, at which
Time, through bodily Infirmities (Contracted by ẏ
Care & Fatigue of Publique Affairs) He Withdrew,
Prepared & Made for his end, & With a Gentle &
Even Gale in much Peace Arrived & Ancord in his
Last & best Port, at Wanstead in ẏ County of Essex
ẏ 16 Sept. 1670, being then but 49 & 4 Months old.
To whose Name & Merit his Surviving Lady
hath Erected this Remembrance

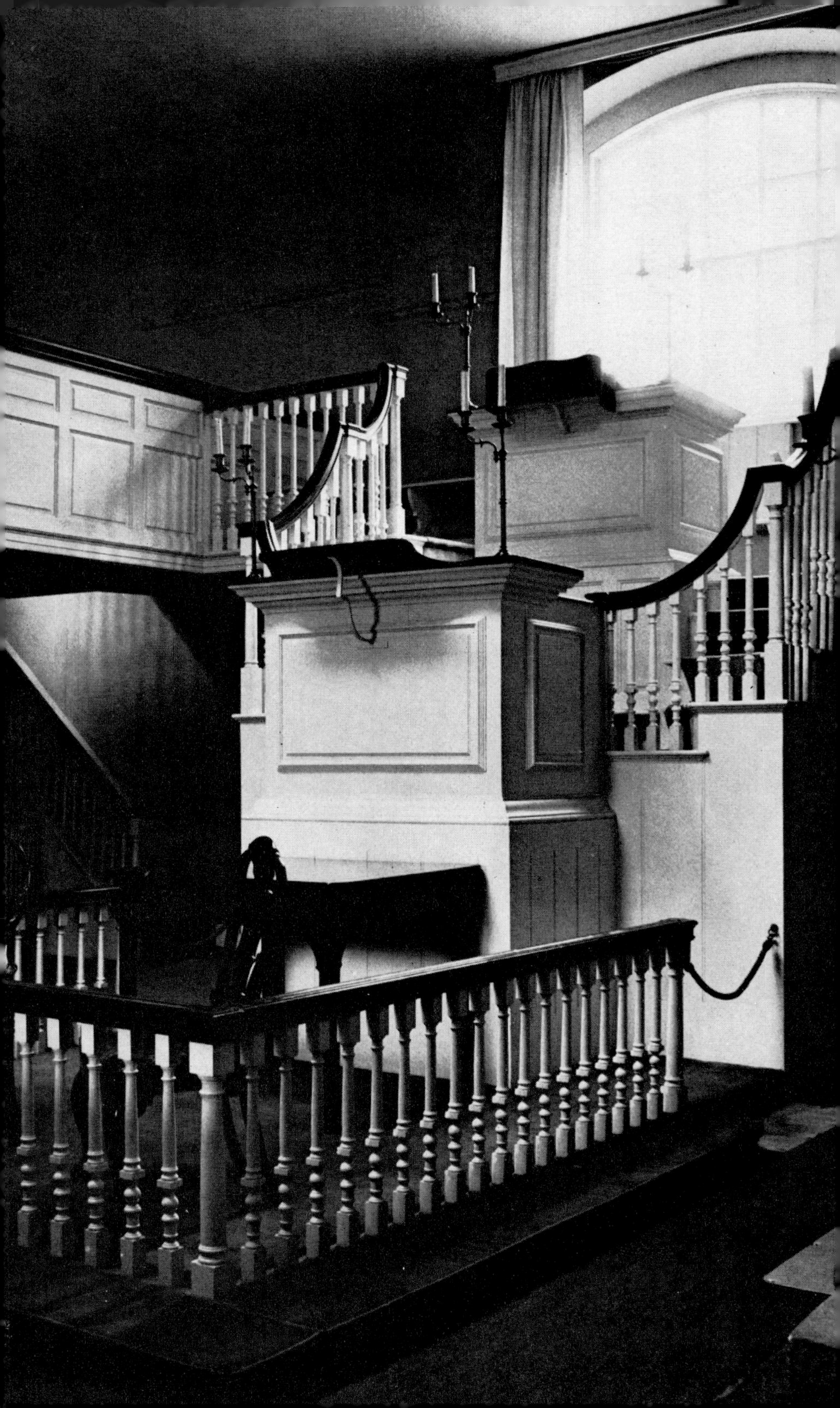

at a cost of £60,000, £40,000 of which was subscribed by a public obviously devoted to Bristol's most striking city church. The tower rises sharply from the lowest level of the city quarter, a landmark through centuries of old maps, city views, water-colours and photographs. It still dominates, bringing into the heart of Bristol a noble stone-symbol of the Somerset hinterland whose culture has played so important a part in Bristol history. But one tall, ill-conceived, domineering building built too near would kill it aesthetically, as the unfortunate new tower-block near St. John's has dwarfed that lovely and unusual church down to the dimensions of an architect's model. Not only is it dwarfed on one side, but it has also been ruthlessly exposed in front by the demolition of buildings to make way for the new development in Nelson Street and Rupert Street, and equally ruthlessly exposed on the other side by the demolition of the old network of lanes and buildings that followed the old line of the city wall. (Conservationists were assured that the dimensions and atmosphere of the lanes and courts would be preserved in the new development; the attempt has been at least partly successful.)

Christ Church, St. Nicholas's and All Saints are more fortunate; their settings largely survive. Christ Church at the top of Broad Street, probably by the busy Bristol architect William Paty, is an impressive church of the 1780s (replacing a medieval one), with a massive tower and lofty spire crowned by an obelisk and ball. Inside it recalls a Wren City church with its white and gold, its vaulted ceiling on thin Corinthian columns and its charmingly theatrical rood-screen like scenery for a Jacobean masque. Like many of Wren's churches it makes its intellectual point but does not tempt one to linger and pray. Southey, born nearby in Wine Street, often stopped to hear the church's famous quarter-boy figures strike the quarter hours. In 1970 the church was given a new lease of security when it was designated as a local centre for religious education.

St. Nicholas dates from the 1760s, again a Georgian church replacing a medieval one. The rebuilding was started by an architect of North American origin, James Bridges; Horace Walpole thought it "neat and truly Gothic". Truly Gothic or not, it is an interesting example of the early serious use of neo-Gothic. Pevsner considered its crypt "one of the most precious survivals of medieval church architecture in Bristol". Fortunately

John Wesley's 'New Room' in Broadmead

the gutted nave was covered over in time, and although the semi-derelict condition of the church was for years an open temptation to the compulsive sweepers away of the unjustifiable Past it now seems safe, as indeed it ought to be in its commanding position. It has now been beautifully restored and made into a museum of local ecclesiastical and civic history. The collection of vestments, church silver, paintings and of superb nineteenth-century water-colours of Bristol churches and other scenes, is dominated by Hogarth's immense religious triptych, painted for St. Mary Redcliffe, long in the City Museum, and now at last in a suitable setting. St. Nicholas's is now a secular shrine for the spirit of the proud old city and a notable addition to its attractions.

All Saints, diagonally across the old High Cross intersection from Christ Church, is a dark, haunting and no doubt haunted church, which never seems to shake off its murk to allow the visitor to admire the fine, rough Norman west bays. A little wan light filters through the plain windows to illuminate Rysbrack's superb statue on James Gibbs's monument to Bristol's most famous philanthropist, the late seventeenth-century merchant, Edward Colston, who was born in Bristol but spent most of his commercial life in London. He died at Mortlake but was brought back to All Saints for burial after a funeral of long-remembered solemnity.

As with his contemporary Wren, if you seek his monument look around you. In Bristol you cannot escape the name of Colston, which was once a popular second Christian name in the city in honour of the philanthropist. There are his two schools, his almshouses on St. Michael's Hill and in King Street, the Colston Hall, Colston Avenue and Colston Parade; and in Colston Avenue Colston himself in bronze leans on a tall cane and broods. On what: the vanity of earthly riches or his involvement in the slave trade? He gave vast sums of money to found charities that survive vigorously today. Yet he was a bigoted High Churchman, who made money from the slave trade and stipulated that the boys at his school were to be Anglicans only and were not to be apprenticed to Dissenters. Can philanthropy make conditions so narrow and still be accounted philanthropy? The sadly beautiful Rysbrack statue of a weary Colston propped on one elbow, with its vase of commemorative flowers dutifully renewed each week after nearly 250 years, is to me the central mystery of this part of Bristol: a symbol of what often seems to be the city's thousand-year-old and always doomed attempt to reconcile the demands of this world and the next.

There is no mystery about the commercial buildings in this central area, however beautiful; they symbolize business and the desire to make business look dignified, though it could be said that the famous bronze 'nails' in front of the Exchange symbolize a certain country cattle market honesty about Bristol business. The tower of All Saints, an early eighteenth-century fantasy crowned by an enchanting cupola of 1807, looks down on the Exchange (1743) by John Wood the Elder of Bath, the most imposing building in the area and a masterpiece of what Osbert Lancaster might have called Slave-Trader's Palladian. It is set back a little from the street-line, but it needs a lot more self-important space around it to set off the robust harmony of its façade and the spatial relevance of two flanking blocks, separated by lanes running down the sides of the Exchange. One flanking block is Carwardine's coffee house (still filling the alley-ways with the pungent smell of roasting coffee) and the other, the old Post Office, has become Martin's Bank, which, with its cleaned stonework, homely white curtains and window-lights, glows at night like a Venetian palace. The whole makes a noble concept, all rather too grand for its workaday setting.

The Exchange apart, though, Bristol's 'City' is small, compact, dignified in its blending of eighteenth-century elegance, Victorian floridness and twentieth-century polished functionalism. There is something of the counting-house, the steel-nibbed ledger *and* the computer in the air, but the dominant atmosphere is of eighteenth-century Quaker-tinged 'trade' at its worthiest and canniest. Something of this old aspect of Bristol commerce lingers on in the Bristol Commercial Rooms in Corn Street, opened in 1811 as a coffee-house and club for merchants. John Loudon McAdam, the road builder, was the first President.

The building by C. A. Busby, later famous in Brighton, has a handsome 'Grecian' pillared façade and pediment, now squashed in between higher buildings. Inside is a large club-room filled with arm-chairs, with a fine ceiling, a central lantern and dome, and a now rather superfluous wind-indicator. Papers and magazines abound (there was a ticker-tape from the Press Association, now gone) and there is still a feeling that, however irrelevant to the great seismic movements of modern finance and speculation, this is how business ought to be conducted.

Membership was over 1,000 in 1920, down to 484 in the late 1940s, up again to 896 in 1951, but down again in 1970 to 500. It stubbornly continues and there is always a small nucleus of loyalists, not necessarily in business, who join to help keep it alive. But the harsh logic of modern business has no place for such institutions.

The mild anachronism of the Rooms is not untypical of Bristol's traditional aloofness from the ruthlessness that has marked London and Liverpool business. Sometimes this has enabled Bristol to consolidate without risk, to avoid the boom and crashes of other trading cities. Sometimes it has prevented Bristol—as in the early nineteenth century—from catching the commercial tides at the full.

This sociable way of doing business was always popular. Wood's Exchange stands on or near the site of the medieval Tolzey, a low roofed arcade along the wall of All Saints, where merchants strolled, chatted and bargained. Later, they would pay their money 'on the nail', that is, on one of the squat bronze pillars still standing outside the Exchange and one of Bristol's favourite conversation pieces (there is always someone who has not heard the story). Wood made the interior courtyard of his Exchange, now glass-covered and used as a civic dance-hall, open to the sky to preserve the informal, gossipy character of the place. In the Middle Ages, and up to the seventeenth and early eighteenth centuries, merchants had fine houses within the city, particularly in Small Street, houses where kings have stayed. Business is still discussed in the local bars and restaurants; Hort's restaurant in Broad Street was a haunt of farmers in town on business in the late nineteenth century. And there is still a tendency for businessmen to stand on the street corners of their little Florentine 'City' and talk shop. The intimate note is kept, too, in Albion Chambers off Small Street, a Dodson and Foggish nest of lawyers' offices and alleyways that lead through to Broad Street. Here, too, are many secret side-alleys and courts, like Tailors' Court off Broad Street, with its early eighteenth-century houses and brightly repainted shell-hoods, and its deep-windowed façade of 1740, replacing a former hall of the Merchant Taylors' Guild, with its great moulded and painted coat of arms suspended in a magnificent shell-hood over the doorway. Here is one of those lost, locked city churchyards—actually the separated churchyard of St. John's—with mouldering tombs and roses that linger deep into winter sheltered by the towering office buildings. Here, one feels, comes a Bristol Lady Dedlock to mourn her lost love—out of office hours, of course.

Bristol was always the banking centre of the South-west, though there were notable old family banks in country towns like Taunton and Langport. John Vaughan, regarded as the father of Bristol banking, lived in the Dutch House in the eighteenth century and conducted his business from there. The first actual bank, believed to have been the third provincial bank in Britain, opened in Broad Street in 1750—when the Theatre Royal opened in 1766 no less than six of the promoters were bankers, evidence that eighteenth-century Bristol was not necessarily the philistine city it appears to be in the Chatterton legend. Against local opposition the Bank of England had opened a branch in Bristol, which in 1847 moved into C. R. Cockerell's severely 'Grecian' building in Broad Street, now less severe since it was cleaned.

In 1878 the West of England Banking Company failed with liabilities of over £3 million, the biggest banking failure of the century. But this was an exception to the rule of success: the Bristol and West Building Society, founded in 1850 by a group of leading business and professional men, is one of the oldest and largest building societies in the country. Today it operates from its new, tall, rather uncompromising tower in the Centre.

As Bristol grows in importance its commercial power-houses are bound to move away from the cramped city quarter, as some have already done. The intimate, gossipy, quirky aspect of its commerce is dying, as it is dying in every old-established business city. Perhaps we should admire while we can the splendid and varied bank buildings: Cockerell's Bank of England, Ponton and Gough's sombre Italian Gothic Bristol Chambers in Nicholas Street, and above all Gingall and Lysaght's fantastic 'Venetian' façade for Lloyd's Bank in Corn Street, an Italian Renaissance palazzo swarming with putti and symbolic figures of commerce, dynamically vulgar and self-confident. There are office buildings in Norman Shaw's manner, in Burgundian red brick, in George V post-office Regency, in Bauhaus austerity: all surpassed in defiant eccentricity by the mad Art Nouveau-cum-William Morris faience-tiled façade of Everard's the printers in Broad Street, which is being preserved while major rebuilding goes on around it in the Tower Lane development.

The old role of the area in civic life has been taken over by the Council House in College Green, but Robert Smirke's Old Council House of the 1820s survives in Corn Street, with its fine brass-railed staircase and elegant Council Chamber, now used for courts and tribunals, and its original Council Chamber above, in Barry-esque House of Lords gilding and panelling. A modest building, the Old Council House was put up during Bristol's long recession in the early nineteenth century when Liverpool was proudly building its massive St. George's Hall. The Law has remained in the area, though: in Pope and Bindon's Assize Courts in Small Street, which used to contain buried inside them remnants of a late twelfth-century house, which survived as a few arches in the Law Library—the arches went in the rebuilding in the early 1960s.

Perhaps the quarter's future lies rather in the cat's cradle of paved alleyways that run through the old markets behind the Exchange, now an Italianate settlement of eating-places, flower and vegetable stalls, butcher's shops, antique booths and sherry bars. The relentless logistics of food-wholesaling have banished the fruit and vegetable markets to a new depot in St. Philip's Marsh beyond Temple Meads, but with luck and goodwill Bristol may keep this area as a sort of piazza of general sociability. It is designated as an 'area of special interest' and it serves an obvious social purpose, a survival of the medieval or Renaissance city centre such as one can find almost nowhere else in Britain today. The little lock-up stalls are Florentine and human in scale. On Saturdays the old market stirs with a kind of medieval apprentice bustle, a Renoir-splash of spring or autumn flowers, trodden vegetables and butchers' sawdust. Implacable steak-drift comes from the Berni restaurants in their converted inns—among them the famous Rummer, where Coleridge's unhappy magazine *The Watchman* was launched at a meeting in 1795—local businessmen congregate for their lunchtime amontillado among the bullfight posters and the young man ventures out with his girl into these simple eating-places where no head waiter will snub him. There is a kind of honest banality about it all, a Dickensian city clerk's bonhomie and bar-banter. Autumn and winter are probably the best times to taste the evocative, Sickert-like atmosphere, when the last chrysanthemums are being sold off cheap, the first eaters are examining the menus and the mist is rising from the Welsh Back.

The atmosphere of the city is not confined within the old line of the city wall. It wanders out into what was long the waste land of Nelson Street and Rupert Street, now filled in with tall new buildings, though not with the raised pedestrian cat-walks above the traffic, which were proposed to carry pedestrians from Broadmead to the Centre, a curious solution to the pedestrian-traffic problem and one I can easily wait to see in operation. Lewins Mead Unitarian Chapel, a dignified plain building of 1787–91 with an uncertain future—no satisfactory suggestion for an alternative use has come up—survives among the wreckage; the chapel marks the beginning of the non-conformist take-over from the Anglican domination of the old city centre. The city atmosphere includes, too, Bristol's famous piece of Ye Oldery, Christmas (possibly originally Knifesmith) Street and Christmas Steps, a gloomy but picturesque, steep-stepped canyon of bookshops, antique shops, clothes and stamp shops, a violin maker's, a restaurant, and windows full of 'girlie' magazines. At the bottom is the surviving fragment of St. Bartholomew's Hospital, founded before 1207, an archway and nearby a statue of the seated Virgin, forming part of a group of timber-framed seventeenth-century houses. At the top of the Steps is the exquisite Chapel of the Three Kings (an unusual dedication), a late fifteenth-century Perpendicular chapel of the almshouses founded by the merchant John Foster; the almshouses, rebuilt in Burgundian style in the last century, are occupied by elderly ladies.

The city atmosphere is taken up again by the district of narrow, hilly streets between Christmas Steps and College Green, an area of great if eroded eighteenth-century character. In Frogmore Street the seventeenth-century Hatchet Inn, once part of a row of old houses and formerly much associated with prize fighters of the Regency, now stands restored and isolated. Orchard Street, arguably the loveliest Georgian Street in Bristol, stands nearly intact, protected over the years by the owners of the land and by the conservationist instincts of the architects and lawyers who occupy most of it. Further up the hillside stands the garish Entertainment Centre, with its neon lights, cinema, dance hall, bowling alley and coin machine arcade, drawing fans not only from Bristol but now from South Wales across the Severn Bridge. Here, too, are Harvey's tentacular cellars, now a wine-museum, and a sombre stone warehouse which, if you are not wary, a local will try to persuade you was once a slave prison. It is a busy, varied area: bowling and films, legal offices, eating, warehouses, Georgian houses, leading to the Soho-ish lower reaches of Denmark Street, with its 'caffs', Indian restaurant, pubs, newsagents, chemists, which in turn leads to Bristol's curious Centre that is no centre, where the commercial, historical and social elements meet, and the statue of Neptune at the Bridge Head gazes out at the all but deserted Harbour. But the Centre is really a modern creation, built over part of the old Harbour and not really part of the old city.

The 'city' shades off into the 'town' on the other side of the Wine Street desert. Between Wine Street and Broadmead lies the cavernous gulch of The Pithay, once a noisome Dickensian slum, later the site of J. S. Fry's chocolate factory until the factory moved to Keynsham between Bristol and Bath in the 1920s. The red brick buildings survived as Her Majesty's Stationery Office until the 1960s. The Fry workers—regularly preached to by Joseph Storrs Fry in his time—took their sense of community with them to Keynsham. The huge cliff-like office blocks in this area are not inappropriate in their context and on humanitarian grounds if not aesthetic grounds are better than the Victorian squalor recorded in old photographs of The Pithay.

Broadmead remains controversial, severely criticized in its early days as the lowest common factor of functionalism. At first there was a sort of Wild West atmosphere, as if rustlers were to hitch their horses to a pavement rail and swagger into the nearest espresso-bar. The multiple stores took up the claims like the medicine men and storekeepers who followed the pioneers West. It was raw and unkempt and the yellowish building material was not attractive. After fifteen to twenty years the buildings have weathered a little, grass and plants have grown, the shops have acquired their regulars. It is at least all of a piece and now that Broadmead and Merchant Street have become traffic-free pedestrian streets, as the Inner-Circuit road system is completed, Broadmead will be more acceptable as a piece of environmental planning.

What was unforgivable about Broadmead was the lack of care for people. The area seemed to thrive on a rapid turn-over (and departure) of customers. There was almost nowhere to sit, nowhere to stroll, no pleasant side roads, no arcades apart from the surviving nineteenth-century Lower Arcade. The service areas inside the squares of shops are still mere backyards; one of the saddest visual ironies is the preservation of the picturesque Quakers Friars group of buildings inside one of these dreadful service areas. It is proposed to plant trees and grass around them eventually to 'improve' the site; but how can those uncompromisingly bleak black walls of shops be improved?

Islands of older buildings that escaped the Blitz, or recovered from it after extensive surgery, survive amidst the efficient banality of Broadmead. Quakers Friars is one: remnants of the Dominican or Blackfriars' houses of Bristol, used as Cutlers' and Bakers' Halls after the Dissolution and today for the City Planning Department's fascinating if rather euphoric permanent exhibition of Bristol redevelopment; and the Quaker Meeting House of 1747–48 used today as a Registry Office. (William Penn was married in an earlier building here in 1696.) Another island is the Merchant Taylors' Almshouses (1701) in Merchant Street, now a branch of Lloyd's Bank; its colourful restoration in recent years won it a Civic Trust award.

The early Victorian Greyhound Hotel survives pleasantly enough, as does James Foster's Lower Arcade (the Upper Arcade went in the Blitz) of 1824–25, one of Bristol's favourite shopping places in the past and superior in some local eyes to London's Burlington Arcade which it much resembles. Today it still seems to be, as it always did, largely occupied by music shops.

Alongside the Lower Arcade stands John Wesley's New Room, built in 1739, the first of all Methodist chapels, and for all its quiet now, disturbed only by the relentlessly rational ticking of the great gallery clock, the powerhouse of the greatest reform movement in eighteenth-century Britain and America. From here Wesley set out on horseback to evangelize Britain, while his associate Francis Asbury sailed for America to become the first Methodist bishop of the Continent. One does not have to be a Methodist or a non-conformist to feel the charge of associative atmosphere in the chapel with its beautiful staircased double pulpit, its plain benches and side galleries (and its rear doors to enable Wesley to escape the mohocking mobs that sometimes invaded the chapel). One feels it, too, in the living quarters above, with the common dining-room and tiny, college-like rooms marked 'John Wesley', 'Charles Wesley', 'Francis Asbury', and now thoughtfully kept as a Methodist shrine, if they will allow the word. The octagon lantern looking from a window in the dining-room down into the chapel is an ingenious method of lighting and of symbolizing the links between the spiritual and the worldly. Wesley, the thinker and pietist is strongly present in his New Room, appropriately set among the Vanity Fairs of our time, as he is present in the historical awareness of Bristol, where Wesley was once a popular second Christian name. The equestrian statue of Wesley in the forecourt of the chapel looks ready to set off again on a new mission.

Broadmead replaces an area that was damaged but not destroyed in the Blitz. It was characteristic of old Bristol and attractive to the urban antiquarian but perhaps not really to be missed more than any other decayed Victorian commercial district. But the destruction of a number of beautiful eighteenth-century houses in the St. James's Barton area slightly to the north of Broadmead is unforgivable. The gradual encroachment of cars and roads on this park-like area in front of St. James's Church and the gradual erosion, despite intermittent hopes of preservation, of the Georgian houses, in St. James's Barton, St. James's Parade and North Street, was one of the unnecessary tragedies of the 1950s. Number 12, St. James's Barton, a noble house of 1728, as we can see from photographs, was typical of the losses involved. Its last owner, a city alderman, had cherished the house, furnished it in Georgian style, and filled the back garden with flowers. The Ministry asked the Corporation to save it and this request was thought to have been accepted. But it came down nevertheless in 1960, an act of ruthlessness much resented in Bristol. The sweeping away of these fine houses is a grim example, not of the orderly segregation of pedestrians and traffic, for which there may be a case, but of the subordination of the human to mere traffic. The new St. James's Underpass, with its red-brick battlemented flower beds and hopeful signs pointing to 'University' and 'Infirmary', is to me the angriest place in the new Bristol. The new buildings looming over the Underpass only add to the sense of urban loneliness.

St. James's itself derives from St. James's Priory, the first monastery in Bristol, founded in 1129 by Robert, Earl of Gloucester; it is probable therefore that its claims to be Bristol's oldest building are correct. The strong Norman arches inside survive from the Priory. But the finest Norman survivals are outside: the lovely West front with its interlaced arcading and an odd and beautiful 'wheel' window with a small lancet in the gable above. This front, with the Chapter House in the Cathedral, are Bristol's Romanesque show-pieces, worth travelling a long way to see. The future of the church seems safe, with something like 3,000 parishioners in the multi-storey flats below Kingsdown and in the vast hospital complex nearby and in residential pockets within reach. The church is as difficult to get into in the day as most other city churches kept locked against vandals. This is understandable, but it is a pity that these churches cannot be opened at announced times, and under surveillance, for interested visitors.

A railed pavement runs alongside the church separating it from the pleasant little park—which used to be bigger—and a handsome, lightly textured insurance office harmonizes admirably with the cleaned stonework of the church. One turns a corner to find the unhandsome and inadequate bus station, a sort of shabby caravanserai for visitors to Bristol, many of whom now come for the day or evening across the Severn Bridge from Wales. The redevelopment now being completed for the area—ten-storey office block, two-level shopping centre, a new pub, church hall and rooftop car park—is at least tidier than the former chaos. But it is not likely to still the suspicion that in the St. James's district particularly Bristol has lost much and gained nothing in return. The seventeenth-century Full Moon Hotel, with its pillared porch, survives to mark the boundary between the old nucleus and the new growth that spread away to the north and the east—other Bristols.

The heart of Bristol, that seemed shapeless and unfocused, can now be seen to have a distinctive shape and boundaries: a boomerang-shaped complex of streets following the curve of the Floating Harbour on one side and the similar curve of a sharp hillside on the other. The covered-in River Frome follows a similar curve but cannot really be called a boundary as the 'city' spreads over it right up to the foot of the Kingsdown hillside. At one extremity the city drew its limits near the late seventeenth-century King Street, leaving the Marsh, surrounded on three sides by the Avon and Frome, to be filled in during the early eighteenth century by Queen Square. At the other extremity near St. James's Barton it dwindled out into country later to be bricked in by the workaday vastness of East Bristol.

The old city lies low in relation to the surrounding areas of the city, but itself is mildly hilly, so that the city steeples form a distinct sky-line of their own, or did until the office towers began to block the sky-line in. From nearbv heights, such as Park Row and Perry Road, the city looks a chaotic jumble of unharmonized buildings, though improved from what it was fifty years ago when factory chimneys and surviving glass-cones cast their smoke-screens across central Bristol. From the low-lying areas to the east, though—and particularly from the railway approaches into Temple Meads—the city still looks the steeple-dominated Bristol of Victorian prints and panoramas.

The swarming Victorian crowds have gone, the elderly bearded men of forty in battered bowler hats, with Charlie Chaplin boots, the knickerbockered boys standing in the middle of the street and trying to stare the cameraman out. But Bristol's City is not so dead as London's outside working hours. The pubs and steak-houses keep the area alive in the evening, and in the day the variety of the streets draws many sections of the population into or through Corn Street, Broad Street, Baldwin Street and the old markets. The office workers sit in St. Stephen's churchyard with their sandwiches. The lawyers hurry through the echoing tunnels of Albion Chambers to and from the Assize Court or the divorce courts in the Old Council House. Businessmen on their way to a self-service lunch in the Commercial Rooms pause to look at the paintings in the windows of Frost and Reed's famous gallery in Clare Street, which specializes—or seems to the infrequent passer-by—in traditional English oils, all stage-coaches stuck in the snow and wherries becalmed on the Broads, and the mild modernism that average Bristol taste reaches to.

St. Philip's and St. Jacob's Church, on the outer limits of the city facing Temple Way, has had a notable revival of life in recent years under its enterprising vicar, Malcolm Widdecombe. As minister-in-charge in 1965 he was given three years by the Bishop of Bristol to prove that the sombre Early English church in its bleak unrailed churchyard should be kept open. Until the First World War, and even after, it was an immensely popular church, the 'Mother Church' of East Bristol, famous for its christenings: it was the 'done' thing for the people of East Bristol to have their children christened at the church and they queued up outside on Sunday afternoons for the privilege. Then the church began to lose its congregation, through time, change and the Blitz. Mr. Widdecombe and his loyal supporters achieved both of their targets, in half the time allotted, by raising £500 a year towards the upkeep of the fabric and by increasing the congregation from 55 to 120; in 1969 they raised £2,000 for missions as well. In the following years their missionary enterprise has increased so that in 1971 they gave over £4,000, over £8,000 in 1973, and in 1974, their Octocentenary year, a colossal £13,000 was given away. The church's main service is the Sunday evening service, to which an average congregation of 300 come.

In addition, the church found a mission on its doorstep. On Christmas Eve 1966 a patrol of young people went out to take soup, food parcels—and copies of the Gospel—to down-and-outs sleeping rough on bomb sites, in parks and on benches in the bus station. Every Wednesday and Friday for about four years a patrol went out late at night (they have fallen off since the vagrants began coming to the church itself for help) and into the small hours visiting meth drinkers and tramps, offering them hot coffee and food, inviting them back to the vestry where a store of clothing is kept, trying to get them into hostels and making appointments at Labour Exchanges. In two and a half years they contacted and tried to help about 200 vagrants in the St. Philip's area, some of whom responded, while others preferred their compulsive and lonely routine. Now that other organisations are doing this work full-time, this particular service has ceased, but the church is still very active in other areas of need. It is appropriate work for a church where Wesley once preached, a church which ministered to working-class Bristol, work which, with its earnestness and lack of sentimentality, has a characteristic Bristol touch about it.

But 200 vagrants in two and a half years in the heart of a prosperous, efficient city! Even when one has subtracted the psychological cases who will always be tramps or down-and-outs, together with the casual labourers, the alcoholics, the refugees from broken marriages, there still seem to be too many. You come across them sifting rubbish dumps for saleable objects in the bombed, overgrown area behind Temple Church; and one wet autumn afternoon I sheltered in a porch of St. Philip's, looking at the superb High Victorian façade of what was Simmonds's brewery in Jacob Street, and was approached by a local tramp who parked his broken down pram full of pieces of old fire-grate, made a bed of dry sacking inside the porch and asked me politely but meaningfully if I had somewhere to go while he snatched an hour's sleep. I had, but he had not.

They huddled inside decayed districts like St. Philip's, as the rebuilding crept around them, like rabbits inside the last stand of corn. Unrepresentative as they may have been, perhaps they served a moral purpose: to remind us that cities are places to live in and that the old, unreformed, underdeveloped Bristol had a tolerance of non-conformers that the new motorized Bristol may not be able to afford. It is a sombre thought to take away from St. Philip's Church and think about on Bristol Bridge, which saw the past begin and waits to see the future happen.

Interlude

FLOWING WITH BRISTOL MILK AND HONEY

PARADOXICAL to the last, Bristol has a reputation outside its boundaries both as a puritanical city with little night-life and as rather an epicurean place, fond of its stomach and especially of its palate, as one might expect in a city that has been the chief English shipping port for the Bordeaux wine trade since the thirteenth century.

What the visitor is most likely to notice, after he has seen the 'nails' outside the Exchange, is the number of wine and sherry bars, the Bristol habit of drinking sherry from the cask instead of beer at lunch-time, and the large number of interesting, moderately priced restaurants. This impression is confirmed each year by the standard eating-out guides in which Bristol regularly takes a high place for the number of recommended restaurants, though after London, Edinburgh and Brighton, and not so much for haute cuisine as for averagely good, reasonably cheap eating. If we eliminate Edinburgh as a capital and a festival centre, and Brighton as a displaced culture-suburb of London, then Bristol appears to have the best eating facilities of any large city outside London.

But is there really a wine-drinking tradition? The wine connection is an historical fact, a present day commercial reality (though not so much wine actually unloads at Bristol or Avonmouth as it did) and it is a rich strand in the mythology of the city. The ship somewhat unprofessionally crashing into the castle walls in the coat of arms is probably a medieval wine ship bringing a cargo from Bordeaux. The city's two oldest wine shipping firms, Averys and Harveys, are such a part of the life of the city that they hardly count as trade-names any longer, but tend to be regarded—or were regarded in the case of Harveys, which has become part of a larger, non-Bristol group—as local families who happened to deal in wine.

Yet another Bristol paradox is that a city in which the ordinary people have obviously not drunk any more wine than in any other city in the country—and really prefer beer or rough Somerset cider, a lot of which is drunk on the Somerset fringes—is nevertheless proud of its connection with the wine trade, which it associated with business success and good living. The teetotal movements of the last century would not have bothered much with so expensive and class-bound a drink as wine and Bristol's non-conformist conscience was undisturbed by this traditional luxury trade. Bristolians may drink more sherry in pubs and bars than other cities; but it is really no more sophisticated about wine than any other large British city and her older wine merchants still do most of their 'quality' business with London.

The Bristol wine trade resulted from the rise to power of the House of Anjou in the twelfth century, when it ruled Gascony as well as England. Henry II's marriage to Eleanor of Aquitaine added to England's Continental possessions many of the finest wine-growing districts of France. Most of the Gascon and Bordeaux wines came through Bristol, partly for geographical and distributive reasons, forming a link that is maintained today by the city's 'twinning' with Bordeaux. Bristol finds Bordeaux agreeably sober and English and Bordeaux finds Bristol agreeably relaxed and chatty. Trade with Spain and Portugal flourished with the exchange of West of England wool and North Atlantic fish for wine, oil, Castile soap and iron. Sherry became the most popular wine in England and Bristol maintained its position in the trade, a position strengthened by the introduction of port as a result of the enterprise of the English merchant colony (which included a number of Bristol men) in Portugal.

The stable progress of the trade was often interrupted by what Bristol wine merchants tended to think of as troublesome quarrels that did not otherwise concern them, such as the Hundred Years War and the threat of the Armada. The Hundred Years War severely restricted the wines from France and England looked for other wines such as malmsey from Greece, but although the Bordeaux trade recovered, by the reign of Henry VII Spanish wines were beginning to outstrip those from France. 'Sack' became the characteristic English wine of the sixteenth century and early seventeenth centuries. (The origin of the word for these white wines from Spain and the Canaries ought clearly to be from

St. Nicholas's Church near Bristol Bridge

Bristol & West

'*sec*', but we read also of 'sweet' sacks.) A reference to Bristol Milk by Thomas Fuller in his *Worthies of England* (1662) shows the early popularity of this particularly Bristolian wine (first mentioned in a document of 1634):

> Though as many Elephants are fed as Cows grased within the walls of this City [Fuller writes], yet great plenty of this Metaphorical Milk, whereby Xeres or Sherry-Sack is intended. Some will have it called Milk because . . . such wine is the first moisture given Infants in this City. It is also the Entertainment of course, which the courteous Bristolians present to all Strangers, when first visiting their City.

The availability and popularity of various wines changed with the fortunes of war and international politics. Spanish wine came in when French wine was cut off. Port came in as a result of good trading relations with Portugal. When we were at war with France in William III's time the duty on French wines became prohibitive; *The Spectator* in 1711 condemned "this plaguey French claret"—rather as dachshunds were hissed at in English streets during the 1914–18 war—and praised "good solid edifying port". Bordeaux still sent its fine wines to our loyal aristocrats, but port was the wine of the eighteenth-century squires who drank their two bottles a night easily enough in the days before port was fortified. French wines remained dear through much of the nineteenth century until Gladstone reformed wine duties in 1869. In the first fourteen years of this century vintage port was Harveys' biggest seller in Bristol and elsewhere, while sherry was somewhat out of favour, having been condemned by doctors as liverish. Claret was also less popular and madeira and marsala more popular than they are today. Bristol cellars were gravely depleted in the 1914–18 war and a period of hectic re-stocking took place in 1919. Casks of wine lay in the roads near the wharves, obstructing the traffic and guarded from looters by police. Harveys record that sherry sales fell off again during the 1920s because of the popularity of cocktails, but in the 1930s sales of sherry exceeded those of port for the first time.

Today, sherry has regained its priority. Harveys re-export one bottle in three of the sherry they import, most of it to the United States where the phrase "Will you have a Bristol?" has become current. Earlier in the century Averys sold four or five bottles of

The Bristol and West Building Society tower in the Centre
The Welsh Back Granary, now a jazz club

port to one of sherry and today it is the other way round. As late as 1926 the sherry shippers were worried about the sales of sherry. In 1923 Averys main business was port, sherry, whisky and brandy with only a very small trade in French wines. Today both firms have adapted to the great increase in wine-drinking on a popular level. Gone are the old high-handed days of patrician wine merchants in Bristol who would not send their representatives to city pubs because they thought publicans would not understand wine, and who would make the publicans use the front-counter like any other casual customer. Bristol Milk-type sherries are still local favourites as you can confirm by keeping an eye on the Bristol Milk casks in one of the bars for half an hour.

It will be interesting to see if firms like Averys (founded 1793) can keep the family dimensions it keeps today in an age of ever larger groupings of small firms; and if Harveys, despite its absorption into a larger, more anonymous group, can maintain the specifically local connection with Bristol (local connoisseurs were known by their personal tastes to heads of firms over many years) that made their reputation for quality in a way that bulk shipping and bulk ordering are not likely to rival.

Everyday Bristol will not care much either way. The city eats in a very bourgeois way still, apart from occasional excursions into the dining-out areas. Food and drink really belong to the history of Bristol commerce rather than to its social and cultural history; but another fifty years of the present growth and popularity of eating out and the city may become the British Lyons or Bologna that some rash admirers say it is already.

III

REDCLIFFE VERSUS BRISTOL—THE INNER SUBURBS

LEWIS MUMFORD pointed out* that suburbs are not necessarily later developments away from the original core of a city, but often developments contemporary with the city itself, expressing the city dwellers' urge to get away from the demanding communal life and the bad air and noise of a crowded city without having to cut themselves off from the amenities of city living.

Bristol shows such a sequence of old, coterminous suburbs growing around the original city centre, themselves becoming in turn as crowded and city-like as the centre. Man's desire, as Mumford added, to live in and away from the city is self-defeating. As the new suburb grows more popular, people follow in large numbers, bringing their shops and businesses with them, and the suburb becomes merely an extension of the city.

The Redcliffe and Temple areas are old suburbs, very nearly as old as the original city around the castle and the bridge. Though they retained a character of their own, they quickly became as crowded as the city itself and ceased to be suburbs, though they still resembled the European 'faubourg', or inner city but outside the city gates, between the centre and the true suburb. The College Green area was a separate but early development, which never really became the core of a new quarter. The eighteenth-century districts that took the place of older streets behind Sir John Young's Elizabethan Great House—which stood where the Colston Hall now stands—quickly became indistinguishable from other parts of the central city. On the other hand, the incomparable early Georgian hillside suburb of Kingsdown, above the St. James's–Horsefair area, always retained something of its suburban air. The late eighteenth-century Brunswick and Portland Squares, to the north of Old Market Street, were intended as part of an elegant new residential district, but quickly faded and

*_The City in History_, 1961, Chapter 16.

became commercial and slummy. The old city was too close and predatory.

These early suburbs shade off at the edges into early and mid-Victorian areas that themselves shade off at their farther edges into the late Victorian and early twentieth-century suburbs that switchback over Bristol's hills and wander out towards the Vale of Berkeley, the Severn coast, the Cotswolds and the first Somerset slopes. What is historically interesting about these districts is that they have never been wholly absorbed into the city centre and have never wholly lost their character as contiguous 'suburbs', unlike, for example, the contiguous Georgian quarters of inner Birmingham which have become wholly commercialized. This is certainly due to Bristol's eccentric geography, to the barriers to uniformity offered by the two rivers, and by the hill-slopes, which in parts of Kingsdown and Montpelier are as precipitous as those of Bath. It is also due, one suspects, to Bristol's 'suburban' instincts, to a certain local patriotism and clannishness that keeps its immediate loyalties for its own district and ensures that an old village-suburb like Bedminster is regarded still as a place different from Bristol across the New Cut.

These areas have not remained static. The Temple, submerged into Victorian industry, then bombed into a coma, still lies partly stagnant. But a large commercial revival has been started with parts of a commercial precinct being built close to the noble ruins of Temple Church. Redcliffe is due for an even larger redevelopment, which pays proper respect to St. Mary Redcliffe Church—in the plans anyway. Kingsdown, after lapsing into a sort of urban gout and near-slumminess, has perked up, painted and restored itself. Portland Square is being rehabilitated. King Street is a 'protected' area and Queen Square may be eased of its noisy road, Redcliffe Way, if traffic is eventually re-routed across a new bridge closing the end of St. Augustine's Reach. College Green and the Cathedral precinct could become peaceful again if the plans for closing Deanery Road, long promised, ever mature. The inner suburbs have, in fact, a brighter future in many ways than the old city centre, part of which has already been rebuilt without style or grace.

Redcliffe was always the most distinctive of them, a place apart from old Bristol. The Fitzhardings, a Bristol family who became lords of Berkeley in Gloucestershire, protected and developed

Redcliffe as a separate township until the growth of Bristol's prosperity identified Redcliffe's interests with Bristol's, and the two were joined by Bristol Bridge. For a time in the middle thirteenth century Redcliffe looked as if it might develop as the city centre instead of the area around the castle: it was level, less crowded and less dominated by the castle. The Avon which flowed past the sandstone 'cliffs' of Redcliffe (there are still caves in the cliffs where sandstone was quarried for glass-making in the eighteenth century, and conducted tours of the caves are made by local history groups) was wider than the Frome and there would have been a deeper anchorage along Redcliff Back than along the Welsh Back on the Bristol side. The new channel for the Frome dug in those years by Bristol men gave Bristol the advantage in harbour facilities. A separatist feeling survived in Redcliffe long after it had been incorporated into Bristol and the great church of St. Mary Redcliffe, deliberately large and ornate, can be seen as a symbol of Redcliffe's claims as an alternative centre for the city.

The church was described by Queen Elizabeth I (or by her speech-writer), as every Bristol schoolchild knows, as "the fairest, goodliest and most famous parish church in England", a claim that might be disputed by those who know the great East Anglian flint churches. It is basically Perpendicular, with an early English and Decorated tower and a Decorated North porch, the hexagonal shape of which is rare and puzzling with its extraordinarily detailed carving of foliage and birds. Was it influenced by Indian architecture via returned travellers, as some have speculated? Or was the influence that of Spain or Portugal? Or was it St. Mary Redcliffe that influenced Spanish and Portuguese architecture? Bryan Little has demonstrated that features of early fourteenth-century Bristol Gothic which appear in the Cathedral and St. Mary Redcliffe appear in certain Spanish late Gothic churches and in Portuguese Manoeline architecture some 200 years later.

The interior is rich and impressive, a forest of tall, slender pillars like Californian redwoods, their summits lost in the intruding mist on winter afternoons. There are fine lierne vaulting, magnificent roof-bosses and splendid monuments, notably those to Admiral Sir William Penn, father of the founder of Pennsylvania, and to the fifteenth-century merchant and Lord Mayor, William Canynges, one of the great semi-mythical figures of

Bristol history, who became a priest after his wife's death and died as Dean of Westbury College in 1474. He has two monuments, one in sombre red and black as merchant and Lord Mayor, the other an austere alabaster statue as priest, in which he looks not unlike the Westminster Abbey effigy of Henry VII, who also managed to combine business and piety. Near his monuments one can feel powerfully the presence of the ill-fated Chatterton, who haunted them. (Chatterton, who made Canynges the patron of his poet-priest Rowley, was born in the shadow of the church and his birthplace survives across the road.) Coleridge and Southey were married here to the Fricker sisters; and Dr. Johnson and Boswell came here after Chatterton's death to see the Muniment Room where the boy-poet had pored over and plagiarized the fifteenth-century church records.

It is a beautiful church but not, to me, a very endearing one. The beauty is rather formal, a little over-restored—there was a massive restoration in the mid-nineteenth century—and over-polished. The dim religious light around its forest pillars is as much Victorian as Renaissance. The church, often spoken of in terms of a cathedral, is not quite grand enough for a cathedral yet a little over-ambitious as a parish church. There is a touch of mercantile complacency and ambitiousness about it, and the aesthetic excitement and religious stirrings I perhaps ought to feel in the tall, yearning Gothic of St. Mary Redcliffe I find rather in the cooler, more spacious radiance of the Cathedral.

John Addington Symonds thought the view from the roof of the Muniment Room better than that over Ghent and Bruges; but then, he was not a notably realistic writer. Victorian photographs of the area, taken from high up on the church, show a Dickensian nightmare of terrace houses, backyard industries, pottery and glass cones, railway goods yards, all under a pall of floating grime and profitable industrial smog. The remnants of an eighteenth-century residential area cowered anxiously behind St. Mary's churchyard in Colston Parade and Somerset Square. Today the Victorian photographer on the same vantage point would see some things that he recognized and more that he would not. The church precinct has not changed greatly, apart from the disappearance of the curious Eleanor-type monument to Chatterton and the overnight appearance during the German air raids of a section of tram-rail impaled in a corner of the churchyard and still there. Colston

Parade beyond the churchyard railings is so far unchanged, with its Georgian houses, its Fry's House of Mercy of 1784, still an almshouse, and a house on the site of the birthplace of Samuel Plimsoll, Member of Parliament and benefactor of sailors. The fine Georgian house on the Redcliff corner was threatened with demolition to make room for a 'Georgian-style' block of flats for church staff, but seems to have escaped this fate.

The glass-cones have gone, apart from the disused base of Proctor's eighteenth-century cone behind a forbidding wall in Prewett Street, the last surviving fragment of Bristol's great glass industry. Despite fears for its future, this base has been attractively preserved as a restaurant attached to the new hotel built on the side. The famous Shot Tower on Redcliff Hill has gone, butchered in 1968 to make a road-widener's holiday. A local plumber, William Watts, built the first shot tower in the world here in 1782, using an existing merchant's house, one of the earliest brick-built houses in Bristol. Molten Mendip lead was poured through a 'colander' in the upper room, falling the height of the tower and the depth of a pit dug down into the rock below to harden, and finally being caught in a vat of cold water. It was still in operation until its demolition, the shot being sold all over the world, both as shot and as screening for fuel rods in nuclear power stations. The company have built a new shot-tower near St. Philip's Bridge, an elegant concrete tulip that rightly won a Civic Trust Award and is a charming addition to the sky-line. But Watts's Tower was a monument of industrial history as well as a handsome building and a city more practically tender of its past might well have islanded it or even moved it elsewhere.

Redcliff Hill itself has gone in the interests of road-widening; a small fragment of shops remained in 1970, including a double-entrance with delicate barley-sugar iron columns either side. There were no architectural jewels here, but what was here was more human than another 3 or 4 feet of bad-tempered traffic and chest-high fumes. On the other side of St. Mary Redcliffe the Ship Inn with its long skittle alley has been attractively 'done up' as part of a new residential group: a neat nest of old people's bungalows and the new Girls' Friendly Society Hostel where the G.W.R. sidings clanked and puffed when Redcliffe was a Doré-scape of chimneys and squalor. Away towards Bristol Bridge is

St. Thomas's Church, a handsome building of the 1780s and 90s, with its fifteenth-century tower surviving and a curious Hogarthian vestry-house built into the angle of the wall and church like a swallow's nest. Here is the Seven Stars Inn, where the anti-slavery reformer Thomas Clarkson heard evidence from sailors on slave-ships; the sand-jetty; the massive warehouses of Redcliff Back, the stone-fronted Wool Hall of 1830, now a warehouse, a clanging iron and steel store-shed, and the group of seventeenth-century gabled houses that remind Victoria Street of its past.

Something of old Redcliffe remains in Guinea Street, running off Redcliff Hill down the slope past the General Hospital towards the Bathurst Basin. Here there is a fine double house of 1718 with a huge Dutch gable, rare in Bristol, and exotic motifs—birds, heads, fruit—over the keystones, and a great stone pine-apple instead of an urn at the gable-top, which one likes to think of as a Bristol touch. On the 'Red Cliff' high above the Harbour stands Redcliffe Parade, two bold eighteenth-century terraces, one late eighteenth-century stretch in white stucco (recently fitted and restored inside as offices) and a further stretch, near St. Mary's, in a lovely smutty red brick of 1768. These terraces are as lovely close to as when seen from Bristol Bridge or glimpsed riding high above the water from other parts of the city. Below them, on a gravelly, cindery waterside stands the Ostrich Inn, a popular lunch-snack place for doctors and nurses from the General Hospital and office workers from across the Harbour. The waterside gives a Rowlandson view of the quays of The Grove opposite, where the sand ships unload. The traffic roars across Queen Square, the gulls lunge after edible debris, a fine stipple of rain drifts across the water, and this part of Bristol, deeply layered with history, lost energies and ambitions, seems a nostalgic world away from the functional banalities of our other great cities.

The new Redcliffe centres on the housing estate of the 1950s built behind the church by J. Nelson Meredith, then the city architect. Apartment blocks of varying heights, none excessively high, and thoughtfully staggered in siting, stand where the Georgian Somerset Square stood and where the eighteenth-century fountain still stands. The future includes plans for a £1½ million office block on the crown of Redcliff Hill, now largely complete, and a new square consisting of the original Guinea Street on one side and new buildings on the other three, with other shop and office buildings. Redcliffe Way is to be moved further away from the churchyard to pass under a new commercial development. There should be more space and greenery in the new Redcliffe, and if any new inner-city residential concept ought to work, this one should, with its natural advantages, picturesque survivals and closeness to the city. If a new population takes root Redcliffe may yet achieve its old ambition to rival Bristol.

The Temple area which adjoins Redcliffe the other side of Victoria Street, huddled between that street and the backwaters of the Harbour, was a sad place in the early 1970s. Already before 1939 it had faded into a drab commercial district. In 1940 the Luftwaffe gutted the ancient Temple Church and shattered the surrounding streets which became a waste land of overgrown alleyways and rubbish tips, with smatterings of warehouses and garages among the desolation. To wander through the churchyard was a melancholy Tennysonian experience; in autumn the clumps of wet leaves cumbered the path through the lime alley and the air was heavy with the smell of ruined hydrangeas. The roar of traffic grinding over the fly-over near Temple Meads contrasted poignantly with the green broken tombstones propped against the river wall of the churchyard. In these derelict corners of Bristol it was all too easy to become obsessed with the dead rather than with the living, though the ruins of the church and its richly ornamented leaning tower—5 feet out of true—were not sad in themselves, and the pigeons at least had not deserted their niches among the delicate stone tracery of the upper levels.

The Temple, now so empty, was once the crowded centre of the Bristol weaving trade, which was early connected with this area and this church. In the thirteenth century the church, although still belonging to the Templars, had become the parish church and many of the congregation must have been weavers. Bristol, more interested in the finished cloth, was never a major exporter of wool despite its closeness to the Cotswolds; but the concentration of weavers, tuckers and dyers marked the beginning of the industrial importance of the Redcliffe–Temple district. The Temple was the birthplace of Edward Colston in 1636 and Wesley preached in the church. Excavations in the early

1970s revealed traces of fifteenth-century warehouses and of wool-drying racks, which confirmed the existence of the district's historical trade.

Today there is little to see here, apart from the church and is it worth describing a church that has largely been destroyed? The tower is beautiful and striking, quite apart from its dramatic lean—there is a story that army sappers nearly pulled it down after the Blitz, thinking the lean was due to bomb damage. Otherwise, there is a derelict row of early nineteenth-century cottages in Pipe Lane; the pretty little Cherry Tree Inn in Rose Street supplies snacks for the goods yard workers nearby; a whole block around and including Dr. White's Hospital, Victorian Tudor buildings of a medieval almshouse (rehoused in Redcliffe) has disappeared awaiting redevelopment. The industrial past is recalled by the splendid old Bristol Tramways generating station in Philip Street, now a wine merchant's warehouse, and the present by the aristocratic wrought-iron gates of Courage's brewery.

An ambitious but slow-starting scheme is planned to restore life to the Temple: the retention of existing warehouses, the rehousing of as many existing firms as possible, the preservation of the church ruins and churchyard as the focus of a new commercial complex of offices and shops, part of which has already been built.

The other great monument of the area thrives still. Temple Meads Station, more than any other in the country, recalls the smut-choked optimism and daemonic energy of the early days of railways. The ghost of the young, inexhaustibly competent Brunel walks here if anywhere. The Great Western Railway and Temple Meads were triumphs unspoilt by delays, frustrations, compromises and conspiracies as some of his other enterprises were. They were young men's dreams realized by the most extraordinary engineering and entrepreneurial talent we have known in Britain, a nineteenth-century epic to compare with Hakluyt's *Voyages*, Marco Polo's *Travels* and the journals of the nineteenth-century explorers of Africa.

The old Great Western Terminus at Bristol was opened in 1840, though the first plan to build a Bristol–London railway had been promoted back in the 1820s. In 1841 a junction was made at Temple Meads with the Bristol and Exeter Railway which had been laid out by Brunel at right-angles to the G.W.R. station.

As a result the enlarged station formed by the amalgamation of the two in 1876 had to be built with platforms curved to conform with the junction lines, a curve which still gives a most striking curved line to the great glass-and-girder roof of the main station. The first train ran from London to Bristol in 1841 with one of the Bristol backers, Thomas Guppy, dancing, it is said, on the roof of a carriage in his delight. Brunel rode on the locomotive platform, driven by his assistant Daniel (later Sir Daniel) Gooch. Brunel's original station faces Temple Gate, where it appears as a symmetrical mock-Tudor façade with angle turrets and a proud carved inscription on a stone scroll: "Great Western Railway Company Incorporated by Act of Parliament MDCCCXXXV." Pugin attacked the mock-Gothic style because it was not his kind of Gothic; but it has a certain dignity unlike the later and feebler mock-Tudor further up the Incline.

Not many people seem to know that inside the original station lurks shyly and shabbily Brunel's train shed, now used as a car park, but easily recognizable from old prints. This to me is the most evocative survival of the early days of railways—were those black smoke-burns on the wall above the end of the shed actually made by Brunel's first locomotives?—possibly of the whole Industrial Revolution, in the country, comparable with the bridge at Ironbridge in Shropshire. Its shallow platforms, Perpendicular arches, and wooden 'hammerbeam' roof letting the light in through ridge-glazing, vividly presents an image of Puffing Billy trains, with their huge wheels to take the 7-foot gauge (one of Brunel's miscalculations about the future, though theoretically he was probably right) and of Bristol's Dombeys and their ladies gathering in a foam of luggage and anxious maids and porters to speed up to London. It all looks very vulnerable, and road-widening enthusiasts among Bristol's planners wanted to pull down the façade to widen the road at Temple Gate. Would the train shed go with the façade? Fortunately a preservation order has been placed on the old train shed. It seems so obvious to preserve it as a railway museum. But the obvious is not always obvious to the civic eye.

A large development scheme for the station is in hand, involving a new multiple-aspect signalling system to replace some fifty-six signal boxes in the Bristol area by a new central panel at Temple Meads. Fortunately, the station is too important, for the time being anyway, to be radically cut down in the general rundown of the railway system. It is still the filter-point for rail traffic from London, Wales, the North and the Midlands into the fastnesses of the South-west. It has an air of importance about it, though like so much else in Bristol it is both metropolitan and provincial at the same time. Although it is a through station it is much like a great London terminus with its lofty roof and wide platforms. Yet it has no restaurant, only a large buffet sometimes closed by nine in the evening.

The station lies in the middle of a huge complex of marshalling yards, sidings, sheds, Post Office buildings, signal boxes and cuttings in which you can see fragments of shattered guards' lamps like fragments of Cretan pottery. Curious old houses, possibly once farm-houses, survive on the fringes of the yards. Shunters still carry out a job that looks as dangerous as it was when *Punch* conducted a campaign against its dangers in the last century. Behind Temple Meads lies the dingy industrial district of St. Philip's, in which the most distinctive building is the castellated façade of John Lysaght's steel works, built presumably in the style of the station. Lysaght was another example, together with Brunel, Humphrey Davy and others, of the outsider—in this case an Anglo-Irishman—making good in Bristol; his bucket-making business rapidly developed into the well-known sheet rolling and galvanizing firm.

St. Philip's is a lost world of yards and sheds, threaded by the dreary waters of the unfashionable end of the Floating Harbour and of the Feeder Canal. In St. Philip's Marsh, between Temple Meads and the Bath Road, a few lonely streets, still with a few corner shops and a pub or two, awaited demolition with fortitude. On the other side of the railway approaches from the north lies a quiet world of early Dickensian terraces, with early Victorian pubs and mid-Victorian school barracks, where the children surely still grow beans on blotting paper. On the wall of a red-brick school beyond a sad, French-looking playground the words "Shaftesbury Crusade", picked out in coloured bricks, have greeted my arrivals and departures: an appropriate slogan for a city with a moral conscience and a great deal of past squalor to be conscience-stricken about.

Between Temple Meads and the late Regency Portland and Brunswick Squares lies a cluttered, largely commercial quarter of considerable interest to students of nineteenth-century cities. "It is very gratifying to know," the *Bristol Times and Mirror* commented in August 1869 (as quoted by Asa Briggs in his *Victorian Cities* in 1965), "that our ancient and well-beloved city is getting on in the world"—getting on at the price of such an area as this, though perhaps it was more tolerable when there was a vigorous street life and a better balance of houses and factories. Today the life has gone out of it, except for a few 1920-ish terraces from which an occasional old man emerges to look round blankly and wonder where it all went. There is a derelict eighteenth-century house near the corner of Kilkenny Street and some imposing Victorian warehouses and factory walls in New Kingsley Road; otherwise it is a wilderness of garages, storehouses, scrap-yards and factories, burdened with a heavy whiff of yeast from the yeast factory by the waterside. The area, known as The Dings and once very tough, a sort of Chaplinesque Easy Street, includes Broad Plain, with its dusty triangle of trees (but no seats from which to admire them) and its row of handsome mid-eighteenth-century houses, one with immense projecting bay windows, one salmon pink with a lovely shell-hood, all commercialized, but all miraculously there against the odds.

Through rising streets the area opens out into Old Market Street—known as 'Old Market'—once one of Bristol's most popular shopping and entertainment centres. It was the old cattle market on the way in from the main Chippenham–London road, a natural link between East Bristol and the city, though many East Bristol people would not come any deeper into the city than Old Market. It was and still is an important bus centre, but the development of the Broadmead shops has drained it of shoppers following a brief revival after the war. Here is the Stag and Hounds Inn, partly pre-Reformation in origin, with its upper storey jutting out over the pavement on slender pillars: the site of Pie Poudre, the Court of Dusty Feet, a medieval court set up to settle fair or market disputes on the spot. A brief ceremony to open the court is held, largely unnoticed by the crowds, outside the inn at 10 a.m. on the last day of September each year. Nearby Kingsley Hall, dating from 1706, has a similar porch on pillars.

In the early 1970s the street, with its empty shops, tottering gables and leaning 'Bristol' mansard roofs, invited demolition. But a new life is confidently planned for it. Already the vast £2¼ million roundabout, underpass and subway system at the Temple Way end is a feature of the local scene: people, as elsewhere, take second place to cars and are obliged to use escalators up to and down from a long passenger footbridge across Temple Way. Old people and mothers with prams understandably hurry through the long, sinister tunnels under the road. The Empire Theatre and the Tatler Cinema have gone, together with thirty other buildings, including 'The White Hart', 'The Bunch of Grapes', 'The Pelican' and 'The Rose and Crown'. A new cinema will be built, with offices, shops and a new pub or two. Further passenger footbridges over the traffic will eventually take pedestrians to the Castle Street area and the new park on Castle Mound. A tall red-brick office block, a new hotel, a new newspaper complex and other developments already dominate Temple Way.

Moving anti-clockwise around the city centre, following the circle of the old inner suburbs, we reach St. Paul's with its two Georgian squares: Brunswick, now a fragment of what it was, and Portland, more or less complete and largely commercial, though still residential either side of the Georgian church of St. Paul's with its charming wedding-cake tower on the top of which one always expects to see a plaster bridal couple. Brunswick Square (1766–84) subject of a tough local fight to preserve it, has kept some of its red brick, pedimented houses but acquired alleys of parking meters and a new low office block, while the impressive Ionic Regency chapel has become a warehouse. Portland Square was laid out in 1790 with stone-faced houses with doorways with Ionic columns. The church, built in 1789–94, is in a vaguely Strawberry Hill Gothic with pinnacles and machicolations. The interior is classical, though with forgetful harkings-back to Early English: a stately, stuffy, civic sort of church, with sword rests and paintings and a splendid Flaxman monument, with a black obelisk, a palm tree and a flag, to Colonel Thomas Vassal who died heroically at Montevideo. It was opened on St. Paul's Day, 1794, for the residents of the new district which was intended to rival Clifton: unsuccessfully, for the squares come from nowhere and lead nowhere. Much of Portland Square has been attractively restored and more restoration is going on. The terraces keep their Regency façades, but as office accommodation. There is little likelihood, as some conservers hoped, of the square becoming largely residential again.

But the squares may yet be the show-places of a revived residential area. A recent low-rise flat-development in the Bishop Street–Martin Street area behind St. Paul's Church, replacing decrepit terraces, has brought residents back to or into the district, though, ironically, many of the nearly 200 flats were occupied in 1970 by people evacuated from a nearby high-rise block regarded as potentially unsafe. The flats in various groupings are clustered around grassy central spaces. Probably they will never fully replace the arms-akimbo, door-step camaraderie and bantering of the old streets. But one only had to look at the exposed backs of the remaining old houses round about, with their domestic rubbish, old bath tubs, broken bicycles, outhouses and outside lavatories, washed up like flotsam around the end of a pier, to understand that the elbowing friendliness of the old way might be a small loss compared with the warmth and comfort of the new flats.

From the fringes of the new development, where the demolishers' bonfires flamed on winter dusks, one could look across the jumble of romantically unplanned rooftops—where Stokes Croft brings the Cheltenham and Gloucester roads into the city—and up to Kingsdown on its steep hill overlooking all central Bristol and across to Dundry Hill. Kingsdown is one of the great aesthetic sights of Bristol and one of the least known to outside visitors: all that remains of a superb Georgian suburb, eroded now by decay and demolition and scarred by a giant functional range of new flats on the first levels of the hill, but still extensive and authentic enough to give an impression of what an eighteenth-century upper middle-class city '*quartier*' looked like. In streets like Somerset Street, with cobbles and only rare traffic, the illusion is complete. Lydia Languish yawns at her boudoir mirror, longing for the evening and the Assembly Room. An ostler hums as he curries a horse in a back-mews. An early chair jolts a painted dowager down to the Hot Well for tea and malice. Kingsdown Parade, with handsome house-front after house-front, looks like one of those backcloths for *The Rivals* used at the Theatre Royal in the early post-war days of the Bristol Old Vic Company. Long gardens lead from the lower end of the Parade up to a noble row of Georgian fronts, now in vigorous restoration, aglow with bright salmon-pinks, dove-greys and ochres on autumn afternoons. Bath can show Georgian terraces finer than those of

Clifton; but stone-faced formal Bath has little plain domestic architecture of the period to rival Kingsdown.

Kingsdown has kept its authenticity—where it has—partly because of its geography: away from main traffic routes and built on slopes (part of a low range of hills that extend West to Clifton and on to Clevedon) so steep that the vertical roads that cut grid-wise across the long horizontal streets are often flights of steps, now weed-grown and chipped. It has survived, too, because for a long time it was 'undesirable' property, fallen into decline like a Regency buck fading into Victorian scruffiness. There was a sprinkling of small businesses, notably an old laundry firm, and some of the houses had become shops. The Montague Hotel, built 1737 and a victim of the Blitz, was the headquarters of the Bristol Madrigal Society for 200 years.

Kingsdown owes much, too, to organizations like the Bristol Civic Society, to the care and concern of local residents and, to be fair, to the reasonableness of the city authorities—when pushed and argued with. Many properties have been rehabilitated with the aid of civic grants. The main controversy in recent years was over the height of the new flats. Ian Nairn, then architectural correspondent of *The Daily Telegraph*, wrote in 1963 of Kingsdown: "The one thing the site cannot stand is a grand gesture." But it was precisely a grand and vulgar gesture of tall towers, masking the Georgian houses behind, that Bristol proposed to allow. After a long dispute over the provision of lifts in blocks that were not officially high enough to merit lifts, the Corporation agreed to four-five storey blocks (with lifts). When built they turned out to be fussy, Meccano-like buildings without grace, raising the old question of why a plain, inoffensive style of functional building has not yet been found in this country. But the residents of Kingsdown Parade and Somerset Street still have their views and the flats blend well enough into the hillside when seen from a distance across the city. The traveller coming into Bristol early by train still sees the windows of Kingsdown flaring in the morning sun.

Below the flats stands what is left of King Square: one intact side of red brick houses of the 1760s, and part of the top side of the square is still impressive though covered with commercial lettering; the Bristol Institute for the Deaf and the Bristol Arts Centre building keep the human element as an acceptable

The Unicorn Hotel and multi-storey car park on Narrow Quay

UNICORN
HOTEL

substitute for the original buildings. In nearby Dighton Street a huge town house of the eighteenth century survives despite fears for its future existence. The flats have kept the names of some of the streets they have replaced, such as Carolina House, and just above them is the charming 'Masons Arms' with its facing of green De Morgan-like tiles.

On the top levels of Kingsdown, a large area of Georgian property in Alfred Street, Paul Street and Oxford Street has gone, decayed beyond rehabilitation according to the authorities. Here an ambitious new housing development, to be called High Kingsdown, is well advanced: a traffic-free settlement of houses with small, high-walled gardens, flats and shops, grouped around and along pedestrian 'walk-ways' with playing spaces for children. This nest is designed to attract a 'professional' community, possibly from the nearby university and Infirmary precincts, people who will want to live near their work and the city's amenities. As an elitist proposal it has already been criticized as high-priced, and therefore privileged, by Labour members of the City Council. But to the non-partisan observer it already looks like an imaginative way of replacing one homogeneous community with another.

High Kingsdown looks down over yet another of Bristol's desolate areas. The Portland Chapel, the second oldest Methodist chapel in the city, closely associated with the one-eyed former soldier Captain Thomas Webb, who caused a stir by preaching in his military scarlet, was closed in early 1970. There are empty, boarded-up eighteenth-century stone houses at the top of St. Michael's Hill opposite the Children's Hospital (its lower windows always full of dolls, gollies and teddy bears to cheer up the gloomy passer-by as well as the children), and as if to cancel out the past as blatantly as possible there is the immense and to many local eyes monstrous outlet chimney built in recent years on the crest of the hill. To be fair, it must be recorded that some Bristolians like it, and have defended it in the Press with Bristol contrariness.

St. Michael's Hill is a curious isolated extension of the old city, climbing a dauntingly steep hill from the church of St. Michael on the Mount Without (Bristol's answer to all those London City churches with odd names). Part of its story belongs to that of the university which has recently bought, pulled down and attrac-

St. Michael's Hill, with Georgian houses gutted and restored by the university tively rebuilt in facsimile some of the eighteenth-century frontages to mask new lecture rooms and offices. St. Michael's Church, with its medieval tower and main body of the 1770s, is a very early version of the Gothic revival, with a spacious, well-lit interior. The trees, lanes and open spaces around it create an attractive breathing space high over the inner city. On the other side of the street are some fine old inns: 'The King David', the 'Colston Arms' and 'The Scotchman and His Pack'. An old sweetshop in a gabled row of houses above the church carries an evocative advertisement for 'Fry's Pure Concentrated Cream'. But the loveliest buildings in a lovely street are those of Colston's Almshouses, founded by Edward Colston in 1691, a low, hipped-roofed, three-sided quadrangle of apartments, with a delicate chapel in the middle of the centre range. Here Bristol charity, Bristol style and Bristol practicality—the almshouses are in active occupation—are expressed with Bristol discreetness. The almshouses can be linked in the pattern of the city's growth of social conscience with the Red Lodge, which stands in Park Row below St. Michael's Hill, between the city and its first extensions. Originally a lodge of Sir John Young's Great House, where he entertained Elizabeth I in 1574, it now belongs to the City Museum and is famous for its superb oak panelling. It was bought by Lady Byron, the poet's widow, for the Bristol reformer, Mary Carpenter, who in 1854 founded there her pioneer Reformatory School for Girls, the first of its kind in the country.

Park Street, the city's most stylish—and impossibly steep—shopping street, the university, Brandon Hill and the surrounding Georgian streets all belong in atmosphere to Clifton. The next distinct early offshoot of the original city is the area around the cathedral and the Lord Mayor's Chapel either side of College Green, though in many ways it seems to look upwards towards the Clifton heights and to have little to do with the sprawling, huddled city below. Already the shops in College Green are indisputably Clifton shops, and the cathedral itself is rich in genteel monuments and tablets to divines and historians, writers and philanthropists, who seem to have belonged to the intellectual life of Clifton and Hotwells rather than to that of central Bristol; and it seemed even more remote from the life of the city in the nineteenth century when the hard-working commercial and philanthropic mood of the city was expressed more in terms of

Nonconformity than of Anglicanism. This aloofness from the city goes back to the cathedral's origins in the Augustinian Abbey founded by Robert Fitzharding in 1140 on a rising plateau well away from the city core. The nave of the abbey seems to have become ruinous before the fourteenth century, although Abbot Knowle, to whom the cathedral owes its magnificent chancel, probably intended to rebuild it. The ruined nave was completely destroyed at the Dissolution and from then until the 1860s the cathedral was a truncated church consisting of a chancel and the two transepts. The abbey became a cathedral in 1542, but its mutilated state seems to have disappointed the occupiers of the see, who tended to use it as a stopping-off place before moving on to a really serious bishopric. Bishop Joseph Butler, author of the famous *Analogy*, was an exception to the practice of marking time at Bristol, though even he stayed only twelve years (1738–50) before moving on to Durham—years notable for his encounter with John Wesley to whom he refused permission to preach in the city churches. The squat, foreshortened, dilapidated cathedral usually stirred travellers to condescension: Defoe thought it "mean"; Celia Fiennes commented on "the Cathedrall which has nothing fine or curious about it"; and an eighteenth-century traveller thought it "the meanest I have seen in England".

G. E. Street's thoughtful and successful new nave of 1868, the restoration of the See in 1897, separating it from Gloucester, and the general nineteenth-century refurbishing has restored the cathedral to life visually; and the exterior cleaning of the last year or so has given it a new charm and lightness in its setting, though some people may have preferred its old weathering and grime. But it is still perhaps not easy for the non-expert to share Sir Nikolaus Pevsner's rapturous enthusiasm for Abbot Knowle's great work of 1298–1330 on the 'choir-limb' of the medieval church. This turned it into a great 'hall' lit, not by a clerestory above the choir as in other churches, but directly from the aisle windows. The aisles are the same height as the central alley (now the chancel), the roof of which is carried direct on unusually high and impressive pillars and arches. Pevsner said, in his Penguin Buildings of England volume on North Somerset and Bristol: "[Abbot Knowle's] work at Bristol from the point of view of spatial imagination . . . is superior to anything else built in England and indeed in Europe at the same time". Sir John Betjeman has described it as "some of the most surprising architecture in Europe". Perhaps this is partly the technical rapture of architectural experts who see and feel more than the layman can. But certainly there is an extraordinary sense of unhampered, harmonious, radiant space; it is a cathedral for the brief, harmonious—intellectual and mystical—Anglicanism of the early seventeenth century, for the spirit of George Herbert. It is a place of some authority as well as of meditation and has spoken incisively in local affairs in recent years through the voice of Bishop Oliver Tomkins. But it remains rather neglected by Bristolians; at most weekday or Saturday Evensongs there are a few casuals like myself listening to the boom and hum of the choir among the vaults at the misty chancel end.

The cathedral by no means exhausts the interest of the College Green area. Attached to the cathedral itself is the great Norman Chapter House, a stone confessional rich with the lozenges, zigzags, spiral-fluting and beading of Norman decoration, symbols of a stylistic culture that easily included Bristol in its Europe-wide embrace. Next to the cathedral stands the 'Norman Arch' or Great Gatehouse, its upper parts much restored in the nineteenth century; Southey recorded in his *Letters from England* that the gatehouse was much used in his time for committing what the law calls 'a nuisance'. The Municipal Library of 1906, designed by Charles Holden, later well known for his London Underground stations of the early 1930s, harmonizes well with the cathedral and the gatehouse; it is a severe, dignified, vaguely fortified building, with hints of Mackintosh's Glasgow Art School present but difficult to identify. The bright, shallow-curved Council House that closes the further end of the triangular green does not really harmonize with anything, though it becomes endearing in time with its flaunting gilt unicorns on the flanking gabled towers and the Merchant Venturer in stone keeping a wary eye on the Finance Committee's activities. Behind the Council House stands Brunel House, a dingy office-building, once the elegant Royal Western Hotel built in 1838–40 to cater for passengers crossing the Atlantic in Brunel's ships, *Great Western* and *Great Britain*. It ceased to be a hotel in 1855—the Atlantic trade went to Liverpool and the *Great Britain* only sailed once from Bristol—and was briefly a Turkish baths and a hotel again before becoming offices. Here stood, despite efforts by Reece Winstone and others to save it, the probable birthplace of William Friese-Greene, the Bristol pioneer of cinematography; and here stood College Street where Coleridge and his Pantoscratic friends lodged.

On the other side of the green from the cathedral stands the modest front of St. Mark's Church, or the Lord Mayor's Chapel, one of the few civically-owned chapels in the country, built as the chapel of the Hospital of St. Mark and bought by the Corporation as far back as 1541. It became the official place of worship for the mayor and corporation in 1721. The chapel was founded about 1230 by Maurice de Gaunt, whose great house stood originally behind the church on a site occupied by the Red Maids' School from the 1840s until just before the 1914–18 war. St. Mark's has a dark Early English nave, heraldic with monuments and escutcheons, a Decorated aisle and a Perpendicular chancel and tower. The Poyntz chapel is a striking late Perpendicular chantry which contains sixteenth-century Spanish tiles, relics of the city's old trade with the Peninsula. It is a dark, challenging church, down a few steps in space and back many centuries in atmosphere: a church in which to thank a watchful deity for the safe return of one's argosies abroad. One re-emerges from the gloom into the bright street. Bristol roars past and it is difficult at times to remember what the green looked like before 1950 when the great trees were cut down, the nineteenth-century replica of the old High Cross removed and the level of the grass lowered in order not to dwarf the new Council House. Then it looked like a cathedral close indeed with its tall, clustering trees. It was a great place for strolling, for meeting one's girl, for taking a rest before tackling Park Street. One of my grandmothers, who lived across the city in St. Paul's, used regularly to sit there for a whole afternoon to watch the people. It was a green heart, a breathing space in a busy city, the essential interval in the relentless rhythm of Bristol. But who sits there to watch the people now? Who meets his girl friend there now? The Victorians' obsession with cluttered, devious space, with nooks and dens, arbours and tree-shaded walks, made it a garden for people. Our obsession with space and pattern has made it a geometrical, depopulated desert, though perhaps when the young trees reach their maturity it will regain some of its beauty.

Queen Victoria on her plinth, the last survivor of the old green, turns her back on it all and looks steadfastly downhill, past the Royal Hotel and the site of St. Augustine's Church, ruined by bombs and finally demolished in 1962, to the Centre, which may be the centre but is certainly not the heart of Bristol. Until just after the 1914–18 war the Floating Harbour came right up to St. Augustine's Bridge near the end of Clare Street. Tudor Edwards in his evocative short book on Bristol (Batsford, 1952) describes the sort of scene Bristolians took for granted earlier in this century: "The ships seemed to be moored in the very streets, and on regatta days in summer, when freshly painted lithe destroyers with bands playing aboard came to rest in the heart of the garlanded Centre, this might have been Marseilles en fête."

Today, Arthur Salmon's "Dutch-like slip of dark water" is covered in by a curiously banal area of roadway and a central island, with grass and flowers, in which nobody sits. Even the name, the Centre, is banal. A newspaper competition in the early 1930s tried to find a more dignified name: Redcliffe Square? Canynges Square? Cabot Way? But most of the competitors settled for what Bristol already called it, the Tramways Centre, or the Centre.

There are only two buildings of any style in the Centre proper: one is the tall, sand-coloured tower of the Bristol and West Building Society, built in 1968. The seventeen-storey building has had some adverse criticism; but its height and slimness are not out of place in a city of tall church spires and towers. The other is the lively, springing new building in front of the Colston Hall; out of place but pleasant in itself. In Colston Avenue, the continuation of the Centre away from the water, stands the pillared Roman Catholic Church of St. Mary on the Quay, built for the Irvingite sect in 1839 by R. S. Pope: recently, plans to pull it down and replace it with a modern church adapted to the new liturgies were withdrawn after widespread protest and disapproval. The old Artichoke Inn has recently gone; the sombre C.W.S. block near the Bridge Head has been demolished to be replaced by an office block in an unusual octagonal design. The three surviving trees in Colston Avenue still shade the statue of Colston. There is an attractive plan for changing the Centre into a pedestrian area with all its opportunities for gardens, kiosks, cafés and entertainments. Certainly it ought to be largely freed of traffic and given over to strollers. At present the crowds gather on the broad pavement outside the Hippodrome Theatre; but there is no real centre. The crowds are all going somewhere else: to the Hippodrome, to the Theatre Royal in King Street, to the Entertainment Centre in Frogmore Street, to the steak-bars of the old flower market, to pubs and clubs and finally to bus stops and taxi ranks. There is little to keep them in the Centre itself, though it could still become the 'centre' in a more imaginative and human sense.

Theatre-goers walking from their bus stops in the Centre to the Theatre Royal turn the corner where the C.W.S. building was, leave the Bristol and West tower and the bewildering chaos of traffic near the Bridge Head, and enter legendary Bristol. It is difficult to write of King Street and Queen Square except in Wardour Street language. The square is the largest Georgian square in Britain, and one of the loveliest, scarred though it is by the busy diagonal road across it and by a few unseemly buildings. King Street is arguably the most interesting and attractive historical street in Britain: fortunately it is now part of a scheduled preservation area, a 'museum street'—though let's hope this does not mean preserving the life out of it—not to be tampered with at the peril of Bristol's soul and pride. Even the most 'forward-looking' Bristolians feel respectful towards King Street, though they did not prevent the Robinson building from looming over it from the other side of the Harbour. It was the first complete street laid out on the flat ground of the marsh outside the city walls. Called King Street in honour of the Restoration, in the 1660s it was new and much wider than the average Bristol street. Its best-known feature visually is the great half-timbered range of houses of 1664 known as the 'Llandoger Trow' from the pub that forms part of it—the name, by no means as old as the buildings themselves, derives from the flat-bottomed trows or boats that sailed across from Chepstow and the Wye Valley where they were built at Llandogo. The towering three-storey building with its gables and oriels is now a Berni restaurant, an acceptable popular use for it.

The half-timbered buildings in King Street are not quite what they seem. They mark a sort of West Country conservatism in domestic architecture: they look Elizabethan or Jacobean, but they all date from after the Restoration. In contrast, Number 6 is a handsome front of about 1700 (built on to a timber-framed house of the 1660s) with a shell hood, once well known as the Bristol headquarters of the British Council. Opposite, St. Nicholas's Almshouses of 1652 have been restored in the 1960s and are occupied. Next door the great Palladian façade of William Halfpenny's Coopers' Hall (1743–44) towers above the street; in 1970 it was gutted and masked in scaffolding as it was being adapted as the new entrance front and foyer for the Theatre Royal. The pokey Edwardian entrance had already come down. The theatre—the history of which is taken up in a later chapter—was closed for nearly two years.

Further up the street towards the Centre stands the former Public Library, a strong, sedate stone building of 1739–40 by Thomas Paty, the Bristol architect. This was one of the first public libraries in the country, famous for its connection with Coleridge, who kept his books out too long and, when asked to return them, remonstrated that he could not get through immense tomes in Greek in a few weeks whatever the library trustees might be able to do. On the corner stand the charming shell-pink-washed Merchant Venturers' Almshouses (1696–99), built for retired merchant sailors and still in use; and at the very end of the street, until it was destroyed in the German raids, stood the seventeenth-century Hall of the Merchant Venturers, established in 1551 and the only one remaining of the ancient guilds. It is now chiefly a charitable society, maintaining the King Street Almshouses, St. Nicholas' Almshouses also in King Street, and Colston's Almshouses in St. Michael's Hill. Master and Wardens hold office for one year and it is still a local honour to be a member. At the waterside end the regular sand-ships add the necessary maritime theme to Bristol's most symbolic street: water, ships, trade, theatre, food and drink, literature, conviviality and charity.

It is no museum, though. There is a newsagent's, a betting-shop, canned music from a morning caff, and there used to be wisps of straw from passing fruit and vegetable lorries. There is not much traffic and often not many people, except when the theatre-audiences pass to and fro, the diners-out make for the 'Llandoger' and other more recent eating places, or the locals for the 'Old Duke', the stylish, intimate Georgian pub opposite the Llandoger. On summer Sunday evenings the street is so quiet you can hear a sedan-chairman stir in his nap in neighbouring Queen Square.

The square, named for Queen Anne after her visit in 1702, is so large that something of its impressiveness is lost through sheer size. When the leaves are out on the trees it is difficult to see the farther sides, and it is certainly possible for a stranger to drive through it by bus along Redcliffe Way and not realize that he had been through a Georgian square. Perhaps this is just as well: the extent of the square and the masking trees hide certain disproportions between eighteenth-century houses on one side, the balconied terraces of the 1830s on the other, that replaced the buildings destroyed in the riots of 1831, and some late nineteenth-century outsiders like the gay but unsuitable Port of Bristol Authority building and a few bricky warehouse fronts. (The riots, the bloodiest event in the history of a city that generally kept the nastier aspects of history subordinate to its business interests, are really part of Bristol's political history, discussed elsewhere.)

The square is rich in ghosts, led socially by William III, whose superb equestrian statue by Rysbrack dominates the centre of the through traffic and was said to gallop round the square at night when nobody was looking. David Hume worked briefly in an office at Number 16, sacked for presuming to improve his employer's written English. Elsewhere lived Woodes Rogers, the privateer, who discovered Alexander Selkirk on Juan Fernandez and, according to an unlikely local legend, brought him back to his Bristol house where Selkirk (also improbably) told his story to Defoe. Burke lodged at Number 19 during the critical election of 1774. On the site of Number 37 stood the first American consulate in Britain (1792), an association which brings into mind those early proud years of the new republic when their consuls and ambassadors dressed in sombre republican black, without court swords, orders or ruffles, to show their republican loyalties in contrast to the monarchistic fal-lals of Europe. Number 37 recalls the Salem Custom House and its receiver, Nathaniel Hawthorne, himself later a visitor to Bristol, and all the other Americans, Henry Adams among them, who came to Bristol looking for their beginnings.

Queen Square, not unlike Portland and Brunswick Squares on the other side of the city, has been by-passed by time and shifts of population. Though built as a residential square, it found no room to expand residentially and quickly became commercial and professional, stiff with lawyers, architects, excisemen and vice-consuls, as it is today. It is enclosed by water on three sides and until Redcliffe Way was sliced across it, was a quiet 'backwater' with railings and walks and Edwardian children trundling hoops and—until well into our century—sheep safely grazing. One of the hopes of the supporters of the plan to put a road bridge across the end of St. Augustine's Reach (thus ending its shipping life) is that Redcliffe Way can be closed and all but local traffic drained away from the square. Perhaps then those unlikely sheep can return to their pastures.

Fine Georgian houses hide in neighbouring streets, particularly in Queen Charlotte Street between the square and King Street. In Prince Street between Queen Square and the Reach there is a magnificent run, as they say in the book trade, of early eighteenth-century houses, tall, ornamented, pilastered, doomed. On one side of the street is the new Unicorn Hotel and its multi-storey car park adjoining behind a huge screen of open concrete lozenges, all fitting admirably into the space left by some old warehouses: too late, alas, for guests to look out of their windows at berthing ships. At the waterside end of Prince Street stands the noble Bush's warehouse of about 1835–36, a brooding, rough-stone masterpiece, which in its semi-disused old age became a subject of contention between planners and preservationists. The preservationists wanted to keep it as an irreplaceable typical building of its time and style (noble as it is, it also looks rather like a mid-Victorian New Model Prison). The planners wanted to cut some of it off to make room for the road-bridge across the Reach. A simpler solution, of course, would be to keep the warehouse and to take the traffic from Queen Square by re-routing all fast traffic well distant from the city centre. In 1974 a happier solution prevailed. The warehouse was gutted, keeping its outward appearance, and rebuilt inside to house offices and new premises for Bristol's famous Arnolfini Gallery—the sort of practical compromise one expects of Bristol at its best.

From the Prince Street bridge, the eye takes in one of the Famous Bristol Views. Some ships still lie along The Grove, the old quay where timber and sand is still unloaded. The circle of Bristol's first, vigorous extensions is complete: the faubourgs—elegant, shabby, busy, dead, decayed, restored—still lead their own lives apart from the old core of the city, though their history is incomplete without that of the great inland port they grew up with and will undoubtedly outlive.

IV

LIFE AND DEATH OF A GREAT PORT

IN THE city's heraldic seal the sailor in his medieval bark still makes port under the battlements of the castle, and Bristol still remembers the sea, though Bristolians do not look very nautical and the trade in the city docks is a mere hulk of what it was when a forest of ships' masts swayed along the quays from the Cumberland Basin to St. Augustine's Bridge and Bristol Bridge. In the early 1970s gulls still lurked for tit-bits from ships, unaware that the city docks might well be empty of sea-going vessels by the end of the 1970s. The coastal sandships unloaded opposite King Street and a few other ships ventured up the Harbour to dock at Prince's Wharf and complete the dockscape as seen from Neptune's statue in the Centre. Neptune now has nothing more nautical than sailing dinghies in his immediate view.

Charles Hill's, Bristol's one remaining shipyard, was busier than it had been for some time, engaged in building oil-rig service ships and starting on the rehabilitation of Brunel's *Great Britain* on her return in July, 1970; though Hill's would have to face the certainty of closing or moving its shipyard before 1980 with the closing of the city waterways to large ships. The Rowlandsonian dockside clutter still lay around, as it does in the famous early eighteenth-century 'primitive' painting of Broad Quay, now in the City Art Gallery, with its Bristol 'sleds' hauling goods over the cellar-riddled cobbles and children see-sawing on wine-barrels, while the quay walls, in curious perspective, seem to be climbing a hill. In the early 1970s there were still a few cranes and bollards, looped chains across the cobbles, rotting lighters bumping wearily into each other in the oily swell caused by the controlled flow of the Avon and Frome through the Floating Harbour. Huddles of tarpaulined dinghies and yachts rode out the winter in the Bathurst Basin and the polished tram-driver's handle in the control cabin of the Redcliffe swing bridge opened the bascule for fewer and fewer ships.

Down at the Cumberland Basin, unawed by the dashing new road fly-over system that has taken the place of the old Ashton swing bridge—and won a Civic Trust Award for its combination of clean functionalism and attractive landscaping—a little W. W. Jacobs world still existed. On a bright autumn morning a man in a blue wharfinger's sweater would come out on to the 'hard' in front of the Old Dock Cottages (1830), with their wall-creepers and white-painted flower-tubs, look at the lock water and go back in again. In the Nova Scotia Inn at lunchtime there were hot pasties and beer, wharfish chatter and old nautical prints and photographs on the walls. Sun, slap of water on lock-walls, autumn flowers in tubs, a berthed tug restless on its cable, surviving fragments of Brunel's locks, the Italian-looking pumping house, swans browsing, mooring buoys bobbing, a slumbering dredger, piles of timber, the great terraces of Clifton condescending from their perches above the Basin, all waiting to burst into activity on the brief tides—this was the lingering maritime scene that many Bristol people feared would disappear for ever with the closing of the city docks.

Yet the possibility that Bristol might one day have to abandon its original docks has existed for more than a century. One of the world's unlikeliest great ports, apart from artificial inland ports like Manchester and Duisberg, Bristol lies about 7 miles from the Channel up a winding, muddy, treacherous tidal river. The river itself lies many miles up the largest inlet in Western Europe, an inland sea full of menacing sandbanks, bewildering navigation channels and brimming tides, the second highest in the world. The Channel was once a graveyard of drowned ships and sailors; cemeteries on both sides of the water abound in headstones over empty graves, recording whole families of seamen "drowned off Hartland Point" or "lost with the S.S. *Resolution* off Mumbles".

But there is no sea-vista from Bristol as there is from New York and Naples, no estuary view as there is at Liverpool and London. The Channel breezes enjoyed by the upper parts of Clifton do not blow down on to the docks, where the air is the more characteristic warm, damp heavy air of the inland West Country. Unlike most sea-ports Bristol has its docks in the heart of the city not away from it in a special quarter as at Glasgow, Southampton and Liverpool. The waters of the Harbour pass under the heights of Clifton and Brandon Hill and lie close to the cathedral,

St. Mary Redcliffe and the once fashionable Queen Square before they come to any district that looks really industrial or dock-like.

This curiously remote position for a large port, which derives from a pre-Conquest desire to use the long river, the Gorge and the surrounding hills as protection against marauding Danish and Turkish pirates in the Channel, has been a problem for Bristol over the centuries. Already in the eighteenth-century sea-captains and ship-owners were beginning to wonder if the strenuous, lengthy and expensive business of docking at Bristol was worth it. There was the wait in the Kingroad for a favourable tide upriver; sailing or being towed by men in rowing boats up the Avon; waiting for a berth in the city; risking your ship's back being broken or timbers strained when the tide went out and the ships settled on the mud; and the unusually high port dues. The tidal variations on the Avon are dramatic and alarming; from a trickle between grey mudbanks to a broad river nearly 200 feet across at places. (Every visitor knows the muddy trickle, but there are local inhabitants who will claim, with more than a touch of dry Bristol humour, that they have lived there all their lives and *never* seen high tide.) The mudbanks are steep and the river winds; one of the most frequent subjects in Reece Winstone's books of photographs of old Bristol is the stranded ship lying broken-backed across the river at low tide. Fog is a hazard, too; after the notorious fog of 1st November 1929 had lifted, eleven ships were found stranded up and down the river. In addition, the twists of the course and the high cliffs of the Gorge, that would suddenly deprive a ship of wind, made it usually impossible for a ship to reach the docks under sail. They were necessarily towed up by horses or by fleets of rowing boats—a favourite subject of eighteenth-century landscape artists, including the young Turner—and the fees, added to the much criticized port and wharfage dues, often made shipowners prefer to lie at the river mouth and unload into lighters, which then had to take their own turn at making their way upriver.

Despite the difficulties of the journey up the river the vigour and enterprise of Bristol commerce made the trip worthwhile nevertheless. The problems of navigation only began to threaten Bristol's prosperity when at the turn of the eighteenth and nineteenth centuries the city started to lose its place as second port of the kingdom to Liverpool, with its miles of accessible estuary quays. In 1804–09, after decades of complacent delays and crippling self-interest, Bristol built its New Cut, a new channel for the Avon, while sealing off the old course of the Avon and Frome through the city as a non-tidal or floating harbour. No longer did the berthed ships break their backs as the tide ebbed from the quays. But then the ships of the nineteenth century began to be too big for the Avon and the locks. Bristol never recovered its leading position among British ports, and never recovered the Atlantic trade lost to Liverpool. But the eventual construction—again after much delay and lack of imagination—of the Channel docks at Avonmouth and Portishead in the latter decades of the last century enabled the city to remain an important port until the present day and the present crisis.

Bristolians tend to be rather apologetic about their river and its perverse habit of being out rather than in. It is not a river at all in its role as the Floating Harbour, and the New Cut is a shabby, muddy canal-like stretch of little charm. Both Frome and Avon are prone to flooding and an elaborate system of sluices and outfalls has not completely tamed them.

Yet it is a lovely river in its upper reaches where it rises in the Cotswolds not far from the source of the Thames, and where it flows past Chippenham and Lacock, Melksham and Limpley Stoke. At Bath it becomes 'picturesque' as it idles under Pulteney Bridge, over the weir and past the Parade Gardens. It is pastoral at Saltford and Keynsham and still pleasant as it winds in to the suburbs, past St. Anne's Wood, Brislington and through the old industrial valley of Crew's Hole, to fork at Netham Weir into the New Cut and the Feeder Canal (and eventually the Floating Harbour) and be swallowed up in the hard-working city.

The Avon becomes part of a scene of great topographical and geological splendour as it passes beneath the towering, quarry-shattered cliffs of the Avon Gorge and the hanging woods of Rownham and Nightingale Valley. St. Vincent's Rocks and the other heights must have been even lovelier 100 years ago or more, before they were so eroded by quarrying; on the other hand, the growth of the woods on the Somerset side has softened the scene considerably from the bare, Alpine look of the Gorge in nineteenth-century photographs. (A monstrous proposal to build a large hotel close to the Suspension Bridge, and thus ruin the Gorge, was finally quashed by the Environment Secretary.)

Here grow a number of specialized or rare flowers and plants, including the Bristol rock cress and the 'Flower of Bristow', a type of scarlet lychnis associated with the city from the Middle Ages, when it may have been brought back by Crusaders or traders from the Levant. The plant does well in July and August in herbaceous borders in and around the city and its colour has been borrowed for some of Bristol University's degree hoods. From the sixteenth century when pioneer botanists like William Turner and John Gerard scrambled about "Saynt Vincentis rock a little from Bristow", naturalists have come to the Gorge looking for rare plants. Young Southey knew the cliffs and riverside well from scouring them for the bee and fly orchis, and in the early nineteenth century Leigh Woods and Nightingale Valley were favourite haunts of a group of young landscape painters gathered around Bristol's talented native artist, W. J. Müller, who died too young to confirm his remarkable promise. Today the Gorge thunders with the noise of heavy lorries along the Portway, the road to Avonmouth. Some of the great slabs of rock have been defaced by massive graffiti in paint, and the foolhardy still try their luck on rock-faces they would shy away from in North Wales.

The Gorge remains a noble and awesome sight, though, until the heights fall away on either side to the flatter country towards Avonmouth and Portishead and Brunel's gossamer bridge disappears from sight as the river twists and snakes. The Horseshoe Bend near Shirehampton is still a navigational problem, though the old *Great Britain* took it calmly enough on her return trip. The name of the Hungroad, where ships moored to rings and chains fixed in the riverside rocks to wait for high tide, survives in Hungroad Cottages. On the Somerset shore Pill, once famous as the home of Channel pilots—they have moved up in the world since and now live in Stoke Bishop or other unnautical suburbs—still looks like a small West Country seaport out of Charles Kingsley. The river passes under the great pylons carrying the M5 road bridge and the motorway on its way to Exeter; then it broadens muddily into Kingroad and the grey slopping Channel.

The development of the port in history is still traceable from what we can see today. The first shipping must have berthed beneath the castle walls, though at an early date the bridge must have prevented larger ships passing it and brought about the construction of new quays along the Welsh Back and Redcliff Backs. The early trade dealt with the south of Ireland as well as with other regions of England; fish and hides and corn were brought from Galway, Waterford and Limerick—in the early Middle Ages payment was partly made in slaves from England—and the Irish trade was always an important one, though no very distinct Irish community seems to have settled in Bristol. The 'Dublin' shed on Broad Quay was a landmark into this century. The early wine trade with Gascony and Bordeaux followed and when this was interrupted by the Hundred Years War Bristol ships went further, looking for wine in Spain and Portugal. Bristol's connections with the Peninsula were close: tangible relics of the link are the late medieval azulejo tiles from Spain to be seen in St. Mark's on College Green.

Despite Barbary pirates and home-grown wreckers, the city's ships ventured out to the fringes of the known world. As early as 1420 they were going regularly by compass to Iceland through the North Atlantic storms. There they may have heard stories of Vinland, the distant Western shore explored several centuries before by Eric the Red, now widely accepted as a pre-Columbian discovery of America. Certainly the possibility of another continent beyond the Atlantic was an idea known about the Bristol waterside before Columbus and before the mythical visit supposed by some speculative historians to have been paid to Bristol by Columbus. In July 1480 John Jay left Bristol in a ship of 80 tons looking for a land, known as the Island of Brasil, reported by Bristol sailors off course. He found nothing, but others followed and it could be that Bristol sailors did land in America before Columbus and the Cabots. One of the reasons why John Cabot came to Bristol was almost certainly because more was known about the possibility and risks of finding land beyond the Atlantic in Bristol than anywhere else. The city was the forge of ideas and ambitions in the search for America, and loyal Bristolians still like to believe that the name of the new continent came, not from the Italian Amerigo Vespucci, but from the Bristol merchant, Richard Amerycke (or Ap Meyrick), friend and patron of Cabot.

The story of the Cabots is Bristol's greatest romance, commemorated in civic tapestries, aldermanic speeches, headmasters' reports, school essays, in the Cabot Tower and the Cabot Ward

College Green: the Council House and Bristol Cathedral

Freed from all storms the tempest and the rage
Of billows here we spend our age
Our weather beaten vessels here repair
And from the Merchants kind and generous care
Find harbour here, no more we put to sea
Until we launch into Eternity
And lest our Widows whom we leave behind
Should want relief they too a shelter find
Thus all our anxious cares and sorrows cease
Whilst our kind Guardians turn our toils to ease
May they be with an endless sabbath blest
Who have afforded unto us this rest.

and the Port of Bristol Authority tug *Cabot.* The epic of the Italian free-lance navigator Giovanni Cabotto coming to Bristol with wife and family, winning the reluctant support of the city merchants and the goodwill of Henry VII, and sailing in his tiny ship *Matthew* to make, on 24th June 1497, the first recorded landing on the mainland of America, is so dramatic that it seems a pity to qualify it. But it was not so romantic as the legend suggests. Cabot was a professional explorer, looking not specifically for a new continent but for a new source of wealth, the spices of the East, as Columbus had. He hoped to use Bristol to help him find it; Bristol was hoping for a share of the wealth and Henry VII was no doubt hoping for the biggest share of all. What Cabot found was not Cathay as he thought but plain, empty New England. He did not stay long and did not bring back much, but he was a famous man; an Italian observer wrote: "Vast honour is paid to him, he dresses in silk, and the English run after him like mad people." In 1498 he set out again with five ships to make the same landfall and sail down the coast. A storm struck the fleet, Cabot never returned and if the others did their crestfallen return was not recorded. Cabot's son Sebastian set sail with the king's backing in 1508 to find the North-west Passage through the Arctic ice. He may have sailed from Bristol but there is no record that he did and none of where he went, though he may have entered Hudson's Bay. He found Henry VIII on the throne on his return and the new king was not interested in Atlantic exploration. The brief Golden Age of Bristol exploration across the Atlantic faded, though there were numerous attempts to revive it in the succeeding years.

In 1576 Martin Frobisher sailed into Bristol from the west with two Esquimaux who paddled their canoes on the Avon for the citizens' interest and then succumbed to the climate. In 1631 Captain Thomas James made a serious attempt to find the North-west Passage that has haunted the English imagination until the Franklin tragedy. In 1603 Captain Martin Pring—whose splendidly ornate monument can be seen in St. Stephen's Church—sailed to New England to found a colony, a voyage inspired by the enthusiasm of Richard Hakluyt, a canon of Bristol cathedral, whose collection of notable voyages is one of the documentary classics of English. Prospects for the colony were good, but on his return Pring—repeating Sebastian Cabot's experience with

Modern office buildings above the Merchant Venturers almshouses in King Street

Henry VIII—found the parsimonious James I on the throne instead of Elizabeth and nothing came of the scheme.

Despite the energy and enterprise of Bristol sailors, or explorers backed by Bristol, colonial ventures in this first phase of the city's part in transatlantic history tended to fade out. Expeditions went astray. Colonies failed. The Spaniards had already appropriated the rich southern part of the hemisphere and British explorers were advised to keep to the fish of the north and renounce the gold and silver of the south. Bristol at first was not willing to invest in America; perhaps what the Cabots had told them about the barrenness of New England persuaded them to stick to the profitable Newfoundland fishing. Perhaps they distrusted Sebastian Cabot who in his later years made himself a figure of mystery and was ambiguous even about whether or not he had been born in Bristol.

The story demonstrates the curiously intermittent nature of Bristol's enterprise over the centuries, the alternation of bursts of energy and daring with long periods of caution, retrenchment and stagnation. In many cases the energy and daring are associated with the arrival in the city of outsiders or foreigners—the Normans, the Cabots, James Loudon McAdam, Humphrey Davy, Thomas Beddoes, Brunel, among others—and the retrenchment and stagnation with the caution of the native Bristolians. It is as if the energy and inventiveness of the natives needed some more reckless outside influence to set them in motion.

Though the city's prosperity undoubtedly declined throughout the Tudor period, by the middle of the seventeenth century Bristol had settled happily enough for calculated risks and began to play its dominant part in the origins of the thirteen American States, in the growth of the tobacco trade from Virginia and in the acquisition of the rich West India trade, mainly in sugar. Numerous Bristol names occur in this busy century of British colonization. Sir Fernando Gorges, of Wraxall across the Avon in Somerset, a West Country gentleman and soldier, was largely responsible for the foundation of the Virginia Company in 1606. He helped finance Pring's voyage of 1603 and also Captain John Smith's famous exploration of New England. Charles I granted Gorges the province of Maine, and despite the initial failure to colonize this tract (which later became New Hampshire and Maine, where he is honoured as founder) he kept urging the settlement of New England. He spent £20,000 on his life-long interest in the colonization, and died at Ashton Court, also just across the Avon into Somerset, in 1647, saddened by the defeat of the king who had shown a sympathetic interest in his work.

A Bristol captain, Thomas James, was the first Englishman to winter in Canada (1631). Another Bristol sailor, Admiral Sir William Penn, captured Jamaica for England in 1655, and in 1681 his son William was granted a lease of land beyond the Delaware by Charles II and sailed in 1682 to take possession of the province which became Pennsylvania. William Penn is connected with Bristol through his marriage to Hannah Callowhill at the Friends' Meeting House—now part of Quakers' Friars—in 1696. Penn, Callowhill and Hollister (another Bristol Quaker name) are the names of streets in modern Philadelphia. By the 1620s Bristol had sixty privateers, many of them belonging to the Merchant Venturers' Society, with government letters of marque to capture French and Spanish merchantmen. By 1670 the city had 6,000 tons of shipping, one half of which was employed in the importation of tobacco. By the end of the seventeenth century Britain's colonies in America had been well founded, largely, some Bristol historians will claim, through the efforts of Bristol men. The tradition of daring voyages was carried into the next century when, in 1708, Captain Woodes Rogers, with Dampier as his pilot, made one of the greatest Bristol voyages, privateering enterprise though it was. During the voyage he rescued Alexander Selkirk from his exile on Juan Fernandez and allowed him a £800 share of the total loot of £170,000.

The links with the origins of modern America are so strong that it is surprising to find that Bristol is on comparatively few American tourist itineraries: London, Oxford, Stratford, but not the city where so much of it began. Perhaps the shadow of the slave-trade hangs over it too dauntingly. If the discovery of the American mainland and the development of the first American colonies are Bristol's bright epic, the city's part in the slave-trade is her tragedy. Bristol played a major part in the trade through the late seventeenth and early eighteenth centuries—in the first nine years of the trade she had sixty ships transporting 170,000 Negroes from Africa to the plantations—until Liverpool's take-over eased the West Country port out of a traffic her conscience, assailed by Wesley, Wilberforce, Clarkson and others, was beginning to feel uneasy about. Retrospectively, it has lent a sinister air to eighteenth-century Bristol in historical novels and colourful history books: in well-researched novels like Marguerite Steen's *The Sun is My Undoing* and other Bristol stories.

Bristol is curiously obsessed with the slave-trade and curiously ignorant about it, boasting about it on occasion like a reformed sinner at Marble Arch. There is still a wide-spread myth in the city that eighteenth-century Bristol swarmed with chain-gangs of naked Negroes. I have heard the barmaid in a quayside pub explain to visitors that slaves were kept in the cellars and auctioned off in the bar-parlour; and I have heard the massive grey stone warehouse in Denmark Street, now a wine warehouse, speculated about as a possible slave-prison. Blackboy Hill, the unofficial but accepted name for the last slope of Whiteladies Road before the Downs, is assumed to take its name from the prevalence of black slaves in eighteenth-century Bristol. A local man, interested in the history of his city, told me that there were a lot of very dark people in Bristol, probably due to the slave trade. Even E. H. W. Meyerstein, Chatterton's learned and indefatigable biographer, thought that the sight of slaves might have inspired the poet's *African Eclogues*.

The slave-trade was, of course, a three-way one. Ships laden with goods sailed to the Guinea coast of Africa where the goods were exchanged for slaves, who were then, in appalling conditions, transported across the dreaded 'middle passage' to the West Indies or to America. The slavers got the best price they could and brought the money back to peaceful, civilized Bristol, where the merchants dined well in Kingsdown and had their daughters taught lady-like accomplishments. Probably no slave-ship with a human cargo ever came to the port; no slaver would have risked the lives of his charges in such a climate.

But this does not mean that Bristol saw no Negroes. A number returned with their masters, when they retired, to continue working as body-servants or as ladies' pages, a fashion of the time. Dr. Johnson had a Negro servant, an ex-slave, whom he cherished and provided for on his death. It has been speculated that at some point in the later eighteenth century there were as many as 20,000–30,000 African Negroes in Britain, and of these many were likely to have been in Bristol or Liverpool, where they would have been conspicuous in the streets. Some were returned to slavery after their masters' deaths. Some were provided for by their masters, a number becoming inn-keepers or prize-fighters, much admired and highly priced in a city always interested in pugilism.

It is possible that the sight of real Negroes in the streets may have helped to prick the city's conscience about the trade. Here were breathing human beings who were otherwise statistics in a slaver's bill of lading. The growth of anti-slavery feeling was slow and confused but genuine, despite the fact that it also coincided with a natural decline in the trade through economic causes. Respectable Christian merchants, like Edward Colston and later John Pinney, believed that God had provided the Negroes for their use, otherwise his displeasure would have been shown in some way. But some Bristolians, notably the Quakers first, then the Methodists, a few merchants and a number of ships' officers who had served on slavers, decided that God *had* shown his displeasure through their own uneasiness over the trade, and the growing feeling against it was focused and organized by the intrepid reformer, Thomas Clarkson, who arrived in Bristol in 1787 full of anxiety at "attempting to subvert one of the branches of the commerce of the great place which was then before me". In fact he was not received all that badly. Many helped him; even the Merchant Venturers allowed him to visit their Hall and consult records. He talked to disaffected sailors in taverns like the 'Seven Stars' alongside St. Thomas's Church, trying to get them, usually unsuccessfully, to give evidence against cruel slaver-captains. Clarkson found Bristol rather ashamed of the trade: "everybody seemed to execrate it, though no one thought of its abolition."

Ironically, the collapse of the trade was due more to economic conditions than to abolitionist agitation. The American War had greatly reduced Bristol's overseas trade and the slave traffic never recovered. It went into a rapid decline in the 1790s as Wilberforce, using Clarkson's evidence, began his long battle against slavery in the House of Commons. The adverse effect of the French wars of the 1790s on Bristol banking damaged what was left of the trade and when Parliament finally decided to abolish it in 1807 Bristol was not greatly stirred; it had already quietened its conscience about a trade that it had been forced to abandon by economic pressure.

The city has still not quite come to terms with its slaving past.

though. The myth of slave-gangs in the streets lingers on as though it were more acceptable than the hypocritical realities of the trade. Some of the dockside alleyways are thick with guilt still, as R. L. Stevenson sensed, and the suspicious streak in the Bristol temperament may have been strengthened by the city's experiences with the relentlessly inquiring abolitionists. When emancipation of the West Indian slaves came in 1833 Bristol's interest suffered a death blow and the city went into the long decline of the early Victorian period, a stagnation already noted by foreign visitors shortly after Waterloo.

The decline was inevitable, perhaps. Despite attempts to build docks at Sea Mills (remnants can still be seen) and at Hotwells during the eighteenth century, it was not until William Jessop's plans for a floating harbour were accepted in 1802—Jessop, a pupil of Smeaton and already an engineer with a national reputation, had first submitted them fourteen years before—that Bristol began to take itself in hand. By then, though, the best of the Atlantic trade was already passing to Liverpool, and the new harbour and the lock system at the Cumberland Basin presented problems of drainage, silting and tidal clearance. The entrance locks were thought too narrow by many users, and when the *Great Britain* left the port in 1844 she had to be helped through the junction lock by a timber cradle and almost became jammed in the north entrance lock.

Nevertheless this was the harbour which saw the building and launching of Brunel's two superb pioneer ships, the *Great Western* and the *Great Britain*, which ironically hastened the decline of the city docks: their dimensions proved the feasibility of large ships and the larger ships inspired by them finally could not get up the Avon. The *Great Western*, launched in 1838 from Patterson's yard, was intended to be the first steam-ship to cross the Atlantic entirely by steam. The idea of the ship is said to have come from a bantering remark of Brunel's when a director of the Great Western Railway expressed concern about the length of the line. "Why not make it longer," Brunel replied, "and have a steam-boat go from Bristol to New York and call it the Great Western?" Thomas Guppy, another director (the irrepressible Guppy, who danced on the roof of a carriage during the first G.W.R. run from London to Bristol) seized the idea and formed the Great Western Steamship Company. The story of the voyage is a small, half-forgotten epic: the doubts as to whether the ship could carry enough coal for the voyage and the fact that it carried more than enough; the fire that made most of the passengers cancel their passages; the race with the heroic smaller Irish Channel steamer *Sirius*, which had set off first but by a shorter route from Cork.

The voyage confirmed the possibility of a regular service by steamship between Britain and America; but again Liverpool stepped in, in the person of Samuel Cunard, and snatched the contract for carrying transatlantic mail. Brunel decided to go one better and build an iron ship with propellers not paddles. The *Great Britain* was launched in 1843 by Prince Albert to notable civic celebrations and public enthusiasm. But she had a rough time getting down the Avon and thereafter sailed from Liverpool. Brunel went on to his giant *Great Eastern*, which was built in London and was generally a commercial failure though it heralded the age of the great liners. His health ruined, worn out by years of daemonic overwork, he died in 1859 aged 53. In the early 1860s Bristol, almost guiltily, set about completing his great Suspension Bridge at Clifton.

The *Great Western* seems almost a toy to us in retrospect. Even the model in the City Museum fails to convey how large she must have seemed at the time, with her 205-foot keel, then the longest in existence. She crossed the Atlantic sixty-four times in all, a lovely ship with her wooden hull and man-o'-war lines. But her owners failed to provide sister ships and lost the mail contract to Cunard. The *Great Western* was broken up at Vauxhall in 1857. The *Great Britain* is more real to us because of the dramatic return of her battered hulk from the Falkland Islands to Bristol in 1970. She was not only the world's first ocean-going propeller-driven iron ship but the biggest ship in the world in her day. Other new features, such as her watertight bulkheads and fold-down masts, made her a marvel of the age.

Bristol Corporation acquired ownership of the docks in 1848, the first city in Britain to do so. The municipal take-over was linked with the Free Trade movement and was strongly backed by the Merchant Venturers and the Chamber of Commerce. Harbour facilities were greatly improved, the dues made relative to competition with Liverpool and other ports. But the great new iron ships could not come up the river to the city docks and Bristol continued to lose trade. In 1851 the steamship *Demerara*, built by Patterson, who had built the *Great Western*, and the largest ship to be built in Britain after the *Great Britain*, was launched and began her journey down the Avon. At a bend in the river she ran aground and was drastically warped as the tide went out (her figurehead on a building in Colston Avenue was a familiar sight in Bristol for many years). Patterson was ruined and the corporation began to think about where they could build new docks.

Argumentative to the last, even when it concerned their own prosperity, the citizens divided into factions over the new docks. The corporation wanted to turn the whole length of the Avon from the city along the Gorge into a floating dock with a lock at the river mouth, while the merchants favoured open docks at what are now Avonmouth and Portishead. The traders went ahead, fought it out in Parliament, won and built the docks, completing Avonmouth in 1877 and Portishead in 1879. The corporation forgot its objections when the liners started coming to Avonmouth as part of a great boom in world shipping in the latter part of the nineteenth century; wheat came from America, frozen meat from the Argentine, cocoa from the Empire for Fry's and tobacco for Wills'. Bristol's new prosperity as a great world port continued unchecked through two world wars with their inevitable booms and on into the 1960s when the development of containers for cargo carrying, with the large ships needed to carry the containers, set problems for Avonmouth and Portishead as well as for the city docks.

Avonmouth is still an important centre for the importing and distributing of grain, frozen meat, phosphates, ores, cocoa beans, woodpulp, timber and tobacco, though some of its former wine trade has gone to Shoreham and some of its well-known banana trade to Barry across the Channel. About 1,800 vessels, with a total net registered tonnage of 5 million, enter the Port of Bristol each year. In recent years leading imports at Avonmouth have included feeding stuffs for livestock, fertilizers, grain, ores, petroleum spirit; exports, much slighter in volume, have included carbon black, manufactured nearby, petrol and cars from the Midlands—all handled by equipment that makes Avonmouth one of the most highly mechanized ports in Britain.

In the early 1970s the 7 miles of quays and wharfs, with their silos and warehouses, were serviced by some 1,375 workers. But by no means all of these lived in Avonmouth, which still looks like a temporary encampment in many ways. Many of the dock workers prefer to live in Bristol and travel out to work, and a number still live in the St. Paul's–Portland Square area where, curiously enough, the Dockland Settlement does its community work. The human history of Bristol as a port is as odd as the geographical and economic history of the docks. There was, for example, never a real 'dockland' in Bristol, a sailors' quarter distinct from the city centre; though there were once some rough pubs along the Welsh Back. The 'Llandoger Trow' itself, before it became respectable, has seen knives drawn in anger. But where were the brothels and doss-houses of other great ports? Probably few or none, as there was no marked cosmopolitan seafaring population to need them. 'Coal out and grain home' was almost the rule of merchant shipping in the later nineteenth century, and ships which brought grain or cargo for Bristol industries to the docks, usually paid off their crews in Bristol and then sailed across to Cardiff in the care of three or four riggers and a ship's apprentice or two, there to take on coal and sign on a new crew, while the old crew, discharged at Bristol, would travel to some other port to find a new ship. This meant that the sailors who did sign on at Bristol were more often than not in the coastal trade and therefore had their homes in the city, often in Bedminster and Hotwells, and particularly in Redcliffe. If not engaged in the coastal trade they would sail on a regular run like the Bristol City Line's transatlantic service, which was always manned largely by Bristol men. Bristol always had quite a large number of seafaring men, but they were usually locals and did not need the various facilities of a dock quarter.

The bustling, colourful, self-confident life of the city docks earlier in this century is still vividly recalled by Bristolians, particularly by those engaged in it such as Captain C. B. Short, former Dredging Superintendent to the Port of Bristol Authority. In an article in the *Bristol Evening World* in 1953 he recalled many details of a lost world: "the reek of bonded cellars when pavement trap-doors are opened to admit casks"; walking beneath the figureheads of sailing ships; the quays covered by barrels of pungent turpentine and straight-sided resin casks, and small boys rubbing resin into their hands as a protection against caning. At The Grove he would see small wooden, square-sterned barques from Norway with a peculiar windmill between the masts for working the pumps. Near the end of King Street little wooden steamers unloaded ice which slithered along wooden shutes over the roadway. Close to Bristol Bridge fruit and vegetables were unloaded and there he would see Breton ketches, their bereted crews unloading ropes of onions. There was an old shipwright's shop near The Grove, full of figureheads, spars, pulleys and pump boxes, and the shipwright himself with axe and adze. On Wednesday or Saturday evenings the local lads would go to the Cumberland Basin to see the Cork and Waterford boats unload their cargoes of Irish cattle and to follow the beasts and their drovers on the long amble across the city to the cattle market at Temple Meads.

As a former ocean-going sailor, Captain Short recalled his emotions on leaving Bristol at the start of a voyage: "Leaving these friendly quaysides was always rather poignant. A winter evening and the cheerfully-lit tramcars and streets, with people hurrying homewards or going out for the evening; the widening strip of water between, and a few hours later, the flare of a city's lights astern." Bristol had a strong hold on its native seamen, he remembered: "Most of the men who served in these Bristol City steamers did so because, in spite of the rigours of the trade, it brought them home regularly to the old city which, each in his own way, they loved."

The dockmasters and lock-keepers, tug-captains and pilots of the port had and have a particularly tricky job to do. At the Cumberland Basin the dockmaster has to handle all his ships, coming and going, within two and a half hours before high water and within half an hour after high water. Every ship likes to leave up to half an hour before high water, if possible, and in the port's bustling days the deft control of all this traffic was a nerve-racking task, complicated by the vagaries of the tides; at most he has a matter of only five hours to clear the ships. A 38-foot ebb tide, plus the natural flow of the river, plus rain freshets could make it dangerous to leave Bristol on high water on a falling tide. High spring tides, which used to flood the many cellars close to the Floating Harbour, might threaten to rise above the maintained level of the water in the Harbour. In these circumstances special stop-gates are closed against the abnormal tide and these cannot be opened again until the tide has ebbed, thus causing a serious hold-up of traffic at a critical moment. The high tide goes up the New Cut and the lockkeeper at Netham, where the Avon splits into the non-tidal Harbour and the tidal Cut, would have to close his gates against it after much agitated telephoning between dock-masters and lock-keepers. Many of these problems have now greatly diminished with the falling away of traffic, but in the great days the dock officers at Bristol exercised a highly skilled and demanding craft.

Although working in the city docks, close to agreeable pubs and the varied life of the city, must always have been pleasant—working 'down de Mouf' at Avonmouth was always regarded as a step down—Bristol dockers, with a good working record in recent times, experienced some hard years early in the century and back in the 1880s and 90s, during the bitter struggles to get better pay and working conditions for them, struggles led by two local men, Ben Tillett and Ernest Bevin. Tillett, born in the Bristol slums, went to sea after a miserable childhood and eventually settled in the London docks, where he helped to organize the 'Dockers' Tanner' strike of 1889, which ended partly through the mediation of the socially-conscious Cardinal Manning. Tillett then came to Bristol to address a dockers' meeting on the Downs, demanding that they should get a proper share of the increasing prosperity of the city. Through the early years of the new century strikes in many parts of the country, as well as Bristol and Avonmouth, paralysed the ports; families suffered and had to rely on poor relief and soup kitchens. The London dockers came out in August 1911 for three weeks, causing chaos among the transport systems. The Great Western staff at Temple Meads joined the strike and soldiers with fixed bayonets guarded the station. Tillett brought the London dockers out again in 1912, but Bevin, the country lad who had come to Bristol and risen rapidly as a union official, recommended to the Bristol dockers that it was not their struggle. Though militant when necessary, he also believed that much immediate misery could be relieved through reasonable negotiation with the managers. He set about reforming the whole system of dock employment by insisting that the dockers should have regular work and pay packets rather than one job at a time.

Dockside 'character' is rare now. A port official saw a sailor with a parrot on his shoulder at Avonmouth in 1970. Breton onion men have been seen at a favourite pub of theirs within recent years, and it is still possible to come across a few sailors lying dead drunk outside a quayside pub late on a Saturday night. The Cumberland Basin operates more or less as it has done for 160 years. To see a ship being 'locked' through on a bright autumn morning is still worth stopping for: children watching from their playground under the fly-over, swung open to let the ship through; swans disturbed at their scavenging; the ship gliding under the Rownham woods and past the terraces and squares of Hotwells, followed by the ghosts of all those ships of the nineteenth century, queuing up for admittance to the heart of the old city.

In early 1970 the city docks still had eighteen berths and about thirty-five cranes and eighteen sheds. But by early 1971 these had dwindled to twelve berths, about eighteen cranes and five transit sheds. By 1974 all this had dwindled again to four berths, a handful of cranes and two sheds.

Already the whole dock complex seemed to be moving back into the world of industrial archaeology, to join the remarkable working and non-working survivals of the great construction work of the middle nineteenth century. Near the Basin, the Underfall Yard, where William Jessop first dammed the original course of the Avon, was developed from 1840 for the workshops and maintenance of the port and still serves this purpose. The old hydraulic engine house in the yard is still in use, and the gridiron, attributed to Brunel and used for minor repairs to ships' hulls, is still in operation, while his system of culverts with sluice-gates is still used for flushing away mud dredged from the Harbour into the New Cut. The Albion Dockyard, the home since 1820 of the shipbuilding firm of Charles Hill, is still active, and has indeed increased its activities in recent years with orders for oil-rig service ships, though eventually the firm will have to face the prospect of moving from the city docks. In the adjoining dry-dock where she was built the *Great Britain* undergoes the first stages of her rehabilitation and wonders about her future. Down-river the Lamplighters Ferry still crosses from Shirehampton to Pill but may be discontinued if the motorway bridge proves a suitable alternative crossing for local people. The great bonded warehouses near the southern approaches to the Basin, though built only as far back as 1905–1919, already rank as pioneer buildings in steel-frame and reinforced concrete construction in the eyes of industrial historians. Fragments of lost shipbuilding slips, traces of road approaches to old ferries like that at Rownham, the Old Dock Cottages, lock-walls, bollards, massive Victorian cast-iron artefacts of all kinds, ensure that if and when the docks cease to exist Bristol will have a unique ready-made museum of British mercantile life.

At the end of the 1960s Bristol faced what could justifiably be called its greatest crisis among all the crises of its erratic economic history: the proposed closing of the city docks and the problem of what to do with the deserted waterways which, more than any other feature, give the city its distinctive visual character and atmosphere. Aircraft may have taken over from shipping as Bristol's leading industry, but it has always been the presence of water, wharfs, cranes and ships in the city centre that has attracted outsiders, charmed foreigners and stirred the secretive Bristol heart. The closing of these waterways to shipping is not just one more inevitable change—to their credit, those who say it is inevitable have not minimized the emotional shock involved. At the very least it will alter the fundamental visual character of the city; at the worst it could, if mismanaged, destroy everything that has made Bristol beautiful in its tumbledown, Gothic fashion. The cranes rising among the church spires will go, together with the sheds and wharfs, the tugs and lighters, and all the vigorous clutter of a working port.

This was not the first blow to the promoters of Bristol's docks in the 1960s. Ambitious local men, foreseeing a future world rôle for the port, devised a project for new deep-water docks at Portbury between Portishead and the mouth of the Avon. This was turned down in a Government White Paper on transport in 1966, together with permission for any new liner port in Britain. After the General Election of 1970 the Conservative Government approved the scheme for the West Dock at Portbury, which will consist of a basin covering 70 acres, with a lock 1,200 feet long. It will be the largest dock in Britain and will have the largest mitre gates in the world. The completion of this important new dock was scheduled for the end of 1975, when ships two or three times the size of those now using Avonmouth Docks would be able to use the new West Dock.

In 1969 Bristol Corporation submitted to Parliament a Bill to cancel historic navigation rights through the city waterways, based on the assumption that the docks, which have been losing money for at least ten years as the result of a marked decline in trade, will have to close within the next decade. Avonmouth and Portishead have been subsidizing Bristol to the extent of £200,000 a year and the Port of Bristol authority say this cannot continue. Opponents of the Bill point out that the plan to close the city docks has come rather late in view of recent improvements, such as the £2,650,000 Cumberland Basin fly-over and swing-bridge, opened in 1965, and the high level bridge to carry the M5 over the Avon, both of which will be unnecessary if the city docks close. According to the Bill ships will immediately lose their traditional rights to sail up St. Augustine's Reach to Neptune's statue. By 1980 navigation rights for the whole of the Floating Harbour from the Cumberland Basin to Temple Meads and the Feeder Canal and Netham Weir will also have ceased.

Supporters claim that closure is inevitable on financial grounds because trade is leaving the city docks: in June 1963 there were eighty ships berthed in the city; in October 1969 there were twenty-eight. It is inevitable, too, they claim, because the age of the small cargo ship is passing in favour of the large container ship and the giant tanker. Symptoms are not hard to find: in 1969 the Bristol Steam Navigation Company closed its direct service to the Continent from Bristol because it was no longer economical, and the Bristol City Line transferred its new container ships to Southampton as Bristol could not handle them. Bristol's road planners were anxious to close St Augustine's Reach so that they could build a road bridge across it as part of the Inner Ring Road system, which they claimed will reduce traffic in the Centre and Queen Square. The devisers of the Bill suggested that the waterways could become a 'new Amsterdam', with tree-lined quaysides, new building development instead of docksheds, marinas for pleasure craft, places of entertainment and gardens, and already several imaginative schemes for this new waterfront have been put forward. The proper development of the disused city waterways as a new social, residential, commercial, entertainment environment, will almost certainly mean the abandonment of the rigid road-grid originally planned for it and increasingly rejected by the authorities.

Opponents of the Bill include businessmen and dock users who claim that the city has not maintained the docks properly, that there are years of life in them still even if trade is reduced, and that cancellation of navigation rights would be disastrous as it would give the authorities and/or developers a free hand to fill in the waterways if they wished. In fact, since the public controversy and town poll of late 1969 and early 1970 the situation has taken a notable turn for the better. Organized opposition to certain parts of the original draft came from the Bristol Civic Society, the Cabot Cruising Club, the local branch of the Inland Waterways Association and the Clifton and Hotwells Improvement Society; none of these bodies opposed the ending by 1980 of commercial navigation in the city docks, though the end of this was much regretted. The Select Committee of the House of Lords, who have been considering the Bill, have recommended that through navigation should remain along the entire length of the Floating Harbour, that St. Philip's Reach should remain a waterway, and that Totterdown Lock (blocked in 1940 as a safety precaution) should be reopened so as to allow passage to and from the old course of the Avon, allowing for the abandonment of the Feeder Canal; all these provisions would be for the benefit of pleasure craft, motor cruisers and inland waterways boats using the Harbour as what is considered by small-boat people an essential part of the waterway link from the Bristol Channel to the Thames via the Avon and Kennet Canal. These recommendations have been incorporated into the Bill for the two Houses of Parliament to debate eventually. Thus the town poll in favour of the original Bill has been reversed by the combined efforts of the societies and clubs which disputed certain points in it. This might be seen as a triumph for unrepresentative but active minorities; but the town poll itself approved of the original Bill on a ludicrously small turn-out of voters. Over the dispute hung the threat of the nationalization of the docks, removed by the Conservative victory of June 1970 but revived by the Labour victories of 1974.

The Bristol Corporation Act, 1971, is only an enabling Act, which makes the point that the Corporation *may* abandon the commercial navigation of the Floating Harbour. No legal action has been taken so far, though it is possible that Hill's shipyard may eventually be notified of the City Council's intention to require closure. It is possible that economic changes and alterations in transport economics may still open the way to renewed commercial use, though not necessarily of the same type as before:

e.g., as a result of the offloading of cargo brought into the lower part in larger ships. The leader of the City Council has said that he is not averse for the moment to further delay in running down the city docks, and one possibility, being unofficially discussed, is that of a barrage lower down the Avon which would stabilise the water level all through the Gorge.

A compromise may yet be reached, with limited shipping using a restricted part of the docks. The *Great Britain* and other old ships may find a home there and the weekend sailors still find their fun messing about in boats. In a letter to *The Times* in November 1969 the chairman of the city's Planning and Traffic Committee pointed out that anyone with local knowledge would know that the waterways formed an integral part of the city's stormwater drainage system as well as a passage for the River Frome and could not be filled in without endangering the drainage system. He assured the anxious that a cruiseway would be maintained through the Harbour and that the Cumberland Basin would still be able to take high-masted ships (for official visits and naval calls, it has been suggested). "The City Council," he added, "fully realized the unique contribution which the historic pattern of waterways can make to our thriving regional city on the threshhold of an exciting era which we hope not only Bristolians but others will share."

History and economic and technological change have brought about the decline of Bristol's port rather than any plot by wicked capitalist managers, difficult as it is going to be to adapt to the new situation. The caution that made the first builders of Bristol settle so far up river and that, as an inherited local characteristic, made Bristol hesitate at almost every stage of its history to take bold steps to improve the port and to shift its location logically towards the river mouth, has been the undoing of the city docks. Fortunately, the same caution ensured that the city was in close touch with its hinterland and with the rest of the country so that it could and can survive without its inner harbour. If we cannot have ships and cranes, timber piles, bowsprits sticking out over the city pavements, and foreign sailors wandering bewildered around Queen Square looking for the red-light quarter, we can, we hope, keep the waterways as a new public amenity for recreation and entertainment as the Welsh Back Granary has been preserved as a jazz club.

The Avon almost empty as traffic piles up along the Portway from Avonmouth

SLOW

T.S. ADVENTURE

Whatever the future, Bristol said an emotional farewell in July 1970 to her pioneering sea-going past: the return of the hulk of the *Great Britain* from the Falkland Islands to her birthplace in the Floating Harbour was the most heavily charged symbolic act for romantic Bristolians since the Americans came to the city in the Second World War and General Bradley set up his invasion headquarters at Clifton College. Thousands of people—the Press differed as to whether it was tens or hundreds of thousands—turned out on a chill, blustery Sunday morning to watch her towed skilfully upriver, surrounded by an escort of official and unofficial boats. They stood in damp meadows, clambered up the signal posts that dot the river-banks, lined the railings at the Sea Walls like Apaches about to attack. They greeted the ship in staid Bristol fashion; some cheering, but most clapping sporadically or waving handkerchiefs in a kind of sympathetic semaphore. Cars and tugs hooted at each other in the natural echo-chamber of the Gorge. Florin-size confetti floated down from Brunel's bridge on to Brunel's ship, each seeing the other for the first time. Signal flags stood rigid in the strong following winds. Turner should have been there to paint it.

It was a situation not without irony. The City Council, cautious to the last, had shown little enthusiasm for this purely private, romantic and unbusinesslike operation, made possible by a gift of £150,000 towards the salvaging from Mr. Jack Hayward, the Bahamas developer, who is also the man who bought Lundy for the nation. The council became rather more interested as the ship on her pontoon came closer and closer to Bristol on her 8,000-mile journey. But the future of the ship, now being restored by Charles Hill's at a cost of at least £350,000, remains uncertain: will Bristol keep her as a maritime museum, or will she go to London where the Honourable Company of Shipwrights has already expressed interest in buying her as a floating headquarters? Local opinion differed sharply, though a poll conducted by the *Evening Post* showed a majority of those polled in favour of keeping her and of the city helping to pay for her restoration. Hesitating between past and future, as so often in the past, Bristol may lose a unique symbol and reminder of her greatness as a pioneering port; and surely, only by keeping the *Great Britain* and other ships in her city centre can Bristol justify her seal with its proud ship sailing into its proud castle.

The Old Dock Cottages near the Cumberland Basin
A sandship ties up opposite the Welsh Back

V

CLIFTON NEAR BRISTOL

CLIFTON is logically the Anglo-Saxon 'ton', or inhabited place, on the cliff. But from its history it could as plausibly be the French 'ton', or exclusive upper-class society, on the cliff. Its popular image for those who do not know it well is still as a place of Georgian terraces, Victorian villas, the sacred Close of the College, whose hush was immortalized by Henry Newbolt, and of retired army officers and colonial administrators. Those who live there know that its typical residents today are more likely to be businessmen, B.B.C. officials, university lecturers and students, schoolteachers and estate agents, with a fringe of young hippies and of staid, middle-aged Bohemians; that it has slummy parts; that it has planning problems; that it is no longer the Simla of Bristol.

Yet within the last ten years I have heard Clifton people in a tea shop in The Mall reminiscing about the old days in "K.L." (Kuala Lumpur, apparently); and within the last fifteen years, glancing through a window of one of the Italianate villas along grey Pembroke Road, I have seen a drawing room hung with assegais and leopard-skin shields. Even as late as 1951 Tudor Edwards was writing in his book on Bristol: "the promenades are still fashionable. On the Downs there is a liberal sprinkling of ex-Indian Army officers, elderly spinsters and widows eking out their limited capital and reading books from the circulating libraries, and prim schoolmistresses with their young charges tripping in echelons along the white roads or running beneath the lime, ilex and plane trees." Most of the circulating libraries have gone; the schoolmistresses are probably not so prim; those Indian Army officers and widows must be getting thin on the ground by now, and it would be difficult to track down that Cliftonian widower from Sir John Betjeman's poem "Bristol and Clifton" who sublimated his grief and loneliness with the minutiae of Low

Anglican sidesmanship—he would be disturbed by the glowing Piper windows, amphitheatre nave and Roman baldachino of the new All Saints Church in Pembroke Road, bombed in the war and restored in 1965.

Yet Clifton remains a separate place despite the pressures towards uniformity exercised by a large, vigorous city like Bristol on its constituent suburbs. Unlike most middle to upper-class suburbs it did not start as a place where Bristol businessmen could live not too far from their counting-houses; they preferred Kingsdown originally, and later suburbs like Stoke Bishop beyond the Downs. Clifton began as a residential quarter, looking down on the early eighteenth-century spa of Hotwells by the river, providing lodgings on the healthier higher slopes for the melancholy succession of dying invalids who came to the Hot Well as to Delphi, hoping for a favourable augury. As the muddy Avon waters got into the Hot Well Water and hastened the decline of the spa, Clifton developed into a health resort in its own right, turning its face now to the Downs and the Gorge, with their fine air and bracing breezes, and their acres of open, furzy downland and the rare flowers that brought the botanists flocking through the centuries. It had its own short-lived Pump Room and its longer-lived Assembly Rooms, now incorporated in the Spa Ballroom alongside the Clifton Spa Hotel.

The spa and Assembly aspect of Clifton declined in turn, but the charm and situation of the district ensured that Clifton survived as a fashionable place to live. Those who came to quiz remained to pray in the burgeoning Victorian churches. The rise of Clifton College in the 1860s, and the development of other schools in such an eminently cloistral district, brought with them the scholastic element that has remained in the local population. Parents came to live near their boys at school. Lawyers and doctors with Bristol practices moved in, and with them moved their servants and coachmen into mews that have become houses and flats in the area near Regent Street and The Mall. The tradespeople, the mercers and drapers and butchers, lived in a little warren of houses arranged in courts off Portland Street. These gloomy Hogarthian courts still exist in the road leading down to the 'Coronation Tap' pub, noted for its cider and packed to the doors at Saturday lunchtimes.

Clifton must have seen its high noon in the 1880s and 90s,

before the car destroyed the peace of the streets, with the college flourishing and Bristol keeping a respectful distance the other side of Whiteladies Road and below the Victoria Rooms. It would have been a microcosm of Bristol itself, but more genteel, more like a quiet country town, with the professions instead of agriculture as the main business of the place. For the wives of the professional men there was a busy life of philanthropy: collecting boxes to be filled for worthy causes, committees to be served, voluntary work of all kinds to be organized over drawing-room tea. One could easily think of this period as typical of Clifton's history. But in fact it has had recurring crises, booms, declines and falls; a place which has no natural product or industry and lives on its appeal as a spa or health resort or social meeting-ground is more vulnerable than most to changes in fashion and to economic fluctuations.

Hotwells itself—Bristolians call it Hotwells, though the long road flanking the river below Clifton is called Hotwell Road—had a sad and erratic history as a spa. All spas offering hope to mortally sick people are sad places, but the Hot Well, close to the muddy river and hemmed in by the walls of the Avon Gorge, was sadder than most.

The pollution of the well water by the muddy river water had always been the spa's great problem. The spa rose rapidly to fame in the late seventeenth century and declined as rapidly at the beginning of the nineteenth; among those who came to visit it were Catherine of Braganza, Sarah, Duchess of Marlborough, Addison, Cowper, Gay, Pope, Sheridan and Mrs. Thrale. Fanny Burney sent her Evelina there: "a most delightful spot; the prospect is beautiful, the air pure, and the weather very favourable to invalids." The waters, first described by the fifteenth-century Bristol chronicler, William Wyrecestre, became known in the later seventeenth century as a 'cure' for kidney troubles and for diabetes; towards the end of the eighteenth century the waters were used to treat tuberculosis, though in all cases one suspects it was really the rest, the fresh air and exercise which effected cures, if any. If the Hot Well was sadder than other spas it was because it was regarded in its time as a last resort when other treatments had failed; many of the visitors really were dying and one set of lodging houses was known as 'Death Row'. Effective or not, the waters were much bottled and exported and helped to give rise to

Bristol's flourishing glass industry in the eighteenth and nineteenth centuries.

It was not all gloom, though; a visit to the spa could be a prescribed rest for a heavy drinker or eater, and there was scandal and cards, an orchestra, riding, boat excursions down the river or across it to eat strawberries at Long Ashton or up to the races on the Downs. In the 1770s and 80s it was a gay place, but the increase in the number of incurable patients and the high death rate began to give the spa an unpleasant reputation. By the turn of the century it was well into its own decline; in 1822 the old Hotwell House was demolished for a new road and attempts to revive the spa failed. The Hot Well survives in *Humphrey Clinker* and *Evelina*, in memoirs of the period and in the many water colours of the curiously-situated spa buildings on their platform close by the river beneath the towering white crags of the Gorge. Today, the charming Colonnade is all that survives of the spa, refurbished and inhabited and more cheerful than when it lodged consumptive beauties, risking the night damp to attend some over-heated Dance of Death in the Assembly Rooms.

Today, Hotwells is one of Bristol's most picturesque and least known districts, with what Pevsner calls "its display of comfortable modest lovable early Georgian brick architecture which even Bristol can hardly match anywhere else". Here is Dowry Parade, built 1764, a terrace of brick houses with wrought-iron balconies; and here especially is Dowry Square, a charming three-sided square of 1725–50 packed with interesting houses, and much and attractively restored through the interest of a local building contractor. The square also contains the oddly classical Clifton Dispensary of 1823 and in one corner the house where Thomas Beddoes conducted his Pneumatic Institution in the early years of the nineteenth century and where, as the plaque says, "Humphrey Davy, 1799–1801, here carried out his researches in the nature of nitrous oxide which led him to suggest a practical means of anaesthesia." In fact Davy and Beddoes probably did not recognize the possibilities of nitrous oxide, 'laughing gas', as a serious anaesthetic, and the whole experiment in trying to cure consumption, asthma and other diseases by the inhaling of gases proved a failure. But the institution, despite its sombre purpose—an offshoot of the Hot Well's purposes—forms an amusing episode in Bristol's rather over-serious history; the seriousness is much enlivened by the stories of the celebrities, including Southey and Coleridge, who attended evening parties to sniff laughing gas from Davy's green bag, and sometimes to rush out of the house and round the square intoxicated by the gas.

Hope Square higher up the hill was badly damaged in the Blitz, though it is now restored in parts; but nearby Albemarle Row (1763) is an impressive red-brick, pedimented range. Less well known are some of the climbing and falling streets such as Ambra Vale, with its tall, knife-edged buildings; Freeland Place, with its pretty, brightly coloured, balconied houses, a number of them occupied in recent years by artists, architects and designers; Crosby Row with its muddy lane and handsome square Regency houses; and the early Victorian streets with their secretive corner pubs, once the conspiratorial haunt of coachmen and footmen from the great houses up the hill. On the Hotwell Road stands Cockerell's splendidly Italianate church of 1829–30, Holy Trinity, gutted in the Blitz and since admirably restored.

In 1712 Hotwells and the small portion of Clifton above had 450 inhabitants. Clifton on the Hill remained little more than a village until 1790, but after that the building of Clifton developed rapidly, much of what we see today dating from soon after that year, with the beginning of the noble, flaking Palladian range of Windsor Terrace, beetling on its crag over the Avon, Royal York Crescent, the longest Georgian crescent in Britain, Cornwallis Crescent, Richmond Terrace and York Place. (There are comparatively few separate Georgian houses in Clifton compared with other Georgian towns and suburbs). The Napoleonic Wars brought financial crashes of speculating builders which left some of the crescents uncompleted through two or three decades. A visitor to Bristol recalled the silent and melancholy spectacle of roofless houses; in 1792, during the upheaval of the French Revolution, there were thirty-four 'shells' in Royal York Crescent. But Clifton grew nevertheless, terrace upon terrace rising above Hotwells to the plateau upon which the Pump Room, Assembly Rooms and shops were eventually built. The old rural roads, like Gallows Acre Lane, and the kitchen gardens and orchards disappeared under the weight of monumental, self-important stone, which spread up to the Downs and across Whiteladies Road, adding early Victorian terraces like Vyvyan Terrace (probably of the 1830s) and Worcester Terrace (completed 1853) to the more graceful Regency terraces below, until by 1841 the population had reached 14,000.

Clifton is an atmosphere as well as a place and the atmosphere has much wider limits than the actual place. The university area, Park Street, Brandon Hill with its neighbouring streets, Great George. Street and Charlotte Street, together with Berkeley Square and Queen's Road and the open space in front of the Victoria Rooms, and the long rising lope of Whiteladies Road itself, with its terraces and villas, restaurants, offices and shops: all belong in atmosphere to Clifton. The Clifton ambience, the sense of a privileged sector, spreads into the sombre grey avenues of Redland and Cotham, and across the Downs into Stoke Bishop. A spur of 'Clifton' runs alongside the Downs through Redland and Henleaze to where the road dips down to Westbury; and the Clifton atmosphere is present down the hill, around St. Monica's Home of Rest and the Badminton and Red Maids' girls schools. Though Clifton kept itself apart and aloof through the nineteenth century—Bristol is retaliating today with its nibbling encroachments—it would on occasion help its workaday neighbour. In 1829 rich, fashionable Clifton sent down blankets, potatoes, coal and clothes to cholera-stricken Bristol. By then it had clearly become a settled community with a sense of social obligation and not just an elegant lodging house for invalids and snobs.

By the beginning of the second half of the nineteenth century Clifton had developed its own distinct culture, predominantly literary and educational in a rather high-minded, dilettante manner, but with links with the physical and natural sciences. It was Conservative and Church of England while Bristol was radical among the people, Whiggish among the merchants and generally non-conformist, and the two places eyed each other with some suspicion. It tended to produce or attract rather over-refined, bloodless writers and poets, like John Addington Symonds or Thomas Beddoes' son, Thomas Lovell Beddoes, who was the sort of poet one might expect from Clifton: minor, eccentric, highly skilled technically but in a 'period' mode. Hannah More, the evangelical-dramatist-schoolmistress, who had been born in Stapleton and had grown up in Bristol, came back to Clifton from her Somerset retreat to die at Windsor Terrace. Lord Roberts's father, also a general, lived in Royal York Crescent, as did the Empress Eugénie when a schoolgirl at Clifton. The Beddoes family, though not native-born, lived long in Clifton at 3 Rodney Place, a discreet terrace near the 'town', and Dr. Johnson's friend, Mrs. Thrale, was at one time a resident. Sydney Smith passed through scattering witticisms. Maria Edgworth, who is today beginning to receive her critical due as a pioneer realistic novelist of Irish life, was a visitor. Coleridge and Southey had many links with Clifton, and Macaulay, something of a protegé of Hannah More, knew it well. Charles Kingsley was a schoolboy there and remembered seeing Queen Square burning in the 1831 riots from the Clifton heights. Benjamin Jowett, F. D. Maurice and T. H. Green and other Victorian intellectuals were frequent visitors to the home of J. A. Symonds's father. As with Bath and Bristol, though, it is difficult to distinguish between the famous who really belonged and those who were merely visiting or passing through.

Certainly John Addington Symonds belonged. His name recurs in any account of nineteenth-century intellectual life in Bristol. He was born there—at 7 Berkeley Square—in 1840 and grew up in the later family home, Clifton Hill House, the handsome eighteenth-century house, now a university women's hostel, facing the riverward end of the churchyard of Clifton Parish Church (a Georgian Gothic church, gutted by bombs and later pulled down completely). His doctor-father, also John Addington Symonds, played a part in the founding of Clifton College, and his son, the historian of Renaissance Italy, was for a time a classics master at the college and played an influential part in the early committee work that went to creating the university college, arousing great interest in the project in his friend and former tutor, Benjamin Jowett.

He came back from Oxford, settled for some years in Victoria Square with wife and family, wrote his Renaissance books and many others, until a serious riding accident on the Downs in 1873 impaired his already delicate health; he developed consumption and gradually retired to Davos, dying in Rome in 1893. He was the most distinguished man of letters to come from Clifton itself and he loved the place passionately, eloquently acknowledging the debt his literary work owed to the lovely physical setting of Clifton and to other early influences, such as the music in the cathedral. He wrote: "At Davos I sometimes yearn for what I always had at Clifton—the sun rising above a mighty city, flooding wood and pasture and sea-going river. . . ."

Clifton made him and unmade him; as he looked at smoky Bristol from Clifton and saw it transformed by sun and clouds into a dream city, so he looked at life and history. Clifton may have made him a writer; it also kept him a minor writer. A sheltered place bred a sheltered talent and nothing much of him remains today except the unread reputation of his *History of the Italian Renaissance*. But his references to Clifton express vividly one aspect of the place: the curious lyrical nostalgia that is so easily felt there, a euphoria compounded of the physical beauty of the scene and of memories of childhoods spent there or of other happy times associated with the district: "Ah how happy I was then! It seems like a dream—so happy!" the Empress Eugénie wrote of her girlhood years there. And Symonds wrote in an enigmatic passage: "Clifton, now as ever, is full of vague yet powerful associations. When will this Circe cease to brew enchantments for my soul? . . ."

We now know, of course, largely from Phyllis Grosskurth's definitive biography of Symonds (1964), that many of those enchantments were to do with his first feelings of that homosexual passion which became the dominating theme of his life, which he wrote about in Havelock Ellis's *Studies in the Psychology of Sex*, and for which he is now better known than for any of his books. One could not categorically say that Clifton had made Symonds a homosexual; but it is arguable that a sheltered, dreamy, rather secret district like Clifton, which had eliminated the visual realities of industry, commerce and poverty, was a place where the romantic homosexuality of an over-literary adolescence could linger on into manhood more easily than down in the realistic neighbour-city.

But this was only one aspect of Victorian Clifton and arguably an untypical one. More representative of the general direction of nineteenth-century high thinking and moderately plain living were the creation of Clifton College and of Bristol University, which in many ways grew from the soil which had nurtured the college, and which still, geographically and atmospherically, belongs to Clifton rather than to Bristol; the founding of the zoo and the construction of Brunel's Suspension Bridge. The bridge is, with Rysbrack's statues of Colston (in All Saints' Church) and William III (in Queen Square), and the chancel vaulting in the cathedral, perhaps the loveliest 'made' thing in

Bristol. While the setting obviously inspired Brunel to his bold gesture—other contenders for the winning design in the 1830s thought the gorge unspannable and had their pylons rising from the floor of the gorge—the proximity of Clifton may well have determined the elegance and simplicity of the design, when it was completed in the 1860s after Brunel's relatively early death: "a work of art thus thrown across such grand and imposing scenery should be as simple and unobtrusive as possible," Brunel wrote.

The history of its construction is long and complicated by delays, like that of many other Bristol enterprises. The great stone pylons were up by 1840 but the money dried up and the ironwork was sold in 1851. Work was resumed in 1861 and completed in 1864, iron chains from Hungerford Suspension Bridge at Charing Cross, taken down in 1861, being used in place of the original ones. Today it is as elegant and breath-taking as it ever was; the vaguely Egyptian pylons are still awesome and it is always surprising to see in old photographs men in the fustian clothes of the 1860s standing alongside the cables and chains which we see today and which still look hardly twenty years old. The original purposes of the promoters of the bridge are still rather enigmatic; as Bristol's outstanding 'sight' it seems to be linking two halves of a great city together over a natural chasm. In fact, it links genteel upper Clifton with the sparse suburbia of Leigh Woods and Failand, though admittedly the development of Nailsea, Portishead and Clevedon as dormitory areas has kept the bridge busy and profitable in recent years. But the size and drama of it do seem out of proportion to its actual usefulness; did the promoters expect the Leigh Woods side of the Gorge to develop as Clifton had done? Busy as it is, its future is uncertain; will commuters use the new motorway bridge now built across the river at Avonmouth instead and will Brunel's masterpiece become another piece of industrial archaeology?

It is thrilling still to stand on the footwalks and feel the bridge tremble to traffic or thrum in the wind cutting up the river. Seen from below, it leaps gracefully across the Gorge; from above, by the Observatory, once a windmill, now a charming camera obscura, or from the limestone rock-slide nearby—polished by generations of small bottoms—it seems to float hazily into the woods of Nightingale Valley. It has a melancholy history of suicides and accidents; some end anti-climactically with safe landings in the river-mud, one Victorian fall ending bizarrely with a woman parachuting safely down on her voluminous inflated skirts.

Bristol Zoo belongs as much to the outside world as it does to Bristol and Clifton, but it is appropriate that it originated in intellectual Clifton—long before the surrounding houses and streets and the college were built—as an expression of that growing nineteenth-century obsession with natural history which culminated in Darwin's theory that human beings were part of natural history too. The Bristol, Clifton and West of England Zoological Society was formed in 1834 by 250 Bristol and Clifton citizens (Clifton became part of Bristol in the following year) who subscribed £25 each (some much more) to buy and equip the gardens, agreeing in their trust deed that no dividends should be paid and that any profits should go to improving the gardens and adding to the 'menagerie'. The 12 acres of gardens were opened in 1836 and progress was steady but slow for some eighty years. Then came a period of decline when the gardens were neglected and used for fêtes and fairs. In 1927 the old purposes, zoological and horticultural, were revived and the zoo as we know it came into existence, with its aquarium, monkey temple and houses, sea-lion pond, elephant house and polar bear enclosure. Aviaries and other animal houses have been added since the war and the zoo has become noted for its skill in breeding animals in captivity.

The balance between animals and gardens is attractive, even for those who do not like zoos; the squeamish can avoid the contagious frustration of the beasts of prey—that endless pacing to and fro of the zoo's unique pair of white tigers—and wander among the flower beds, stepping over a somnolent pelican or two or admiring the blush of flamingoes in their paddling pool. At weekends in summer the zoo is unattractively crowded; but on weekdays, especially early on a bright morning, it has a charm hardly rivalled among British zoos. It belongs to the Clifton ambience in so far as it echoes the Victorian taste for dabbling in zoology: a monkey here, a tiger there, a pair of zebras, and generally one or two of each as in some genteel upper middle class ark, with appropriate but undemanding labels to read before going home to lunch in Manila Road. Uncrowded, it is a restful place, where one can think unfashionably of the days when we ruled so many of the countries from which these animals came—unless we are roused by the distant banging of desks and the clatter of form-changing across the road in the college, another notable Victorian attempt to civilize the primitive instincts.

Clifton College was one of the new mid-nineteenth-century public schools founded for the sons of the professional and upper-middle classes at the time of Britain's maximum world power, to provide administrators, soldiers, bishops and pro-consuls for the Empire. But it was also founded for a more immediate, local purpose: to improve the educational situation in Bristol after a disastrous period earlier in the century when some schools had closed and Bristol Grammar School had gone through a very bad time under a rascally and for a long while immovable headmaster. The wealthy of Clifton had hoped that the grammar school would become a boarding school and when this did not happen they decided to found a school of their own after the pattern of Dr. Arnold's Rugby, a school that would offer "for the sons of gentlemen a thoroughly good and liberal education at moderate cost", as the original prospectus put it.

The school got its first headmaster, Dr. John Percival, from Rugby and appointed him at the age of 28 to make their new college into a school for future leaders of the country and rulers of the Empire. They were to be not only gentlemen but also Christian gentlemen and the school chapel was to be the focal point of school life. The third element in character training was to be organized sport, then a relatively new concept in school life. Percival was liberal in that he did not believe in teaching character through fear of punishment but preferred good relationships between masters and boys; but the boys, often more snobbish than the masters, made their own rules and gradually established sport as the dominant theme of the school's life.

The Clifton College ethos at its most ritualistic is preserved in the poems of Sir Henry Newbolt, himself a Clifton boy who in his inner mind never really left the school, and who wrote in his *Memoirs*: "My vision of Clifton Close is not merely an individual experience. It is a touch, a password between all who have seen it." He was a pretty awful poet but when the passion for his Clifton days was upon him he created a surprisingly powerful nostalgic myth of public school life. The "breathless hush in the Close" in *Vitai Lampada* may not have been entirely spontaneous

—you might have to answer to your house captain if you did not appear breathless enough—but it was no doubt a real experience of Newbolt's. Newbolt loved Clifton, but he also harmed its image by exaggerating and romanticizing the more sentimental aspects of his relationship with the school.

Clifton did not become quite the self-denying Christian and gentlemanly establishment its founders had in mind, and towards the end of the nineteenth century it had its rather more than full share of the arrogant imperial fervour of the time. But in its early years following its foundation in 1862 and since the imperial obsession died in 1914, Clifton was a rather advanced liberal-minded school. It made a point of accepting a number of Jewish boys in their own house, an almost provocatively liberal gesture in vaguely anti-Semitic Victorian England. Percival instituted a tradition by which senior Clifton boys interested themselves in the welfare of poor boys in the city; there must be a number of elderly Bristolians today who remember this link and may have played friendly cricket with Clifton boys in their own Close. Percival also started a modern side and the military and engineering side which created the school's strong military tradition—Haig and Birdwood were old boys, and a statue of Haig dominates the Close. There was an emphasis on science probably unique among Victorian public schools.

These innovations were regarded askance by some parents, who particularly disliked the important place given to day boys and the close links with Bristol. In 1871 the assistant masters—a radical lot—presented a memorial to the governors in favour of the college being thrown open to "boys of all classes without regard to social position". By 1945 9 per cent of entries over 11 came from city elementary schools. In June 1965 the college was taking guest boarders from local comprehensives as an experiment and by January 1969 nearly 180 of the 600 pupils were day boys. Had not Dr. Percival himself said that of all forms of education that which combined a good day school with a good home was the best?

In June 1969 the college embarked on a twenty-year major rebuilding programme, and at the centenary celebrations in 1962 there was much emphasis on its liberal, forward-looking character. In the early 1970s a school council was due to be created and service in the cadet corps to be made optional, the alternative being social work of some kind. And today the college sends fewer boys into the army and government service and more into industry, technology and science.

Charles Hansom's grey, battlemented 'Greyfriars' buildings, the chapel with its lovely blue octagon tower, and the noble Close, haunted by Newbolt and the colonel whose Gatling jammed, to some extent falsify the realistic attitude of the college to its job. If Clifton does seem—even to the doctrinaire disapprover of the system—tolerant, liberal and flexible compared with other public schools it is surely because it lies so close to busy, realistic Bristol, whereas so many of our public schools are situated in the countryside or in relatively small towns.

Whatever changes have taken place since it was founded as the College of Science and Literature in 1876, Bristol University belongs more to the Clifton ethos of education as a principle of life than it does to the Bristol ethos of getting on in the world. The impetus given to educational progress in Bristol by the arrival of Percival at Clifton College helped on the long-mooted plan for a university in the city. In 1872 Percival published a pamphlet pressing for a local university, partly supported by the city and partly from outside, and offering a liberal education rather than a purely technical one. In Clifton support came from J. A. Symonds's father, the formidable doctor and man of culture and from people like Catherine Winkworth, the religious writer and translator of German hymns ("Tr. Winkworth" echoes from our school hymnbooks); in Bristol from Lewis Fry and Mary Carpenter, the social reformer; and in Oxford from Benjamin Jowett, Master of Balliol and friend and mentor of the Symonds family. As the translator of Plato, Jowett naturally saw the new university as including the whole range of ideas and as an extension of the Balliol 'idea', and if Bristol University today attracts so many would-be entrants—by 1966 it was ranking closely behind Oxford and Cambridge as a first choice—it may well be because of its broad appeal and liberal range of studies, dating from its foundation. There is nothing of the exalted technical college about it, and even today it tends to attract the sons and daughters of the administrative and professional classes. Its buildings and halls of residence, and particularly Sir George Oatley's great Gothic tower (completed 1925), resemble more those of the neo-Oxbridge universities of Eastern America, with their cult of

Learning, than they do those of most other non-Oxbridge British universities.

The university college opened in 1876 in two houses in Park Row—gone since 1970—with eighty-seven day students and 234 at evening classes. The medical school, founded in 1828, became part of the university college in 1893. It had an engineering department, still one of its glories, from the start, and it was the first university college to admit women. Henry Overton Wills helped it on its way to full university status with a gift of £100,000 and became the first Chancellor in 1909. The second Chancellor was Lord Haldane, then Minister of War in Asquith's Government, and the third for many years was Winston Churchill.

It remained a quiet university for many years, known more for its engineering and dentistry than for its humanities. In later years it has had distinguished names: D. G. James, L. C. Knights, Frank Kermode, Henry Gifford and Christopher Ricks in its chairs of English; David Douglas, redoubtable medievalist, in that of History; and August Closs in the chair of German. Most distinguished of all, perhaps, was the late Cecil Powell, Professor of Physics from 1948–63, Head of the H. H. Wills Physics Laboratory from 1964 until his death in 1969, and Nobel Prize winner in 1950 for his development of the photographic method in the study of nuclear processes and for his discoveries concerning mesons. Powell and his school of experimental physics and their photographic techniques gained a world-wide reputation. His Nobel Prize obviously gave him the opportunity to move to higher positions in more prestigious universities; perhaps he found Bristol, his laboratory and team sufficiently attractive to stay. Here, as in other aspects of the university, many of Jowett's hopes seem to have been realized: universality combined with close links with the city and the power to attract and keep distinguished scholars and scientists.

The number of students has increased from about 1,500 twenty years ago to 6,400 today; with those from other colleges in the area this makes a large student population and the whole district is now obviously a university town. The new Students' Union building in Queen's Road, opened in 1965, is bulky but not unattractive (its restaurant was quickly nicknamed the Avon Gorge) and aptly symbolizes the new importance of the student in university life. There has been relatively little student unrest so far; partly, no doubt, because there is no obvious campus in which to gather and demonstrate, and because the students are widely dispersed in hostels and lodgings; partly, possibly, because of the cool emotional atmosphere of the city; partly, certainly, because the university in recent years has wisely developed a system of departmental rather than professorial control and thus defused a lot of potential resentment against remote authority. When the previous Chancellor, the Duke of Beaufort, retired he was succeeded by someone in whose choice the students, refusing to elect royalty, aristocrats or businessmen, had taken part. The first combined choice was an imaginative one: Dorothy Hodgkin, notable chemist, Nobel Prize, Order of Merit.

Town and gown relations seem good, though there is some hostility among local property owners from the way the authorities have extended the university outwards from its original nucleus into neighbouring areas like St. Michael's Hill, where it was claimed that they did not pay proper prices for properties taken over; though the attractive replacement and restoration, as promised, of some Georgian houses as university buildings has eased the tension to some extent. The blocking in of the hilltop fortress of science buildings around Royal Fort House has displeased many local people who feel the individual buildings could have been better designed. The university, which is advancing into Clifton proper, will have to be tactful if it is not to endanger the generally good relations between the city and its university.

Clifton has always had its building and development problems, though. The stone-faced fronts of the crescents flaked in the soft, damp air. Property values rose and fell. Even by the 1890s some of the villas were too big for single houses and were being divided into flats. The surface dignity endured, but the 1914–18 war threatened Clifton as the Napoleonic Wars had done. Property deteriorated for lack of maintenance and after 1918 there was a movement of wealthier Cliftonians across the Gorge to the exclusive Leigh Woods estate. By the end of the 1939–45 war Georgian Clifton, according to the *Western Daily Press* in 1964, had become "a neglected run-down suburb of Bristol, in scarcely better state than Kingsdown". Rows of houses were sold for less than they had cost 150 years before. A few conscientious owners began to paint and improve and by the end of the 1950s Clifton was showing signs of its former style. Property prices increased, and it

The cranes at Charles Hill's shipyard frame the Cabot Tower in the morning haze

began to appeal to certain potential residents with its pleasant setting, its centrality without being overwhelmed by traffic and its relative inexpensiveness. It was regarded as a private place, where there was still old-fashioned service in the shops; though even in 1964 journalists were still noting the crumbling masonry, gardens knee-deep in weeds, rents of £6 a week for flats whose tenants had to share toilets, baths and kitchens. There were stories of wild student parties and stories of pensioners living in the shabby basements of once elegant villas. Traffic increased. In 1966 the Bristol Junior Chamber of Commerce, in a survey, found parts of Clifton in a bad state of repair and demanded that close control should be exercised over piecemeal developments. In 1966 the area had a population of 15,584 with 77·9 per cent of the property rented: a dusty contradiction of the old image of select, rentier Clifton.

Clifton is a problematical place to live in today; the developers want to come in, reasoning that there is a lot of decayed and unsuitable property to be replaced. The residents, proud of Clifton's special character, want to keep them out. In 1969 residents of Pembroke Road were turning down offers of £2,000 for their back gardens, fearing they would be used for garages or blocks of flats. But Clifton remains an exciting visual experience despite its problems. The shabby parts are not obvious and the modern depredations still slight. There has been much refurbishing of old properties, such as the charming mews houses in Litfield Road. At Portland Street there is a very neat and harmonious terrace of six houses built in 1963, and on the corner of Wellington Street and Royal York Crescent a whole section of decayed and blitzed terrace has been restored. Round here there is a hint of young executive socializing, a revving up of posh sports cars outside Sunday lunchtime pubs.

For the visitor Clifton could be said to start in Park Street, that handsome and exhausting hill that climbs from College Green, long a moderately fashionable shopping street, now more popular with its restaurants and cafés and at present worried about a number of empty shops, undoubtedly the result of the headlong uphill traffic and the near impossibility of crossing the street. The blitzed gaps have been discreetly filled in and the gutted buildings restored, notably C. R. Cockerell's Masonic Hall, built in 1821–23 for the Literary and Philosophical Society, and a somewhat

Clifton Suspension Bridge by day and night

mysterious reminder today of the 'different' and unique ritual used by Bristol Masons. Off Park Street lie Charlotte Street, one long climbing and rigidly elegant terrace of 1788; and Great George Street with a number of stone houses by William Paty, also from 1788, including Number 7, the home of the West India merchant Pinney, and now a city museum of Georgian furniture and objects. Here, according to one tradition, Wordsworth and Coleridge met for the first time. Between the two streets stands St. George's, an imposing classical-fronted church of 1823 by Sir Robert Smirke, challengingly poised at the top of a long flight of steps; its rather sombre interior has just undergone a redecoration and general brightening up. Behind these fine streets rises Brandon Hill, with its views over the city and surrounding country, and its Tudor-Gothic tower of 1897 in memory of Cabot. Local housewives long exercised their sixteenth-century privilege of laying out blankets and sheets on the hillside to dry after washing.

George's handsome bookshop dominates the top of Park Street, its second-hand department rich in cheap standard texts from the coming and going of students. Berkeley Square, behind the Cadena Café (which used to have a splendid tea-shop orchestra), dates from about 1800 and is slightly dull, if one dare say that about Georgian architecture, more a set-piece than a natural piece of town planning. It is now increasingly a university enclave—the university has filled in the fourth side with a vaguely appropriate block—where it was once residential: in 1913, according to Wright's *Directory*, it housed six or seven clergymen, some of them vicars of city churches. The university refectory, originally built as the Museum and Library in 1867–71 and gutted in the Blitz, is one of the most loyally Ruskinian buildings in the country, a copy-book piece of Venetian Gothic. Facing the Victoria Rooms across one of Bristol's recurring open spaces stands the Royal West of England Academy of Art, architecturally one of the city's most bizarre buildings with its mixture of styles. The Victoria Rooms themselves, built by Charles Dyer in 1839–41, honour a fine late Greek Revival design and make a most attractive grouping behind the sprawling Edwardian baroque of the Edward VII memorial fountain.

Behind the university and the grammar school, and almost out of the Clifton ambience into Kingsdown, stands the Royal Fort, a superb Georgian house of the 1760s, built on the site of a Civil War fort and now housing the music department of the university. Handsome in itself, it conceals inside some of the loveliest interior decoration in the city, exquisite plasterwork by Bristol stucco workers, now charmingly picked out in dark greens and white, and realistically carved wooden swags of fruit and leaves and symbols of the chase.

Despite the popular image of grey elegance and solidity, Clifton is in fact a place of many contrasts. It is both the great theatrical set-pieces of Royal York Crescent and Windsor Terrace on its cliff over the Gorge, and at the same time the narrow Dickensian side-streets, with their antique shops and corner pubs, near Dover Place and York Place. It is the rows of squat Victorian villas with their roughstone facings and wormy rusticated stones; and it is the dainty, balconied white houses of Canynge Square near the Downs, redolent of the first romantic, feminine years of Victoria's reign. Within minutes one can leave the busy streets of Clifton's shopping centre and stroll past the curious, convex, hemispherical porches, with their different-coloured doors, of the Paragon (1809–14) and glimpse at the end of the crescent a quiet garden on the edge of the Gorge: a tree with a gouty branch propped on a crutch, a stone bowl filled with damp leaves. Clifton is both the beautiful descending curve of Sion Hill with its late eighteenth-century houses and village green atmosphere, and the shabby backwaters of Quay Steps off Blackboy Hill, an area for which redevelopment was demanded in the local Press in the late 1960s. It is the 'period' pleasures of the camera obscura on its knoll above the Suspension Bridge, offering in its plaster mirror a curiously surrealistic multi-dimensional view of "the waving of foliage and the coming and going of ships", as the notice outside says; and it is the slummy terraces of Caledonia Place.

The hushed Anglican respectability of Christ Church in Clifton Down Road, a finely spired and aspiring piece of Victorian Early English (1841), contrasts with the un-Cliftonian gloom of the Roman Catholic Pro-Cathedral of the Apostles in Park Place, a strange building (1834–38), ambitious but unfinished for lack of funds and then compromised over, so that the eaves of its basilica roof rest directly on the top of the huge capital-less pillars. The Pro-Cathedral has now been replaced by a new full cathedral in Clifton Park some distance away, possibly the first Catholic cathedral in the world to be designed for the new liturgical requirements, and undoubtedly the most original and striking new building erected in Bristol since the war. A fine old Bristol row among local Catholics as to whether or not the cost was justified went on in the local Press. In the end, the relatively low cost of £600,000 inspired the headline phrase "the bargain cathedral". The design has roused less controversy: two overlapping hexagons arranged so that 850 to 1,000 people can attend without anyone being more than 45 feet from the altar. The cathedral owes little or nothing to Gothic tradition, but there is an immense and exciting sense of space and light inside, a white radiance broken by only two stained-glass windows. The pyramidal or fortress-like exterior still arouses hostile comment. The interior seems an unqualified success, a notable addition to the city's 'quiet' places, such as Wesley's chapel and the chancel of the Anglican cathedral.

Clifton is the noble group of houses on Clifton Hill: Clifton Hill House, once the home of the Symonds family; the Bishop's House (1711), replacing the one burnt in the 1831 riots and then the Palace on Redland Hill, destroyed by German bombs; the mid-eighteenth-century house, now the Chesterfield Nursing Home; and Goldney House (1720–32, and 'Burgundified' in the nineteenth century), now, like Clifton Hill House, a university women's hostel (the famous grotto in the grounds was reported in June 1970 to be in need of a clean-up). It is also the plainer houses in nearby Constitution Hill, where Number 37 in particular, tall, thin, Hogarthian, has been thoughtfully kept up. It is very much the row of imperious early nineteenth-century houses along The Promenade fringing the Downs: Dorset House (1830), Trafalgar House (1830-ish), Camp House (1831), and Litfield House (1820–30).

Clifton may have been dead through the 1940s and 1950s; today it is certainly alive. What once looked and felt like a genteel country town, a suburban Barchester, has become a kind of good-humoured Chelsea, both around the university area and in Clifton proper, in Regent Street, The Mall and Princess Victoria Street. Maxis and minis (if these terms mean anything by the time this book appears) rather than Red Indian head-bands; boutiques, bistros with the *carte du jour* chalked on blackboards; art shops, craft shops, arty-crafty shops—all these blend tolerantly with the pompous dimensions of Francis Greenway's Clifton Club buildings (1806) and the richly atmospheric William IV chemist's shop on the corner of West Mall, with its jars of coloured water and its finely preserved apothecary's fittings. There are delicatessens, shops with old Bristol prints and shops with carved Swedish smørgasbrød sets, a Victorian castellated schoolhouse turned into a public library, banks with gilt lettering attached to Regency stone-facings, little general shops, a butcher's which not so long ago announced breast of lamb free to pensioners, and curio shops stiff with shakos and Iron Crosses. The young seem to favour the Albion Inn and its cobbles on Saturday mornings while the polo-necked bohemians and the cheerful chappies prefer the cider at the 'Coronation Tap'. But the middle range of the population seems to consist mainly of young, maxi-skirted and blue-jeaned couples, with their bright, classless infants, shopping for the Saturday spaghetti and vino.

Yet within minutes the lyrical Downs are reached. This is Bristol's lung, a green expanse of over 400 acres, riding along the crest of the city from the 300-feet-deep Gorge at one end to its gentle slope into Westbury at the other: a vast unfenced city park unique in Britain, except perhaps for the open spaces around King Arthur's Seat in Edinburgh, yet surpassed in the area by the huge Ashton Court estate of 840 acres, acquired by the corporation for public use in 1960. Here Prince Rupert led his defeated army out of Bristol in 1645 at the end of the long and bitter siege of the Royalists' western stronghold; here the early non-conformists, banned from their meeting houses, held open air services. In the eighteenth century there were fine nursery gardens and orchards around the edges of the Downs; it is pleasant to think of the charming nursery that survives incongruously near the Victoria Rooms as a relic of this tradition. There were pleasure gardens and rural inns, and in the genteel Regency period, as Clifton grew in popularity, riding on the Downs was much cultivated, as it is along the Lady's Mile today. They were the scene of popular horse races, such as that depicted in the fine racing scene by the Bristol woman painter, Rolinda Sharples, now in the Bristol Art Gallery. They were also the haunt of petty thieves and highwaymen, and roughs from Kingswood who burnt down the hated tollgates, and the scene of public executions, the last recorded one taking place in 1783. By the end of the eighteenth century, though, the cult of the Picturesque had claimed the Downs and a nineteenth-century guide wrote: "The adjacent scenery is eminently beautiful, comprising magnificent cliffs, noble woods, exhilarating downs, verdant and bowery meadows. . . ."

Despite their popularity, the Downs were in growing danger of encroachment; quarrying and mining had always been practised around the edges. Houses were built, large tracts were enclosed for fields in 1809. Then the Merchant Venturers Society, Lords of the Manor of Clifton, scenting danger, began to take counteraction. In May 1861 an Act of Parliament secured Clifton and Durdham Downs as open spaces for the citizens of Bristol for ever. When they can get to them, that is; fast traffic along the straight Downs Road, elaborate traffic islands, and more to come, have been subjects of complaints in the local Press in recent years. For Bristol does not neglect them; football posts mushroom on Saturday afternoons; brisk men with pipes stride over them on crisp winter mornings; there is cricket in the summer and there are riders in the autumn.

It will need a real effort to vandalize and commercialize Clifton out of existence, but no doubt there will be those willing to do it if the watchdogs relax their guard. Already brash little encroachments have been made, and as in so many British towns and suburbs, with their low, open dimensions, one high-rise tower of flats or offices in the wrong place will ruin the visual aspect of the district. At present the mixture of quiet residential streets, fine architectural ensembles, good shopping and the lively, tolerant variety of the social life, make it still a delectable place. Despite its legendary associations with maiden ladies of means and half-pay colonels, it is a more practical and resilient place than it looks. It has, after all, its industrial monuments: Brunel's great bridge, the fragments of the Clifton Rocks Railway, which used to climb the sides of the Gorge from the river-level; and, if one knew where to look, a handsome, ruined, red-painted chocolate machine of the 1930s, tucked away in a niche in a wall near the zoo—still there in the summer of 1970, since removed, alas. Perhaps Clifton needed the banality of that chocolate machine to counter the vaguely guilty melancholy of the long, grey, acacia-scented avenues, as it needs its new, bright young population to bring it eventually, adapted but not destroyed, into the new century.

Interlude

BRISTLE

'BRISTLE' is what Bristolians tend to call their city and their native speech, Bristol writer Dereck Robinson claimed in his amusing booklet *Krek Waiter's Peak Bristle* (The Correct Way to Speak Bristol), published in late 1970. To my ear, though, some Bristle people over-emphasize the 't' and call the city 'Brist-tol', as my grandmother used the over-genteel form 'Awrrthurr' for her husband's name rather than the natural Bristol 'Ahrrthurr'. Mr. Robinson's book, light-hearted though it is, made one important, perhaps not deliberately intended point: that Bristol speech is more a slovenly degradation of the English language than a picturesque dialect. Geoffrey Woodruff, a Bristol schoolmaster, who has studied it and lectured on it with popular success, calls it 'Bristolese', which carries the same connotation of a debasement rather than an enhancement of the language. It is perhaps not surprising then to find that there appears to be no printed material on the dialect, apart from some newspaper cuttings, and a short article in *Punch* in August 1960. Perhaps Bristol is ashamed of the way it speaks?

Paradoxically, this is not entirely true. Bristol mocks its speech but is really rather proud of it and goes out of its way to speak it loudly and deliberately in the street. It is not uncommon to hear two professional-looking men indulging in a slanging match in Bristolese about whether or not one has parked his car in the path of the other. To the outsider this might sound like a public row; the passing Bristolian knows it is part of an elaborate local joke. The disadvantage in this for the serious student of the survival of English dialects is that it is almost impossible to know when the dialect is being spoken as a joke and when it is a surviving natural way of speech. A Yorkshireman or North Midlander who says 'Anyroad' for 'Anyway' is probably using it naturally. A Bristolian who says "Snow?" (Dost thee know?) may or may not be using it naturally, though when one hears it from elderly Bristolians on street television interviews one can be certain it is genuine. Then one can hear an old-age pensioner complaining about bus fares to the interviewer: "It cosses (costeth) me one an' farr to get into town."

'Bristle' is more an accent than a dialect, a way of pronouncing standard words rather than a special set of local words and phrases. The outstanding characteristic of the dialect was always the survival of the second person singular of the personal pronoun, though in the peculiar form "thee bist" rather than the standard "thou art" (still used in the North). This led to local jokes such as "thee cassn't see as well as thee cousst, casst?" (thee canst not see as well as thee couldst, canst thee?) and such usage was certainly alive well into this century. Where it survives today (apart from being a deliberate joke) it does so fragmentarily and unconsciously, as Welsh-language idioms survive in wholly English-speaking parts of Wales: a boy who may otherwise speak modern English may say to other boys "Swanny 'elp?" (Dost thee want any help?). There are local words like 'skag' for a tear in cloth; 'spreath(e)' for rough, chapped skin in cold weather (I used this naturally in childhood, though living away from Bristol); 'scrage' for abrasion; 'croupying' or 'coupying' down, for crouching down; 'dap' for plimsoll, pump, running shoe (also usual in South Wales); 'dap' also for put something down carelessly ("I dapped it down somewhere"), for a short errand ("Just dap down the shop for me"), or knowing where to find something ("To dap our hand on it"); 'shrammed' meaning numb with cold; 'French toast' for a piece of bread and butter toasted on the dry side. Some of these words may not be unique to Bristol, and some are certainly shared with South Gloucestershire or North Somerset; they do not really constitute a full dialect, compared with Lowland Scots, or Newcastle, or rural Yorkshire.

'Bristle' is more a matter of mispronunciation. Geoffrey Woodruff links the accent with the local proneness to bronchial troubles and catarrh, common in a warm, damp climate like Bristol's. Liverpool and Glasgow, also westward-looking ports, have similar sounds, he points out. Catarrh makes for difficulty in speaking and for a certain strained aggressiveness of tone, characteristic of Bristol speech, and to typical sounds like the glottal-stop dropping of the 't' in water or the 'tt' in butter. Another characteristic which suggests difficulty in articulation, due to nasal or bronchial blockages, is the substitution of 'd' for 'th', as in 'dis' and 'dat' and the greeting shouted by passing gangs of dockers at each other (I heard it near the Bathurst Basin in November, 1970): "Ah-roy denn?" (All right, then?). These sounds, or lack of sounds, combined with the West of England 'burred' use of the 'r', make Bristol speech a trial for visitors.

The most famous Bristol trick of speech, though—apart from the use of 'thee'—is the legendary adding of an 'l' to words ending in vowels; traditionally Bristolians are supposed to say "Americal, Africal, Australial . . ." and to refuse to recognize any difference between 'idea' and 'ideal'. The name Bristol itself is assumed to come from the adding of this terminal 'l' to the old name Bristow (from Bridge-stow). Phonetically, none of this is quite true. The sound the Bristolian adds is really a deep 'aw' sound, which almost but not quite becomes an 'l' in the depths of the palate. He talks about a 'cameraw' not a 'cameral', and this explains why he also *drops* the 'l' from the ends of words where it legitimately exists, as in 'cathedraw', or, paradox of paradoxes, 'Bristaw' itself! Having added, as the legend has it, the terminal 'l' to make Bristol, he then drops it to say "Bristaw": which suggests that it was not an 'l' in the first place. The confusion between 'idea' and 'ideal' arises, not because he says 'ideal' for 'idea', but because he pronounces both words 'idee-aw'. The exceptions are where the word ending with a vowel is followed by a word beginning with a vowel; so that we do certainly hear "cameral obscuraw" (the camera obscura near the Suspension Bridge) and "Americal and Africaw". The myth of the terminal 'l' is widely believed, not least by Bristolians themselves.

Does one hear today "a dear little bit" for a very small piece of something? Or the charming "dateth" (or "datef"), as in "What's today's dateth?", a piece of linguistic pre-echo from, one supposes, the ordinal 'th' (the dateth is the eighth)? Or the time-usage, heard even among the well-spoken: "I'll see you at five and twenty to, all right?"? What does survive vigorously is the harsh, aggressive Bristol accent, which packs harmless words together and emits them in staccato bursts of lost or squashed consonants, as in "W'as 'a m'ar dee, denn?" (What's the matter with thee, then?); or the perhaps rather fictional use of 'diesel' noted by Derek Robinson, as in "diesel get my fist up thy frote" (Thee shall . . .); or the memorable Bristol word 'Gharff!' used by a football crowd to express its disapproval of a player.

This is an idiosyncratic Bristol dialect of its own, and it seems as strong as ever in the streets. But time and state education are against its survival. Schoolchildren can be taught to take a pride in a rich idiomatic dialect like Northumbrian or Scots; but teachers can hardly encourage their pupils to continue to speak what is basically a maltreatment of English. Well, das wa' 'tis, innut denn?

VI

THE BRISTOLIAN—VERY SPARYNGE OF HIS HATT

THERE is a Bristol story—there are a number of them, all, one suspects, created to puzzle the visitor—about two city draymen who, having survived the Western Front in the 1914–18 war, return to Bristol, resume their jobs and pass each other one day in the street. As the lumbering horses approach, pass and draw away, the draymen nod to each other. When they are well apart again, one of them calls dourly over his shoulder: "I thought thee was bloody dead, Bill." It takes a Bristolian to tell it and possibly a Bristolian to understand it, so rich is it in layer upon layer of local experience and assumptions beneath the bare details, like the more Jewish of Jewish jokes.

There is, for example, the curious neutrality and waggishness about death. Bristol is rich in graveyard humour. An uncle made a point of telling me, the Bristolian who had forsaken his city, in great detail about who had died in the neighbourhood since my last visit; and a solemnly waggish cabbie grandfather, who did side business carrying surplus relatives to funerals, used to carry a tape measure in a pocket and mournfully measure fellow cabbies with it in city bars. It is an attitude only possible in a long-settled community that remembers its dead. In cities with large immigrant populations from other cities the deaths of neighbours' parents or grandparents would not be remembered because they had died in another town. When generation after generation dies in the same city, as in Bristol, the fact of death becomes both familiar and less solemn, and a startlingly flippant attitude towards it can develop, as in many long-settled villages. That Bristol shares this attitude shows how closely the city has lived to its rural surroundings over the centuries into recent times.

Then there is the refusal to show surprise or emotion. Neither the war itself nor the fact that both men, obviously old friends, have survived it, are regarded as justification for breaking one's usual reserve. This is the suspicious caution of the countryman; but it is also the inherited caution of a city that has risked its prosperity on the Atlantic, on Cabot's voyages, on Brunel's Great Western Railway and pioneer steamships, and is currently risking a large sector of its future prosperity on the Concorde venture. It is the caution of bookies or auctioneers or poker-players and involves a good deal of bluff. It might seem that the man who finally speaks has lost the game of bluff. But probably it is he who has won by thinking up the devastating comment and being too far away for his friend to reply. The element of verbal abuse is strong in Bristol humour ("Theece want thee ruddy 'ead read," is the type of friendly banter between friends that often disconcerts strangers to the city). The prevailing tone of harsh banter and mock-insult has led many visitors to conclude that the Bristolian is unfriendly and pugnacious.

It is aggressively unsentimental; the two draymen may be good friends and genuinely glad to see each other alive. But they will never in a lifetime admit it or say a sentimental word to each other. Geoffrey Woodruff, the Bristol dialect and character expert (to whom I owe much here and elsewhere), has observed that the aggressiveness in the local character rarely comes to blows; the disputants insult and threaten each other, but always from the other bank of a canal or the other side of a busy street: "Ah-roy denn, ah-royt. S'wanna make summat of it? Take dee [thee] coat off den. Wass th' matter wiv dee? Yurr [here], I'll be over durr to dee in a minute, mate. . . ."

The aggressiveness is sometimes so rough and personal at the edges that one suspects that in the past it must have reflected real violence. It sounds like an echo of a time when the population crowded into the foul huddled slums of nineteenth-century Bristol, when the city was notorious for mobs and general roughness (though today its crime rate tends to be slightly lower than that of comparable large cities). There is a vindictive do-you-down tone about it that has played a part in making the Bristol character not much liked outside the city. There were many strikes in nineteenth-century Bristol and fist-fighting was always a popular local sport. Possibly it reflects the two-class rather than three-class basis of the population; there was no real aristocratic class and the class struggle would be more sharply focused between the working people and the middle and mercantile classes.

But the story of the draymen also reveals an element of uncertainty, an under-confident anxiety about being caught out, put in the wrong or made to look foolish. The draymen are creating a humorous situation for themselves and for anyone listening. But they are also using it to forestall any outbreak of emotion, any public demonstration involved in meeting a friend thought to be dead. It is situation humour rather than verbal humour, which is less strong in Bristol than other large cities. Thus in Bristol banter there is a tendency to repeat old jokes rather than coin new ones; there is no metaphorical wit as in Liverpool, or cheeky hyperbole as in inner London.

All these are again characteristics of the countryman, but in this case imperfectly adapted to city life, unlike the Cockney or the Mancunian who has become completely urbanized. There is almost a certain sadness in the Bristolian's uncertain position between country and city, and his natural caution is increased by his sense of not quite belonging to either way of life. The characteristic local response to a question or a challenge or a startling piece of news is "Ar!" (which might well be the city's motto). And when the caution, the uncommitted response and the verbal aggressiveness are put together one might hear the sort of exchange noted by Geoffrey Woodruff as quintessentially 'Bristol':

"Ar!"

"Wassat?"

"I said bloody AR!"

The country element appears in the lack of verbal subtlety compared with the strong sense of humorous situation; in the slow timing; in the tendency to laugh at one's own waggishness, unlike Cockneys and Liverpudlians who keep a straight face at their own jokes; in the many stories arising from ritualistic occasions like weddings, christenings and burials. And it may appear in the observation, made by some visitors, that Bristol girls are more lively and responsive than the men, as countrywomen, in a primitive economic context, are often more energetic and sharp-witted than their men.

There is also a type of Bristol 'funny man', almost a Bristol Cockney, a fast talker, a recognized wag with special privileges in mock-insult and sarcasm. A 'Bristol' joke I have observed myself is when two accepted wags occupy seats some distance from each other on the top deck of a city bus and exchange dead-pan badinage without turning their heads. A wag can be so accepted and admired that he really does not have to do anything funny to get his effects.

The local humour remains private and domestic on the whole. There are few Bristol jokes that 'travel' as Liverpool jokes do; and there are no Bristol music-hall, radio or television comedians of note, though the city is full of wags who come into their own at dances and office parties.

They figure, too, in the distinctively Bristol form of gossip, a stolid interweaving, over beer or sherry, or in the stone-faced terrace houses, of family relationships and the eccentricities of friends and neighbours. You listen with mild interest, and then you begin to realize that some of the people being talked about as living presences have been dead for decades, grandfathers and great-uncles, who came from the country, lived in Bristol all their adult lives and always dreamed of going back to Midsomer Norton but never did. You may even find not only Great Aunt Hannah and her father entering the conversation, but W. G. Grace and Ernie Bevin and the last Duke of Beaufort but two with them. Old controversies and scandals, old characters, old names for places that are often private Bristol jokes—'Screws 'Ole' for Crews Hole, the early industrial district in East Bristol, 'Magpie Park' for the island in Colston Avenue (from the *Bristol Magpie* newspaper, once published nearby), and 'Skivvies' Island' for the centre of the Centre, where the domestic servants once met their followers: vague memories of these haunt the collective mind of the city, outwardly engaged in catching buses, building aircraft and making cigarettes.

It is in more intimate social relationships that Bristol people display those characteristics of formality, banter and lack of sentimentality noted by people who come to live there, and often expressed in letters from them to the local newspapers. Certainly they do not go out of their way to make themselves affable to strangers, but they do not to themselves either. The first breakthrough with them is often made by returning their banter in kind; when they turn the banter against the stranger he can be assured he is on the way to acceptance. These are not merely personal comments; Bristol is aware itself that it has not had a good Press in the past. Daniel Defoe noted:

> the tenacious Folly of its inhabitants; who by the general Infatuation, the Pretence of Freedoms and Privileges, that Corporation-Tyranny, which prevents the flourishing and encrease of many a good town in England, continue obstinately to forbid any, who are not Subjects of their City Sovereignty (that is to say, Freeman) to trade within the Chain of their own Liberties.

The "Irish Gentleman", who recorded his *Journey through England in the Year 1752*, commented: "Their Souls are engrossed by lucre, and [they] are very expert in affairs of merchandize; but as to politeness, it is a thing banished from their republic as a contagious distemper."And an actor, who visited Bristol in 1780, and did not do well in the city, noted: "What right had I to expect being attended to where Savage died neglected in gaol and whence Chatterton fled to perish prematurely in London?"

Yet by one of the paradoxes that make any attempt to summarize Bristol's character seem like a string of contradictory sentences, no city in the country has so long, durable and deserved a reputation for organized and effective charity. A local review of charities "for the sick and poor", commissioned by the Corporation in 1968, listed about 150 such charities still in existence, and a substantial number of them still active. These ranged from the Gloucestershire Society (1657), said to be the oldest county society in Britain, to the Good Neighbours Trust formed in 1960 to provide some financial assistance for the "sick and aged, the physically and mentally handicapped, the unfortunate and deprived". (The report noted that "appeals for tremendous sums of money which on occasion lack a personal touch are less favourably received by the Trustees", an interesting comment in an age of vast, disconcertingly vague, world-embracing charities.) All Saints Almshouses of 1350, Trinity Hospital of 1395, St. John's of 1475 and Foster's Almshouses of 1481 all survive today, as do the lovely Colston's Almshouses (1696) in St. Michael's Hill, and the attractively restored St. Nicholas Almshouses (1652) in King Street, both of them assisted by the Merchant Venturers Almshouses Charity. Unlike some old institutions, these have not been allowed to die when decay or damage have afforded an excuse. Alderman Steevens' Almshouses (1679) in Old Market Street, destroyed by a landmine in the war, have been rebuilt to house fifteen old people, and the inhabitants of the Temple (or Dr. White's) Hospital, founded in 1613, have been moved from the old hospital, now pulled down in the general devastation of the Temple district, to a new building near St. Mary Redcliffe. In 1970 there were nineteen old almshouse foundations flourishing in the city.

The corporation report concluded: "The charities of Bristol are in general well run and continue to play a most important part in the life of the city. Loneliness has replaced hunger as arch-enemy, and this is a field in which the charities are playing a vital part. . . ." The report did, however, recommend that very small, or unused, or moribund charities, such as those for dying trades like coopers or some of the tiny parish charities of a few pounds each, should be amalgamated for greater efficiency, though a surprising number of these small sums are still in demand for immediate relief of hardship. Many, though, are attached to old city parishes that have lost or are losing their parishioners. Similarly, one wonders if there is really any justification for the continued separate existence of the various Colston charities, for which active appeals are made each November: the Anchor Society (1769) for "elderly people in distress"; the Dolphin Society (1749) for men and women whose income does not "exceed £208 p.a. and are 55 or over"; and the Grateful Society, which pays "annuities to ladies who have suffered financially". The old political differences between the societies—the Dolphin was Tory, the Anchor Whig and the Grateful non-political—have long disappeared, and in 1968 the Grateful had surplus funds and was looking for a project on which to use them. The advantage of amalgamated charities is demonstrated by the efficiency of the Bristol Municipal Charities (1836), which administers charities of which the corporation was formerly the trustee, notably Bristol Grammar School, Queen Elizabeth's Hospital and the Red Maids' School. Bristol can still think up new forms of charity: in 1970 eleven Bristol landladies offered homes to men just out of prison under a scheme started the year before by the Bristol Association for the Care and Resettlement of Offenders. Early reports quoted examples of middle-aged recidivists finding home comforts and affection for the first time since childhood, if then.

Charity and commerce? Caring for old people and ignoring neighbours and strangers? Is this Bristol paradox too paradoxical to accept? Not really perhaps; the organization of charity is often

Sion Hill near Clifton Suspension Bridge

undertaken by people of conscience who find it difficult to express personal emotions directly. This does not detract from the sincerity of the charitable—though one might question the motives of an Edward Colston who made so many bigoted conditions about who was fit to receive his charity—and it might help to explain the remarkable amount of organized charity in a city reputed to be rather cold in its human relations. Bristolians give charity well but receive it badly; the old working-class dislike of official charity, of welfare benefits and the dole, is still active. So is the working-class and non-conformist distrust of moral or psychiatric advice; local psychiatrists and psychological workers report a cautious, suspicious attitude to their work. Non-Bristolians who are acquainted with the local banter know that the 'looney-bin' attitude to mental illness has not quite died out.

George Müller, who founded his homes on the belief that God would provide—and claimed that God always did provide—was one of a number of men of faith from outside Bristol who brought a fiery evangelical spirit into a city that, left to itself, might have ambled on in the undemanding Anglicanism of the past. But the outsiders—George Whitefield and John and Charles Wesley above all—found and focused the latent elements of evangelical non-conformity under the unemotional Bristol surface. As so often, it was as if the Bristolians needed the pressure of a less inhibited outsider to enable them to discover their own character. There was a ripple of Lollardry in the Middle Ages, especially in the Weavers' Guild in the Temple, and later William Tyndale was tutor at a manor house at nearby Little Sodbury. But the city's religious emotions were as cautious as its political commitments and only five Protestant martyrs could be winkled out of the canny populace in Mary Tudor's reign. It was not until Archbishop Laud's time that religious dissent became marked, with the formation of a group of Puritans around the grocer Anthony Kelly and his formidable wife Dorothy, who married the Puritan Matthew Hazzard after her husband's death. The Puritans' part in encouraging the defenders of the city against Prince Rupert's siege was acknowledged by a wave of persecutions of all non-conformists during Charles II's time—though the Duke of Beaufort wisely prevented the citizens from supporting the Duke of Monmouth later. Meeting houses were closed and the

Meridian Vale, within a few minutes of busy Queen's Road, Clifton

dissenters had to take to the Downs and the surrounding hills for their worship. George Fox came to Bristol in 1656 and was married in the old Broadmead Chapel in 1669. The Quaker influence under Fox, and later the Penns, Hollisters and Callowhills and other families, became a significant part of the city's religious character, though the Quakers have never been very numerous. The spiritual needs of the people seem to have been more complex than Quakerism but less complex than Anglicanism; when Whitefield and the Wesleys arrived in the following century it was as if Bristol had been waiting for their kind of unfanatical, warm, conscientious evangelicalism. There has been a Methodistical air about the city ever since as if Methodism, more than any other creed, is essentially the Bristol form of Christianity. In practical historical terms, though, the popularity of a 'reformed' type of low Anglicanism was much helped by the weakness of Bristol's episcopal status over the centuries, and local Anglicanism never became as remote from the city as the bishops themselves did; Hannah More was a notable figure in the reforming Anglican evangelicalism of the turn of the eighteenth and nineteenth centuries. Relations between Anglicans and nonconformists remained uneasy or remote, though, for a long time—perhaps into the nineteenth century—as a result of the persecutions of the dissenters in Charles II's reign.

George Whitefield, born in Gloucester though his mother was Bristolian, was moved to bring the Gospel to the brutal and degraded colliers of Kingswood "by seeing the white gutter made by their tears which plentifully fell down their black cheeks as they came out of the coal-pits". Like John the Baptist he made way for a greater than himself when he asked John Wesley, himself recently 'reborn' through his London experience of Christ's presence, to join him in 1739. Wesley's famous sermon on Hanham Mount was given in April that year and he later preached to crowds increasing from 2,000 to 10,000, though he long had reservations about open-air preaching and about the growing practice of laymen preaching. In 1739, too, he had his encounter with Bishop Joseph Butler, author of the famous *Analogy of Religion* (1736), who refused him permission to preach in the city churches—a sad misunderstanding as both men were great reformers, Butler rescuing the church from intellectual unbelief as Wesley rescued it from spiritual apathy. John Wesley's career embraced the whole of Britain and extended to America—his brother Charles settled in Bristol for many years—but he regularly returned to the city and it was at a house in Dighton Street below Kingsdown in 1784 that he appointed Thomas Coke first bishop of the American congregations, the crucial act of separation from the Church of England. Bristol took to Wesley, one suspects, because he could speak in their own combative language when necessary. When Beau Nash tried to warn him off Bath and met him with "My name is Nash", Wesley replied: "Sir, I dare not judge of you by common report. I think it is not enough to judge by."

Other denominations and sub-sections of denominations arose—the Moravians flourished from 1748—but the religious pattern remained constant through the nineteenth century: upper and professional-class Anglicanism, middle and lower-class nonconformity. The *Western Daily Press* took a census of all those who attended churches and chapels on Sunday, 30th October, 1881: of a population of 266,000 there were 48,596 in attendance in the morning and 60,856 in the evening, figures that seem to support the city's reputation for church and chapel-going and for the lugubrious Sunday bell-ringing that so depressed one of my grandmothers. But the paper also found that on a December Saturday night in the same year 98,226 people, including 12,440 children, were in the pubs between seven and 11 p.m.—more than a third of the population!

To what extent Bristol is still a church and chapel-going city in an increasingly secular age is difficult to assess, though a writer in the British Association's Bristol Handbook of 1955 thought there was more church and chapel activity than in any other English city and noted that in 1955 a large group of city councillors held regular meetings for prayer and discussion before civic events. A large amount of space is given in the local Press to church affairs and to announcements of Sunday services and until recent years at least the inner suburbs still thought very much on a parochial basis. Church-based scout groups and organizations like the Boys' Brigade were always strong, as was the Salvation Army, which received a friendlier welcome in Bristol in its early years than it did in London. Clergymen like the Reverend Mervyn Stockwood, a Bristol clergyman from 1936 to 1955, now Bishop of Southwark, and the Bishop of Bristol (until 1975), the Right

Reverend Oliver Tomkins, have played a conciliatory part in social problems, and the Bristol Council of Christian Churches has interpreted the prevailing ecumenical spirit in practical terms. The more abstract reaches of theology have not much appealed—the Anglo-Catholic revival did not make much impact and Pusey was met with threats when he preached there. On the other hand Roman Catholicism has flourished in Clifton since the creation of the new See in 1850.

The reputation for pride and aloofness is well documented, though. A Stuart visitor found them "rather admiring themselves soe that an ordinary fellow that is but a freeman of Bristoll, he conceits himself to be as grave as a senator of Rome, and very sparinge of his hatt". Despite Bristol's world-wide trade over the centuries no large colony of foreigners ever settled in the city. It has never had a large Jewish population, though there was an influx of refugee Polish Jews from the Tsarist pogroms early in this century (my father got pocket money for lighting their fires on the Sabbath eve); though this may be as much due to lack of opportunity for characteristic Jewish trades as to coldness or hostility.

There was a substantial Italian colony before 1914, living mostly behind St. James's Church in the North Street area. They brought with them many of their national customs, the women wore peasant costume and immense black nailed boots, and man and wife would often live on the proceeds of a hurdy-gurdy, or a barrel organ, which they would hire by the day or the week from an entrepreneur, and play in the streets with the baby held in a sling across the front of the organ. There is now quite a substantial Italian colony again, largely connected with the restaurant trade, some, like the Bernis, having settled here many years ago. Like other Italians in Britain, they maintain a diplomatic balance between their own way of life and fraternizing with their English neighbours. The Roman Catholic Church of St. Mary's on the Quay seems to be their cultural centre; here you can see posters in Italian announcing dances and parties, always with a footnote in English inviting their English friends. There were German bands playing from their music stands at street corners, and there was a small Scots community and a Scottish Presbyterian Church. Some of the Scots were 'Scots duffers', credit tailors with extensive business out in the surrounding villages to which they travelled by pony and cart to collect the payments. They were respected as almost the only form of credit available to many people and were regarded as being very tolerant in not pressing the hard-up for payment.

The largest 'foreign' colony, though, has always been that of the Welsh. In the eighteenth century Bristol was in many ways the 'Welsh metropolis' and was long the economic capital of South Wales before the rise of Cardiff in the later nineteenth century; Welsh cattle and produce were being ferried across the Channel in the trows, or flat-bottomed barges, from Chepstow several centuries back. The relationship has not been a happy one —"There is a lot of Welsh blood in Bristol," a local wag told a *New Statesman* writer in 1969, "most of it on the pavements on Saturday night." The antagonism is only rarely violent; it more often takes the form of a distrust of the Welsh by the Bristolians (the Welsh seem to have no particular feelings against Bristol people). By a geographical and ethnic freak two widely differing types of temperament have been brought together: the expansive, mercurial South Welshman and the reserved, cautious Bristolian. It is like bringing a colony of Florentines to live in Oslo. The Welsh have provided local politicians, trade union leaders, teachers, church organists and choirmasters and even Lord Mayors. But they have always been regarded somewhat askance. My own relatives never ceased to commiserate with us for our sad exile in Monmouthshire an hour away by train, or to be surprised when they visited us to find not a coal mine within 20 miles. (Indeed, until the 1950s, there were coal mines nearer to the centre of Bristol than to Cardiff or Newport.) The antagonism may not have much longer to live. The Severn Bridge has brought many more Welsh into Bristol for a day's shopping or an evening at the theatre or the Entertainment Centre. The transferring of South Wales depots of national distributive firms across to Bristol since the opening of the bridge has no doubt increased the Welsh population. The bridge has even tempted some Bristolians to visit the Wye and Usk Valleys and to penetrate as far as the Gower or Pembrokeshire for holidays instead of the ritual visit to Weymouth or Teignmouth.

Bristol has possibly shown more tolerance towards its coloured citizens than it has towards the Welsh. There is no colour problem yet, as there could be said to be a colour problem in Birmingham and Wolverhampton. By 1963 there were 7,000 coloured people in the city (there may be 12,000 or more now), mostly West Indians and mostly living in the Lower Ashley Road and Newfoundland Road area of St. Paul's, and up the hill in the former middle-class residential area of Montpelier. Here a self-contained coloured community has settled into City Road and Grosvenor Road, around St. Agnes' Park and on the fringes of Portland and Brunswick Squares. There is no obvious friction, though there have been the expected complaints about late-night parties and noise. The old women stand in their doorways looking complacently enough on the coloured children being called home for the night. There is comparatively little history of coloured people in Bristol, despite its maritime past and despite the myth of the city swarming with Negro slaves in the eighteenth century; Bristol has had no multi-racial tradition as Cardiff has. But there was no real trouble until May 1963 when the coloured residents boycotted the city's bus service because of the company's policy against employing coloured labour. This was an unhappy episode. The company held to its policy and the bus crews were nearly 100 per cent in support. Bus crews and one depot threatened to strike. The matter was taken up in Parliament by local M.P.s. The Bristol Council of Christian Churches offered to mediate; the Bishop preached against racial discrimination; Sir Learie (later Lord) Constantine came down to observe. Letters to the local Press angrily picked sides, and comparisons were made with the experience of out-of-work Welshmen, who came across in the 1930s and were not made welcome, not because they were Welsh but because it was felt that Bristolians should have first choice of the jobs available.

John Morgan, writing in the *New Statesman* at the time, said there was an impression, "which the West Indians confirmed, without being able to explain it, that Bristol was a more difficult city for coloured people than others". But this hardly seemed true. The parallels with the Welsh immigrants in the 1930s suggested that the hostility of the bus crews was not so much racial as economic, based on a fear of losing jobs and a feeling that Bristolians should be considered first. The prejudice was against non-Bristolians rather than against coloured people, and a survey of housing and racial attitudes in the city, made in 1965 and discussed in the magazine *Race* in July, 1970, confirmed that such prejudices were closely related to housing and economic pressures —it has been estimated that about one-fifth of the present population of St. Paul's is immigrant.

In August 1963 the bus company's colour bar was ended and a statement of policy agreed between the company and the Transport and General Workers' Union, and in 1967 there were about fifty coloured bus conductors and drivers employed. The local papers made a point of printing photographs of amicable multi-racial conductor-driver teams. The report of Lord Hunt's Committee praised Bristol's "healthy multi-racial attitude". There has been no comparable incident since, though there were some robbing and stabbing incidents in 1970 involving coloured youths.

There is usually a public argument of some kind going on in the city. The early 1930s saw the famous battle in which a group of citizens rallied to found a new local evening newspaper when the existence of the old local ones was threatened by a war of expansion between distant newspaper tycoons. Prominent people were canvassed for money, a staff was quickly gathered and the new paper, the *Evening Post*, was launched to an immediate circulation of 70,000. Gratifyingly, in a world where the tycoons usually win, it eventually outlived its rival evening, which had been laid cuckoo-like and unwanted, as Bristol saw it, in the local nest. In the late 1950s and early 1960s there was a bitter argument about comprehensive schools in the city's education system; some people were expressing party views, others strongly personal feelings for or against comprehensiveness. But the creation of a number of multi-lateral or bi-lateral schools in the early 1950s made the change-over to comprehension easier than in many places and the argument calmed down considerably. Instead the argument has switched to the future of the city's seven direct grant schools. In September 1969, 85·4 per cent of the children admitted to maintained secondary schools went to comprehensives. In July 1970 Bristol appeared largely committed to comprehension and against the return of the eleven-plus examination, though there was still some uncertainty about the status of the existing local authority grammar schools. The acceptance of comprehension may be due partly to the proved value of the comprehensives themselves, partly to the presence of Clifton College and seven direct grant schools, which give a fair alternative choice to comprehension. It may be, too, that the city's underlying radicalism and relative freedom from class divisions smoothed the way. But the fate of the direct grant schools in any attempt to 'localize' them became an issue again in the mid-1970s. The fact that Bristol's education system is now run by the new County of Avon, with its strongly Conservative rural hinterland, will almost certainly prolong the argument between comprehensive and selective education.

Bristol's touchy, radical, rather self-opinionated but at the same time rather self-doubting character is revealed over the centuries in its relation with the great men and events of the city's history. Bristol's relations with its famous M.P., Edmund Burke, are particularly interesting. Burke, an Anglo-Irishman with no personal connections with the city, was one of the two local M.P.s from 1774 to 1780 through the most difficult period of the American War. Burke was 45 and at the height of his oratorical and critical powers when he was chosen as candidate with Henry Cruger, an American-born Bristol merchant, to oppose the Government's American policy which seemed to be threatening the city's prosperous trade with America. The retiring members, Lord Clare (after whom Clare Street was named) and Matthew Brickdale, a city merchant, both supported the Government's tough attitude towards the rebellious colonists, and Burke was a well-known enemy of the Government. The polling went on, in the fashion of the time, for twenty-three days, after which Cruger and Burke were elected and chaired through the streets. Burke was one of the first politicians to use the hustings to get into close contact with the people. And it was while the new Members were thanking the crowds that Burke made his crucial statement on the duties of a Member of Parliament. Cruger said simply that "the electors have a right to instruct their members". Burke disagreed: "Parliament is not a congress of ambassadors from different and hostile interests, but a deliberate assembly of one nation, with one interest, that of the whole. . . . You choose a Member indeed; but when you have chosen him, he is not Member for Bristol, he is a Member of Parliament. . . ." He quickly found himself in trouble. The merchants thought they had the greatest orator in the House in their pockets. But on issue after issue—America, the Irish trade laws, the law of debt, religious toleration—he either went flatly against his constituents or was not energetic enough in his support of their views. He rarely visited Bristol and had no electoral organization to keep support for him alive. In 1780 he withdrew to fight another seat.

It is easy to represent this disagreement as one between a high-minded statesman and a body of venal and self-important merchants. But Burke is seen today as a much more complex figure than he seemed to the nineteenth century. He was a professional politician, interested in staying at Westminster, enjoying power, aristocratic society and the world of influence. Some of his motives in the American crisis were suspect because he derived part of his income from being the London agent of the city of New York. He hardly ever visited Bristol after his election. There was a touch of Anglo-Irish blarney about him. Some of his contemporaries thought him a little mad and Dr. Johnson said to Boswell: "If a man will appear extravagant, as he does, can he wonder that he is represented as mad?" He melodramatized and over-simplified the American conflict in his speeches. G. M. Young noted that "from the age of 40 onwards (i.e. before the Bristol election of 1774) Burke was a tormented, impoverished and suspected man". Young also noted that Burke was not untainted by Rousseau's ideas and drew a critical picture of Burke's system of ideas as based on his fear of social disorder. He was a curious man for Bristol to elect and it is hardly surprising that he was not re-elected in 1780. Bristol may have been rejecting a great man but its action was wholly consistent and not without a certain practical logic. The statue of Burke in Colston Avenue, with its lifted hand (and hat concealed behind the back ready for the trip back to London) seems too eager to teach the citizens their business.

If Burke's election speeches in 1774 were, as Lord Acton described them, "an epoch in constitutional history" in which "Burke laid down for ever the law of the relations between members and constituencies", the Bristol riots of 1831 were an epoch in electoral history, a warning to the rulers that the ruled could destroy law and order if angry enough. The riots were the bloodiest event in the history of a city that on the whole kept the more violent aspects of history under control, though the Bristol mob had an unsavoury reputation. The trouble was partly the result of general discontent during the early arguments over the Reform Bill, partly Bristol's specific discontent with the recession that affected the city in the early decades of the century, and partly a popular vendetta against an unpopular, reactionary

Recorder of the city, Sir Charles Wetherell, who strongly opposed the Reform Bill. His unwise arrival to open the assizes on 29th October brought a night of terror and civic disorder to the city, and particularly to Queen Square, where more than 150 people were killed or wounded, and the Mansion House, the Customs and Excise Office, and other public buildings, and some fifty houses, destroyed or gutted by fire. The riots spilled over into Corn Street in one direction and in the other to College Green, where the Bishop's Palace next to the cathedral was destroyed. Four ringleaders were hanged, and twenty-six others condemned to transportation or imprisonment, and the cavalry commander at the scene, Lieutenant Colonel Brereton, who had tried to placate the mob instead of dispersing it, killed himself before being court-martialled for neglect of duty.

It was an event untypical in many respects of Bristol. Extraneous elements and emotions were present: roughs from the Kingswood mining district, hooligans from the docks, political agitators from elsewhere stirring up long pent-up resentment against civic, commercial and ecclesiastical privilege. It long remained a dark memory, a reminder of what the passive local temperament could do when roused. (The memory stirred again during the 1939–45 war when there were rumours of simmering discontent with the war in the blitzed and shaken city.) Possibly the violence of October 1831 explains the relative lack of interest shown locally in the Chartist movement, though it was also true that Chartism flourished best in areas dependent upon one or two basic and vulnerable industries. It may also explain the subsequent lack of fire in nineteenth-century politics in Bristol, which produced no Bright, Cobden or Chamberlain and where the great men of the day were the industrialists, like the Frys and Willses, and the philanthropists like George Müller.

Among the outsiders who came to test their wits against the canny locals was John Loudon McAdam, the pioneer of modern road-making, who came to Berkeley Square in 1801 and quickly improved the "wikked ways" around the city. But in 1825 he discovered a plot to have him dismissed from his position as surveyor to the Bristol Turnpike Trust and he left in anger to supervise the macadamization of the streets of London. Brunel got the better of the place from the start, though it is to Bristol's credit that it went along, though with misgivings, with the wild schemes of that very un-Bristolian genius. Probably the inhabitants recognized that the vast and apparently fantastic schemes were nevertheless well founded on the basic laws of engineering and painstakingly documented. Bristol was only a part of Brunel's life-work, but it was the scene of his early triumphs, the Great Western Railway, the winning design for the Suspension Bridge, and the steamships *Great Western* and *Great Britain*. And the winding down of the city docks symbolizes the ironic fate that has overtaken some of Brunel's major prophecies about the technological future: the disappearance of the giant luxury ocean liner and the scaling down of railways in favour of roads. If Brunel haunts anywhere it is surely the dwindling marshalling yards and emptying wharves of Bristol.

We have to move into this century before we come again to a major political figure. Ernest Bevin was one of the few outsiders who was completely accepted by Bristol. Often thought of as a Bristolian, he was actually a Somerset countryman who came to the city as a boy. He worked in a variety of jobs, from baker's assistant to tram conductor to mineral water carter, a job he kept until he became a full-time trade union official. Bevin's career in developing the Dockers' Union, in championing his fellow-carters and the other irregular jobs around the docks not provided for at the time in the trade union movement, his building up of the giant Transport and General Workers' Union: all this is part of social history, as his work as Churchill's wartime Minister of Labour and as Attlee's Foreign Secretary is part of national history. But he never forgot his Bristol background and the man cannot be understood apart from his connection with the city: his attendance at various non-conformist chapels, his Sunday School teaching, his identification of Christian social work with his kind of socialism, his relentless self-education, his concern about the poor and the casual workers, the widows left without support, the poor education facilities for workers' children, his friendship (later much qualified) with flamboyant Ben Tillett, the Bristol dockers' leader. He expressed some cool Bristol reserve about the necessity and conduct of the 1914–18 war; his practical idealism and honesty, combined with a certain ruthlessness and aggressiveness, reflect what was best in Bristol socialism in his day and help to explain why after 1918 the Socialists became the largest party in the city and ruled it for many years. The burly peasant speaking from his mineral cart, remembered by elderly Bristolians, has become a local folk-hero, a lumbering Sancho Panza of Socialism, keeping the Don Quixotes, such as the Bristol M.P. Stafford Cripps, in touch with the realities of the class struggle.

The long relationship between Stafford Cripps and his constituents in Bristol East (and later Bristol South East) is something of a mystery. While Bevin's character and background merged easily into the local scene, Cripps's upper-class academic socialism seems unlikely to have appealed to proletarian Bristol. But his lucid, unsentimental explanation of the National Government's difficulties in 1931 impressed voters and he had no difficulty in retaining his seat right up to his retirement through ill health in 1950. When he was expelled from the Labour Party in 1938, over official Labour apathy to the growing Nazi threat, many of his Bristol supporters went with him and for a time there were two Labour Parties in the city, one official and one unofficial in support of Cripps. There must have been a warmer and deeper common touch in Cripps than was recognized by those who caricatured him as a sour Puritan.

Only one politician since Bevin and Cripps has stirred similar feelings of loyalty in Bristol, Anthony Wedgwood Benn, who succeeded to Cripps's seat in 1950. In 1955 a petition, signed by the Lord Mayor, aldermen and burgesses of Bristol, was presented to Parliament asking that Mr. Wedgwood Benn should be allowed to renounce his father's title of Viscount Stansgate when he succeeded to it, and to continue to sit in the House of Commons. His father died in November 1960 and Benn was expelled from the House. In April 1961 more than 10,000 Bristolians signed a petition that Benn should be allowed to continue as M.P. for Bristol South East. He was unanimously chosen again as Labour candidate for the by-election to replace him, and said at the time: "I am asking the people of Bristol to take a risk and I am also taking a tremendous risk myself." He was re-elected with a 13,000 majority in May 1961 but was dramatically refused entrance to the House of Commons; a petition to an Election Court went against him. On the day that the Peerage Act was passed in 1963 he immediately renounced his title. On 20th August 1963, unopposed by any official Conservative candidate, he was triumphantly returned with a 15,000 majority and was cheered as Burke had been. Bristol acted, as Mr. Benn recalls it, in the "best West Country radical tradition", though the public display of emotion and loyalty was somewhat out of character. Since then Mr. Benn as Minister of Technology and subsequently as Secretary for Industry has been closely involved with projects such as the Concorde, considered by many people vital to Bristol's future; though when the glamour and excitement of the anti-peerage battle died away his views on the central importance of technology in Britain's future again became a subject of controversy locally.

Benn's majority was halved in the 1970 General Election, when two Labour seats, North East and North West, fell to the Conservatives. With three Conservative and three Labour MPs, the city returned to the status quo before the Labour landslide of 1966. The February General Election of 1974, by which time a major constituency revision had reduced the city's seats to five, resulted in two Conservative seats and three Labour. In the Election of October 1974 Bristol North West was lost by the Conservatives to Labour, resulting in four Labour seats and one surviving Conservative seat. Both the changes of allegiance and Mr. Benn's majority, which sank in 1970 and soared again in 1974, probably reflected the city's changing views of the devotion of either party to the cause of Concorde. In local politics the changes brought about by the creation of the new County of Avon left many Bristolians confused. The City Council and Lord Mayor were retained (but not the Sheriff), but many important functions went to the Avon County Council, among them planning, education, police and fire services. The weakened City Council remained under Labour control, while the new Avon County Council had a Conservative majority, reflecting its strong Conservative hinterland in what was formerly Somerset.

Bristol is not prone to hero-worshipping, and if it does allow its emotions to run away with it the hero may quickly find himself the target of retributive criticism soon after. Even W. G. Grace was not quite the hero in Bristol that he was to the country in general. The brilliant young cricketer, the most brilliant of the cricketing family of Dr. Henry Mills Grace of Downend, a village then just outside the city boundary, grew up to become the dictator of Gloucestershire County Cricket Club, resenting any interference in his picking of the team, and regularly choosing public school and university players rather than local men. He played to large crowds outside Bristol but to relatively small crowds in the city itself and his rigid insistence on class divisions between the gentlemanly amateurs and the lubberly professionals eventually alienated the city altogether. The game was more democratic under Gilbert Jessop and later under Wally Hammond. But social division lingered on in Bristol sport, with cricket and rugby the sport of middle-class North Bristol and Clifton and soccer the popular game of proletarian East and South Bristol.

The most famous and easily recognizable living Bristolian is a challenge to the student of Bristol character. Cary Grant, born Archibald Leach in Bristol in 1904, has become the archetypal Anglo-American Hollywood actor, who had to act when playing an Englishman in a film. But some local patriots believe they can detect a Bristol voice under that unmistakable and unclassifiable mid-Atlantic accent. But it is perhaps in his style of acting more than anything else that the Bristolian comes out. He is a master of impudent, slightly aggressive male banter, of the cheeky courtship of sophisticated women stars in films; but he has never been a completely convincing serious romantic or dramatic actor. The Bristol pattern of temperament seems to hold sway even after forty years in Hollywood.

How long the local character can remain itself is uncertain. Bristol's chief idiosyncrasies of character may already be dying. With the vastly greater mobility of the population, and the influx of workers from outside, such as the Derby workers at the Rolls-Royce section of the British Aircraft Corporation works at Filton, local exclusiveness is broken down. The introduction of cross-city bus routes in addition to the old wheel-spoke routes has opened up parts of the city to each other; originally you went from your suburb straight into the centre and back, unaware of the adjacent districts. The new motorways will open up the city to the rest of the country and the Severn Bridge has already destroyed much of the city's remoteness and secretiveness. On the other hand, the inner ring roads and high-level link-roads may restore the old isolation of certain districts in their rôle as uncrossable barriers, and thus preserve the local character longer than one would imagine possible in a rapidly conforming age.

It would be a pity if it died altogether; it may not be obviously attractive on the surface, but it was always richly bizarre and amusing and had a kind of rough, inarticulate, no-nonsense integrity about it. Like a linguist completing his study of a rare native language just as the last speaker of it dies, the student of Bristol character may find it has gone just as he thinks he has discovered its secret.

Interlude

A BRISTOL 'CHARACTER'

MY CAB-DRIVER grandfather was a Bristol 'character' living on that shabby-genteel fringe between poverty and austerity which accounted for such a vast section of the population of Edwardian England. He rented a hansom and a four-wheeler, had his place at a 'stand' in St. James's Barton, but obviously did quite a lot of extra business with funerals and weddings, and trips to country places like Almondsbury Hill on the Gloucester road to take trippers "to see the sheep on the Welsh hills" across the Severn; though people who recalled such outings did not recall seeing any Welsh sheep. His job brought him into touch with the raffish levels of society: sailors on a drunken tour of the city pubs, bookies' runners, travelling actors (generous with their tips), petty criminals, even a professional burglar whose tool-kit my grandfather looked after when the burglar went away on one of his regular absences. A cabbie could not be moralistic about his fares; it was too precarious a living.

He was basically a respectable man, though; hard-working, conscientious, a good family man in a heavy Victorian manner, often slightly under the influence of brandy and hot water or snatched rums between fares on winter nights—a hazard of the trade—but never noticeably drunk. He talked affectionately to my grandmother in a very Bristolian way, ticking her off with mock-testiness, talking wistfully of his *next* wife, muttering "I'll 'ave to 'ave thee shot", being rude to her relatives or his own if they stayed too long by ostentatiously taking his boots off and dumping them in the hearth to warm for the morning. But there was a close bond between them and she waited in the dark front room behind the curtains for him to return from a late fare. He was devoted to his horse, which he also grumbled at but never neglected. Sometimes, when he was tired or too full of brandy or rum, he would leave the cumbersome cab outside in the street all night, unharness the horse, lead it through the carriageway to the

Picturesque street names: There and Back Again Lane, near the university, Zed Alley, near the Centre

THERE AND BACK AGAIN LANE

ZED ALLEY

London Coffee House 1713
TEA BLENDERS
ALL SAINTS LANE
56 CORN STREET

stable at the back of the house and put it to bed—or through the hall and kitchen if the man who rented a stall in the stable had thoughtlessly left his cart blocking the carriageway. Like so many typical Bristolians he was not a Bristolian, but had been born the son of a gentleman's coachman and a chambermaid outside Bath, though he probably grew up in Bristol. He was a great wag, known and liked in a wide area of the city, and he died at 49, probably worn out by the irregular life and over-exposure.

The whole community of pre-1914 cab-drivers, disappearing even then as the motor-cab and motor-bus took over, symbolized very neatly many of the chief aspects of the Bristol character. They chaffed and threatened each other in 'Bristolese', but there was a very loyal and orderly feeling among them. Strict order was observed in moving up in the queue at the stand when a driver 'took off' with a fare. A driver keeping out the cold in the local pub would be summoned by his mates when it was his turn to take a fare, or his friends would move his cab up in the queue for him.

They stuck to their regular cab-stands through many years and much vile weather, and became well known to regular clients. They liked to give the impression that they owned their cabs and were independent; but most of them bought their cabs on tick and had to have them painted once a year in order to have their credit renewed. Often enough their payments fell behind and they had to go to a moneylender's in Newfoundland Road. Though their hours were long, so were those of all other workers, and the cabbies enjoyed a certain freedom, with a variety of customers, company in the cab-rest, an open-air life—too much so—and no boss. The cab-rests, or shelters, had a memorable Edwardian smell to them; compounded of smoke from a coke stove, cheap tobacco, beery breath, drying horse blankets, sawdust. There was always a fairly up-to-date *Wright's Bristol Directory* on the table, a necessary tool of the trade and probably a free copy from the publishers. The cabbies were chroniclers of the city and the time, but their chronicles were not recorded and preserved as they would be by sociologists today.

For some years up to 1910 my grandfather was the sole occupier of the old cab-stand near St. James's Churchyard; the motor-cab had swept his friends away. With them, and their jokes and gossip and dialect, went many of the richer aspects of the old Bristolian character.

The symbolic heart of the city. From left to right: the old Council House, Christ Church, a bronze 'nail', and a wing of Wood's Exchange

VII

PATRON OF SOME OF THE ARTS

BRISTOL has been no Weimar or Florence—two modest towns that in their day surpassed much larger cities in cultural creativity and patronage—but it has had a lively connection with literature, a respectable one with painting and a theatrical history second only to that of London. Its connections with science have been less obvious; London, Cambridge or Oxford, with their laboratories and concentrations of like-minded experimenters, have tempted scientists away from their native places, though the distinguished physicist Cecil Powell did break the pattern by staying in Bristol during the later part of his career. But the young Humphrey Davy, the greatest scientist to work in Bristol, stayed only two years before moving on to fame in London.

It is a city that looks as if it ought to be literary and artistic. The country comes right into it at Clifton, the Downs, the Avon Gorge and the old village suburbs like Westbury, Stapleton and Ashton, providing the sort of semi-rural, semi-urban environment—such as Hampstead—that enables writers and painters to be mildly bucolic yet not too far from their publishers and dealers. As a city full of rich and generally literate merchants it ought to have provided at least a few patrons to succour starving poets; but their absence was so conspicuous that Chatterton, Bristol's folk-hero, had to invent one in the figure of the fifteenth-century merchant William Canynges to patronize the imaginary poet-priest Thomas Rowley, whose works Chatterton obligingly wrote in retrospect. The merchants were too busy, or too worried about wars and trade and the anti-slavery campaigners to indulge the luxury of patronage; nor would most of them have understood the economics of artistic patronage. Merchants like Pinney, whose house in Great George Street is now a museum of eighteenth-century objects, would plough some of their profits back into gracious living as well as into the business, but the oddly intermittent productivity of a poet, or the long, unprofitable labour of an historian or a philosopher would not have seemed a good investment to them. The geniuses they did help—Cabot, Brunel, Davy—were always possible sources of profit. The merchants and bankers did patronize the Bristol theatres, though, and they played a big part in the notable act of civic pride that saved the Theatre Royal during the Second World War.

The city's reputation for philistinism, still alive, was much exaggerated by the nineteenth-century romantic legend of poor Chatterton starved by philistine Bristol aldermen. That he was not helped by patrons is a freak of cultural history, though he also did his worst to alienate potential patrons through his venomous satirical writings. Had he lived twenty years later in the first flush of Romanticism he would undoubtedly have been taken up, encouraged, exploited and probably ruined, as were those other 'natural' geniuses, Burns and Clare. In fact the city did, in its cautious way, support a number of incautious enterprises, from the lectures of Coleridge to the Great Western Railway of Brunel. The merchants, like all patrons, helped the geniuses to create the works of art or science they themselves could not create, though they could imagine them. Perhaps they were 'using' other men's genius for personal profit and psychological fulfilment; but they were also expressing, obliquely and at one remove, the banked-up romanticism which is the hidden side of the Bristol character.

"I know of no city so mercantile that is so literary," Robert Southey, one of Bristol's most famous native-born writers, said in respectful retrospect. Certainly our literature touches its history at many points. William Langland, author of *Piers Plowman*, is reputed to have had connections with the city. The fifteenth-century poet, Lydgate, wrote a poem called *The Child of Bristow*, and William Wyrecestre, the fifteenth-century chronicler, was Bristol-born and minutely recorded the town of his day for the benefit of local historians ever since. Grocyn, the Reformation scholar and friend of Erasmus and More, was brought up and educated in the city. Pepys came to Bristol in 1668 and "walked with my wife and people through the city, which is in every respect another London, that one can hardly know it stands in the country. No carts, it standing generally on vaults, only dog-carts." John Locke, born at nearby Wrington in Somerset, seems to have known Bristol well for he recommended a visitor from abroad to "see the Hotwells, St. George's Cave, where the Bristol Diamonds are found, Ratcliffe Church, and at Kingswood, the Coalpits". Addison's mother was the sister of a Bishop of Bristol and there is a tradition that he wrote some of the *Spectator* papers in a summer-house on the St. Anne's estate at Brislington. David Hume, historian and philosopher, was briefly in 1734 a clerk with Michael Miller, a merchant of Queen Square. Pope paid a visit to the Hotwells in 1739 and in a letter to Martha Blount described the "twenty odd pyramids smoking over the town" (the glass-cones) and coined his famous and evocative phrase about the docks, "a long street full of ships in the middle, with houses on each side, looks like a dream". Charles Wesley, the hymn-writer, lived in Bristol at Charles Street, St. James's, for more than twenty years. Richard Savage, the satirical poet and youthful friend of Samuel Johnson, died in a Bristol debtors' prison in 1743 and thereby augmented the city's reputation for slighting genius—"Thou blank of sciences, thou dearth of arts," Savage called it. But the merchants seemed to have treated him well, possibly deceived by his false story of noble birth and persecution by a heartless mother. He was buried in St. Peter's churchyard, later blitzed, at the expense of his kindly gaoler. Despite Johnson's vivid *Life*, Savage's reputation has not worn well in English literature.

The connections of Chatterton, Hannah More, Wordsworth, Coleridge and Southey with Bristol were important and need to be dealt with in some detail. Among slighter links one of the most curious is that of Mrs. Mary 'Perdita' Robinson, born at Bristol in 1758, actress, mistress of the Prince of Wales, and later (though not in Bristol) minor novelist and poet under the pen-name of 'Perdita', her most famous rôle.

Maria Edgworth, the Anglo-Irish novelist, lived in Clifton for a time in the 1790s. De Quincey passed through. Southey met his hero, Landor, in Bristol in 1808. Thomas Lovell Beddoes, the nineteenth-century poet, was the son of Dr. Thomas Beddoes, Davy's patron at the Pneumatic Institution in Hotwells. Shelley, Longfellow, Dickens, Carlyle, Ruskin, Thackeray, Tennyson passed through or stayed briefly. The connection between Tennyson, the historian Henry Hallam, and Hallam's son Arthur, has given a literary myth to Clevedon down the Channel, though Tennyson had in fact written the famous section of *In Memoriam* about the Wye filling the Severn before he had actually visited

Clevedon. Jowett, Walter Bagehot (who came of a West Country banking family of Langport in Somerset with commercial interests in Bristol, where Bagehot had some of his education), F. D. Maurice and other nineteenth-century intellectual figures had brief but significant connections with the city.

Despite these links there are comparatively few Bristol episodes of any importance in our literature. Shakespeare set only one scene in Bristol, *Richard II*, Act III, scene I. Bolingbroke enters with Bushy and Green, gives orders for their death and denounces his enemies in a speech containing the fine phrase about those who have eaten "the bitter bread of banishment". It is a pity that Shakespeare, for whom Bristol would have been the nearest port to Stratford, did not find more action to set there. There are satires on the Hot Well in Smollett's *Humphrey Clinker* (1771) and in Fanny Burney's *Evelina* (1778). But to me the most memorable literary episode set in Bristol is contained in chapters 38 and 39 of *Pickwick Papers*, in which Mr. Winkle flees to Bristol from the imagined wrath of Mr. Dowler in Bath, puts up at the 'Bush' (where the flamboyant Lloyd's Bank now stands in Corn Street) and wanders out to look at the city "which struck him as being a shade more dirty than any place he had ever seen".

He looks for Clifton, but loses his way in the narrow streets and steps into a surgery to ask the way. The surgeon turns out to be Bob Sawyer (late Nockemorf) who is trying to make a go of a run-down business by an ingenious method of 'puffing'. A small boy in grey livery and a gold-laced hat is employed to deliver pills and medicines to the wrong houses and call for them next day, explaining the error as due to Sawyer late Nockemorf's immense business. Winkle learns that his beloved Arabella Allen is staying with a maiden aunt in the district—a house in Westbury is traditionally associated with this incident—and Sam Weller, who comes to haul Winkle back to Bath on Pickwick's orders, agrees to search for Arabella. He ambles across the windy Downs, has a haunting conversation of sullenly mutual insult with a groom in a back lane, and by novelistic chance meets his own beloved, the servant girl Mary. Weller, Pickwick and Winkle, aided by Mary, take part in a nocturnal adventure during which Winkle declares his love to Arabella, Pickwick unwittingly flashes a dark lantern on to the neighbouring houses, and a "scientific gentleman", writing in his study, comes out into the lane to see if the mysterious light is a meteor, a glow-worm, fireflies or fireworks. He collides with Sam's fist, sees stars, writes a paper on the effect of electricity which stunned him for fifteen minutes, and makes his name as a light of science. Sam picks Mr. Pickwick up on his back and they scurry back to the coach and the 'Bush'.

It may seem odd to describe this as the most memorable literary episode involving Bristol when the opening chapters of *Treasure Island* exist. But I have always felt that Stevenson's Bristol scenes, fine as they are, could have been set in any eighteenth-century port, Plymouth, Liverpool, London or Leith. Dickens, the journalist of genius, has seen Bristol at camera flash-point. Sawyer's lodgings, were possibly in the tangled streets behind College Green, existing until recent years. The surly groom who threatens Sam and resents his cockney banter, and the equally surly manservant who tells his scientific master he suspects the lights in the lane mean thieves (and is told he may go downstairs): these are authentic Bristol characters. The breezy Downs, the semi-rural group of villas, the clash of Cockney and Bristolian (Sam meets his match in aggressiveness for once), Sawyer having himself called out of church (St. George's, Great George Street?), are all unforgettable; though it is a minor episode, the sort of gratuitous fun Dickens could not resist in his earlier days. To us it is like a daguerreotype in its frozen authenticity, a record of a Bristol sleepy and shabby during its long slump between the closing of the slave trade and the revival of prosperity in the latter half of the century.

Is there any literature which is specifically 'Bristolian', that could not have existed without Bristol as Dickens could not have existed without London or the Brontës without Yorkshire? Clearly no; nor did Southey's 'literary' city produce any one indisputably great writer or any one undeniably great book. But Bristol did at times create intellectual ferments that stirred writers to activity. The first was its part in the early Atlantic voyages, which led to various accounts of the expeditions, notably those collected by Richard Hakluyt, prebendary of Bristol Cathedral in the late sixteenth century. His work was taken up in the next century by Samuel Purchas, whose *Purchas His Pilgrimes* (1625) was to prove so potent an influence in the creation of *The Ancient Mariner*.

There was a minor ferment centred on Hannah More and her influence on writers like Southey and the young Macaulay, and the influence on nineteenth-century writers of her linking of creative literature with philanthropy and humanitarianism. A more important ferment was associated with Wordsworth and Coleridge and their Bristol publisher, Joseph Cottle; here Bristol played an important rôle in the greatest revolution in our literature. And one last, rather academic ferment involved J. A. Symonds, Jowett, F. D. Maurice and T. H. Green and resulted in solid educational creations like Clifton College and the university college.

Chatterton stands apart from any ferment or movement in Bristol itself, though he is part of the very early Romantic movement, which included Macpherson's *Ossian*, the Gothick novels and some of the poems of Collins, Gray and Cowper. He has his champions today as a serious candidate for poetic greatness, but his reputation has dwindled greatly since the turn of the century when he was still Wordsworth's "marvellous boy who perished in his pride", not only in England, but also in France, where De Vigny's ludicrous play perpetuated the legend. In the eighteenth century the Shakespearian editor Malone said he "was the greatest genius England has produced since Shakespeare". Southey, Byron, Scott, Moore and Campbell praised his powers. Coleridge dedicated his *Monody* to him and Keats his *Endymion*. Even Samuel Johnson said of him, on his visit to Bristol in 1776: "This is the most extraordinary young man that has encountered my knowledge; it is wonderful how the whelp has written such things." Stanley Hutton, who recorded many of these eulogies in his *Bristol and Its Famous Associations* (1907), obviously agrees, finding the dirge from *Aella* ("Oh sing unto my roundelay") "not unworthy of Shakespeare himself". Today few critics would think of him as other than a potential poet. In his work as it exists there is considerable technical mastery and an undoubted gift of language, but in the content only echoes of what he had read.

Chatterton belongs to literary history rather than to literary criticism, and here his relationship with Bristol is of great interest. The city cannot really be blamed for his tragedy; he was in many ways a deprived child, an eighteenth-century Rimbaud finding in the lethargic Bristol of his day—he was born in the schoolhouse in Pile Street near St. Mary Redcliffe in November 1752—the villain responsible for the early loss of his father, a schoolmaster and a sub-chanter in the cathedral, for his poor circumstances and his lack of appreciation. His experience of Colston's School, where like many other fatherless boys he was sent to learn a commercial career, only confirmed his hatred of the local bourgeoisie, as did his apprenticeship to the attorney Lambert in Corn Street, where the underemployed youth studied and copied medieval legal documents. They were all passive villains, obstacles to his fame and to the free expression of his ego, and it is possible today to sympathize with them.

But the greatest villain was St. Mary Redcliffe Church itself, which Chatterton could see from his home, still preserved among the desolation. Today, with the church cleaned, spired and restored, it is difficult to imagine how sombre and 'Gothick' it must have looked to the imaginative boy. Here in the Muniment Room he found more medieval documents to copy in preparation for his later forgeries, which deceived Horace Walpole. Here he found the tomb of the merchant Canynges who became the patron Chatterton could not find, as Thomas Rowley became the poet Chatterton could not be. The poems are a remarkable example of precocious talent, but we should not necessarily accept Chatterton's own belief that they were literature, nor the praises of the later Romantic poets as altogether unbiased. Chatterton had become to them a political figure, a symbol of genius crushed by the sort of repressive society the French Revolution destroyed, and which the English revolution would destroy in time. Bristol itself was beginning a radical change in appearance and mood in the very year, 1770, that Chatterton poisoned himself in London at the age of 17. Old churches and gateways were demolished, new streets were laid out, including Redcliffe Parade near St. Mary's Church. With the loss in trade due to the American war went some of Bristol's smugness. The influence of Hannah More and the anti-slavery campaigners had brought a more tolerant and humane atmosphere, which might, had he lived longer, have placated and encouraged Chatterton. It is no longer possible to accept the Chatterton myth without qualifications. Greater, fulfilled poets survived neglect and opposition; every city had and has its philistine elders. But it is possible to regret his bad luck and to feel the pathos of his story, especially in St. Mary Redcliffe.

Bristol gave a cool reception to the bicentenary of his death in 1970. Letters in the local Press attacked the city's apathy, but other letters defended it. There was a small exhibition in the City Museum.

Bristol was kinder to the slender talent of Hannah More, the leading bluestocking of her day and a writer whose influence has survived better than anything she wrote. Philanthropist, poet and dramatist and religious and philosophical writer, friend of Garrick, literary lioness and a high-minded and pioneering educational reformer, she was born in Fishponds in 1745 in a house that still stands near the church. She and her elder sisters opened a school at 6 Trinity Street, College Green, in 1758. The school was a success, but eventually, freed from ties to the school by an annuity from a defaulting but conscientious would-be husband, she went to London, met the Garricks and their distinguished friends, and had a popular success when Garrick staged her play, *Percy*. Garrick's death affected her deeply and she turned to writing religious and moral works, the money from which she used for philanthropic purposes. She retired to Barley Wood at Wrington in Somerset and did valuable social and educational work among the backward rural people there, bringing their condition to public notice and paving the way for other reformers in the field. A widely distributed pamphlet, *Village Politics*, was reputed to have allayed some of the unrest caused by the French Revolution in England. She retired to Clifton to die, left a fortune of £30,000 after her death in 1833 and every word she wrote is utterly forgotten, though her letters are still interesting to read. Her name lingers on attached to a school and a further education centre in modern Bristol.

Bristol was readier for Wordsworth and Coleridge when they arrived in the 1790s than it had been for Chatterton in the 1760s. There is an old tradition that the two poets met in the Great George Street house of the West India merchant John Pinney in the autumn of 1795. Mary Moorman, in her life of Wordsworth, does not mention this meeting but assumes they met either at Coleridge's lodgings in College Street behind College Green (now demolished to make a car-park) or at a political club in the city where Coleridge was lecturing. She does of course mention that it was Pinney, urged on by one of his sons, who rented Racedown House in Dorset to Wordsworth and his sister and thus started the poet on his long spiritual convalescence after his devastating experiences in revolutionary France. Wordsworth's links with the city are purely accidental: links with friends, with Coleridge and with Joseph Cottle, who published the *Lyrical Ballads* in Bristol in 1798 and in whose back parlour at his bookshop in Wine Street Wordsworth wrote down the lines about Tintern Abbey he had composed in his head while walking down the Wye Valley. He apparently had no feelings about the city either way, though we know Dorothy found it a bewildering place. He passed through, stayed for odd weeks, but formed no permanent connection with it.

Coleridge's connection is much more sustained and complex; he was undoubtedly the greatest literary figure to live there and write there. He married, unhappily, a Bristol girl, Sarah, sister of the Edith Fricker whom Southey married so happily. Both marriages were lotteries, chances taken as part of the idealistic 'Pantisocracy' scheme dreamed up by Southey at Oxford, where Coleridge met him. The community was to consist of twelve educated, liberal men and their wives, and was to be set up on the banks of the Susquehanna river in Pennsylvania. The melodious name of the river haunted Coleridge for several years and Cottle in his *Memoirs* thought that it was the main reason for choosing that location. They would labour for two or three hours of the day to provide their simple needs. Their wives would look after the household and the children, and their plentiful free time would be passed discussing philosophy in an atmosphere of complete religious and political freedom. Each member was to provide £125 as capital to start the settlement.

It was not such a fantastic idea as it may seem to us. The idea of founding a better way of life was strong in post-Revolutionary Europe and America was the natural place. Such idealistic, philosophical communities were indeed set up; Hawthorne made one of them the subject of *The Blithedale Romance*. Southey was making a last Romantic gesture before succumbing to the lure of his rich uncle's invitation to Portugal and of the steady monotonous security of a full-time literary life. Coleridge was fantasying a better way of life than his hitherto chaotic career and his already disappointing marriage. Why did the plan fail so quickly? Partly it was lack of money. Partly it was the responsibilities undertaken by Coleridge and Southey in marrying the Fricker sisters. But it was also, as Cottle drily suggests in his *Memoirs*, the influence of Bristol itself: "Bristol was now found a very pleasant place. . . . The solicitude I felt lest these young and ardent geniuses should in a disastrous hour, and in their mistaken apprehensions, commit themselves in this their desperate undertaking, was happily dissipated by Mr. Coleridge's applying for a loan of a little cash—to pay the voyagers' freight? or passage?—No—LODGINGS." (All the Pantisocratists were lodging at this time at 48 College Street). They could not afford to go to America and soon they did not want to go to America. Coleridge gave numerous lectures on theology, on the slave trade, on the History of Mankind—all strongly anti-Pitt—in order to pay for his lodgings and marry Sarah. These were on the whole well received, despite the fact that at least once he forgot to turn up for his lecture on the Roman Empire. He founded his short-lived liberal, anti-Pitt newspaper, *The Watchman*, and ran it from Bristol, for as long as its ten numbers lasted.

He was perhaps finding something like a pantisocratic society ready-made in Bristol: an agreeable city, without the literary and political factions of London, an intelligent if unimaginative audience, a wife, possibly a permanent home, and above all a patron in Cottle who offered him, as he offered Southey, 30 guineas for a book of poems, thus launching both on their literary careers. Coleridge, who responded with immediate delight and immense complacency to the least promise of security, soon lost his pantisocratic ambitions, though perhaps he turned to Nether Stowey and the benevolent Thomas Poole for a local version of the ideal philosophical community. Would he have had a different career if he had settled in Bristol as literary journalist and lecturer? Or would the agreeable complacency of Bristol have calmed his inquisitive intellect? (It was in Bristol, ironically, that he met Josiah and Thomas Wedgwood, whose annuity of £150 a year for life sapped his creative will as it eased his personal life.) Probably he was destined to be what he was. We do not apologize so much for Coleridge today. The cult of the Great Work has faded and the inspired fragments he left us are no doubt greater than any of the Great Works he so enthusiastically planned.

Coleridge owed more to Bristol, though, than the relative peace of his time there, the friendship of the Wedgwoods and the patronage of Cottle. Although *The Ancient Mariner* was conceived while he walked with Wordsworth and Dorothy on the Quantocks and written in the miserable cottage at Nether Stowey, it is also closely linked with Bristol. In *The Road to Xanadu* John Livingstone Lowes detailed the extraordinary range of reading matter, much of it borrowed (for too long) from the King Street library, memories of which went into the poem. Coleridge's eldest brother was an officer in the East India Company's service. Another brother, Francis, was a midshipman. Livingstone Lowes commented: "Surely, if the youngest member of the Devon brood showed himself later curiously at home with unfamiliar nautical terms and the unwritten legends of the sea, it is not a matter to be wondered at. Nor would it be remarkable, either, if sailors' talk in the ancient port of Bristol had also played its part."

The factual background to *The Ancient Mariner* is that Coleridge had been living in an old city closely linked with the sea, that he had been reading books from a Bristol library, including the narratives of Bristol explorers such as Captain Thomas James, that Bristol was full of sailors' yarns (had not Selkirk himself, according to local tradition, lived in Bristol and told Defoe his story there?). Livingstone Lowes, a man of his pre-Freudian time, did not dabble in psychological speculations about Coleridge's inner life, whether Sarah Fricker was the albatross around Coleridge's neck, or whether the albatross was his sense of guilt at his slavery to opium (or Bristol's guilt about human slavery?). But he accepted that Bristol played a significant part in the poem, and we can perhaps see this connection as one at least of the many levels of meaning in it. Perhaps the Mariner's relationship to Bristol is that of Joyce's Finnegan to Dublin: a nightmare allegory from the collective unconscious of a haunted city?

Little of this would have been understood by sane, solid Joseph Cottle, the bookseller-publisher, the agent, the catalyst between genius and publication, one of those ungifted Bristolians who recognized and encouraged the gifts of outsiders in their city. Not that he thought of himself as ungifted; he wrote epic verse that earned him some savage sarcasm from Byron in *English Bards and Scotch Reviewers*. He was waggish, heavily humorous. He saw through the pantisocratic folly, but nevertheless recognized Wordsworth and Coleridge for what they were—though he was not so perceptive in awarding equal stature to Southey. He seems always an older man than the poets, though he was Wordsworth's age. He published the first printed productions in volume form of Coleridge, Southey and Lamb, and he published the *Lyrical Ballads*, and that is a kind of poetic fame.

He seems to have been as generous towards Wordsworth and Coleridge, rounding up the poems for the *Lyrical Ballads*, hurrying between Bristol, Nether Stowey and Alfoxden, lending them money, letting them use his bookshop in High Street as a waiting-room or club. He seems to have been the first of the many props and go-betweens that Wordsworth and Coleridge complacently relied on through their lives. Sadly, Cottle later turned against Coleridge when he came to write his *Early Recollections* (1837), resenting scoffing remarks about him by Coleridge that had become known to him; the over-melodramatic image of Coleridge as an opium-sodden weakling owes a lot to Cottle's descriptions of him. Cottle fades out after 1800 into the respectability of Knowle, where he died in 1853; but he left an impressive footnote in English literature.

Southey, the odd poet out of the trio, and Bristol's most famous native-born literary writer after Chatterton, is a more shadowy figure. He was born in Bristol, grew up there and always spoke of it with affection. He spent some of his childhood at his admiring grandmother's house in Bedminster, then rural, and there was always something in Southey of the clever, indulged, pedantic child. He quickly lost his early sympathy with the French Revolution, and his interest in the Pantisocracy scheme succumbed to his rich uncle's invitation to Portugal and promise of a legacy if he would study law. He remained true to literature, though. His happy marriage and his industriousness, his passion for books, the need to support not only his own family but also Coleridge's neglected wife and children, left cuckoo-like upon him, quickly turned him into the highly efficient and distinguished hack of the long years at Keswick. Of his voluminous work little remains of interest, despite the claims of the Southey 'lobby' that always exists: the *Life of Nelson* for its style and as a record of the early growth of the Nelson legend; a few short poems; the *History of Brazil* and other historical works as sources of rare material; the translation of *El Cid*, recently re-appraised and admired by scholars in Spanish; and the *Letters from England*, written by Southey masquerading as a Spaniard and still interesting, particularly for their rather startingly realistic and unromantic picture of the Bristol Southey knew. Critics, and notably Geoffrey Grigson, have traced Southey's lack of warmth and of lyrical feeling to his childhood years spent away from his mother with an eccentric aunt, years he survived at the price of spontaneous emotions. But the man has been treated unfairly by history. Despite his kindness to his own family and to Coleridge's—warmly reciprocated by them and especially by Coleridge's brilliant daughter Sara—he appears almost as a villain in some books on the period. Byron's mockery of him in *The Vision of Judgment*, and his mock-dedication of *Don Juan* to Southey as Poet Laureate, have rubbed off on to Southey's personal reputation. But he was by no means so emotively Tory and reactionary as his detractors claimed. Southey's conscientious craftsmanship, personal moderation and kindness and sense of responsibility, and his inability to put much feeling into his writing (except in a moving fragmentary poem on the death of a young son) could all be seen as Bristolian characteristics. He might perhaps have written more memorable work if he had, after all, sailed for the Susquehannah.

The same dogged industry, the same inability to make any lasting contribution to literature or history are characteristic, too, of John Addington Symonds, whom we have met as a significant figure of the Clifton intelligentsia of the later nineteenth century. His *Civilization of the Renaissance in Italy*, and his many other books and essays about Italian literature and art served their purpose until they were superseded. He knew he was really not a poet and lamented the fact. But his nostalgic references to Clifton and Bristol, often written from his consumptive's eyrie at Davos, are worth tracking down. Coleridge's gifted wayward son, Hartly, may have been born in the city, or in Clevedon. The talented young poet, Isaac Rosenberg, killed in the First World War, was born in Bristol but left while still a child.

The failure of subsequent Bristol writers to use the city as literary material raises the question: is Bristol perhaps too picturesque for literary purposes? It was, after all, the squalor of London that inspired Dickens and the squalor of Dublin that inspired Joyce. It is Bristol's physical and moral squalor in the slave-trading days that has inspired a certain number of novels, particularly those of Marguerite Steen, who lived for a time in one of the surviving eighteenth-century merchants' houses in

Prince Street. Novels like *The Sun is My Undoing* are almost too rich in local colour, though solidly researched and good reading. Modern writers, including those of Bristol origin, seem to have made little or no use of the city, apart from Peter Nichols, formerly a Bristol teacher and actor, who wrote a number of television plays before making a hit with his stage-play, *A Day in the Life of Joe Egg*. This story of a couple learning to accept their hopelessly spastic child is set in Bristol, though the local setting is not over-stressed, and the edgy, very moving self-mockery of their dilemma by the husband and wife makes good sense in the context of the Bristol character. Exterior shots for a film of the play were taken in Bristol in early 1970. In November of the same year Nichols's television play *Hearts and Flowers* was more specifically Bristolian in its characters and its exploration of the effect of a sudden death and a funeral on a family. The cliches, the stifling of tears, the family jokes, the formality of the funeral tea: these were all marvellously local and placeless at the same time. His stage-play *The National Health* opened at the National Theatre in October 1969.

Poets seem to find the city more amenable. Two of the most evocative Bristol poems of recent years are Maurice Carpenter's *The Descent of Chatterton* (1950), a powerful vision of Chatterton's revolt against Bristol as a permanent revolt against calculation; and Jack Beeching's *A Bristol Graveyard* (1950), a neat, Betjemanesque evocation of what must be the Temple churchyard. Local poetry pamphlets appear, but even in *Unicorn*, a collection of poems by Bristol poets, published in 1960, only a few poems (notably Maurice Carpenter's charming *The Bristol Unicorns*) are on local subjects. The best known Bristol poem remains John Betjeman's word-picture of the flooded Avon, the star high over Bristol and the "tall embattled church-towers of the Bristol waterside"; though the images are rather imprecise and generalized as if Betjeman, though a great admirer of the city, had not been able to focus his images of it. Bristol has perhaps been too agreeable, too bland, too diffident to foster that love-hate relationship between a native and his native-place that produces the memorable literature of cities. There is a new theme for a Bristol writer today, though: the disappearance of the old, mellow, complacent Bristol and its threatened replacement by a vast, road-throttled super-regional capital. Some new Joyce should send a

Bristol Stephen Dedalus wandering elegaically through the streets before they vanish altogether.

If there are reservations about Bristol's importance as a literary city, there can be few about its status in theatrical history. Through the eighteenth and nineteenth centuries it ranked high if not highest among provincial cities for its theatrical activity, and in our time it has arguably taken second place to London only through the presence of its ravishingly lovely Theatre Royal, the oldest active theatre in the country, and through the activities of the Bristol Old Vic Company, which also acts at the Little Theatre, and the drama department of the university, the first academic drama department in Britain. The Theatre Royal stood at the centre of all this; a fine theatre attracts players and audiences, though there were bad times when the theatre fell into disrepair and was for long a stopping-off place for touring melodramas (up to 1914) and for touring revues (up to and during the Second World War). We should not forget, though, the efforts of Muriel Pratt to make a success of a serious repertory company just before the First World War, the outbreak of which frustrated the enterprise. In 1943 the theatre stood empty and desolate but undamaged by the blitz and it was a serious possibility that it might be used as a warehouse or pulled down. But enthusiasts rallied, preserved and restored it and leased it to C.E.M.A., which became the Arts Council. It reopened in May 1943 and various companies kept it going until 1946 when the Old Vic formed a 'colony' in Bristol as the Bristol Old Vic, a name it has kept as the London Old Vic has disappeared into the new identity of the National Theatre. The first post-war years had a pioneer excitement about them under the first director, Hugh Hunt (1946–49). One remembers the Lear of William Devlin, the succession of well-known players who came to the company—Quartermaine, Edison, Pamela Brown, many others. The theatre had its crises: financial, directorial, constructional, but audiences and local backers took a proprietorial interest in helping where they could.

The theatre opened in 1766; it is the oldest theatre in the country with a continuous (if occasionally interrupted) existence as a theatre, and the only one that fully illustrates the development of the English stage since it was built. The designer was the Bristol architect, Thomas Paty, and the auditorium is believed to be the

The 'Llandoger Trow' in King Street

LLANDOGER TROW
Sherry Bar

first of the horse-shoe shape in England. It was certainly sumptuous for its period and today, though much smaller than surviving Victorian theatres, it still looks imposing. Its greatest drawback is not its size—the new provincial theatres springing up all over Britain are modest in size—but its beauty. People visiting it for the first time find it difficult to keep their eyes on the play and not on the green and silver splendours of the auditorium and the glittering plaster stars on the steeply inclined nineteenth-century ceiling. The glamour of the interior sometimes acts against the realism of a modern play, and there is no doubt that the theatre is particularly suited to Restoration and eighteenth-century comedy—even the very minor ones that have been revived on occasion—and to Shakespeare's comedies, brilliant productions of which have been a characteristic achievement of the theatre from its rebirth on. It is less suited to spectacle—a play like Shaw's *Caesar and Cleopatra* tends to wander outside the sight-lines—and to the curtainless, unlocated contemporary play. But perhaps the regular playgoers take the visual beauty of the theatre for granted and are not distracted?

The new theatre quickly became part of the city despite considerable opposition from Puritan Bristol which saw in it "a risk of ruining the morals of our youth, impoverishing our tradesmen and artisans, promoting the arts of intrigue and seducing the innocent". Most of the great stage artists of succeeding years, with the exception of Garrick, appeared on its stage: William Powell, James Dodd, Mrs. Barry, Sarah Siddons (whose ghost used to be said to haunt the theatre), Jenny Lind, Taglioni, Grimaldi, Henry Irving, Ellen Terry, Edmund and Charles Kean, the Kendals and the Bancrofts, William Charles Macready himself, who as stepson of Sarah M'Cready, an energetic early lessee of the theatre, began his career there. She did not have an easy time; Bristol's nonconformist conscience was uneasy about its theatres, though fortunately she had "bespeak" support from the mayor, the city's M.P.s and the Duke of Beaufort. Badly behaved audiences, even during Macready's farewell Lear in 1850, were always a menace, and opera tended to be regarded as more respectable than drama. From 1845 her stage manager was James Henry Chute, who believed strongly in provincial companies in their own right, independent of touring stars. He refurbished the theatre and brought in new players, among them Marie Wilton (Lady

Queen Square, with the Custom House (left) *and Rysbrack's statue of William III*
Berkeley Square near the university tower

Bancroft), Madge Robertson (Dame Madge Kendall), and the young Kate and Ellen Terry.

The Theatre Royal was not, of course, the only theatre in Bristol's stage history, though it dominated it. In the British Association handbook on Bristol (1955) R. I. James gives a hilarious account of the Jacobs Well playhouse, the city's first permanent theatre, opened in 1729 half-way up a steep track above the Hotwell road. Linkboys were necessary to guide playgoers to it and "every actor prayed for a full moon on his benefit night". There was a little beershop adjoining and drink was served continuously through a hatch to the audience. Crowds used to gather in front to watch the audience arriving and then move round to the back to cheer on the actors who, in order to re-enter from the other side of the stage, had to race round the back of the building. Later in the nineteenth century the King Street theatre was felt to be inconveniently remote from the residential areas of Clifton, Cotham and Redland, and Chute built a new theatre in Park Row closer to these areas. It opened in 1867 as the New Theatre Royal, later the Princes Theatre, destroyed in the Blitz and still missed.

Through the 1950s and 1960s the Bristol Old Vic maintained its reputation as the most rewarding company outside London, with the Birmingham Rep its only rival. A series of successes, such as Julian Slade's musical *Salad Days*, were sent up to London to repeat their success; others that went to London were the 1962 version of *War and Peace*, the musical *Fiorello* (1963), *A Severed Head* (1963) from Iris Murdoch's novel, and a great success, Frank Marcus's *The Killing of Sister George* (1964). Of this period J. C. Trewin has commented: "I think one of Bristol's great discoveries has been its director, Val May. . . . He became director in August 1961 when he was 34 and today, at a time when Rep directors have been treated like football club managers, he is still in King Street and with a national/metropolitan reputation. . . . Certainly one of the best and most liked directors in Britain." (Val May's departure from the Bristol Old Vic was announced in 1974.)

Is there a 'Bristol Old Vic style' in acting and direction? It is tempting to think that the dimensions of the Theatre Royal and the consequent close relationship between actors and audience have developed a more conversational style than one finds at the Royal Shakespeare Theatre in Stratford or the National Theatre in London. The impeccable low-key diction of players like Eric

Porter, John Neville and Dorothy Tutin (who started or first made a name at Bristol) may owe something to this—and to Hugh Hunt's care for good speaking—and may explain their versatility in switching from full theatre projection to intimate television acting. King Street has, too, excelled at a quiet, scenically limited type of production which has made it seem to some of us like the last haven of thoughtful production in the English theatre. But neither J. C. Trewin, nor Professor Glynne Wickham, who runs the university's pioneer drama department in the adapted Vandyke Printers buildings in Park Row, think that there is really a Bristol style. Too many of the players—Yvonne Mitchell, Paul Rogers, Donald Sinden, Derek Godfrey among many others—had been elsewhere first or have moved on too quickly elsewhere to have developed a specific King Street manner; and most provincial repertory theatres have dimensions similar to the Theatre Royal. Professor Wickham believes that Bristol's main contribution to the theatre has been the number of new plays and playwrights it has fostered: Harold Pinter's *The Room*, John Arden's *The Happy Hours* and *The Business of Good Government*, Peter Nichols, Charles Wood, Tom Stoppard, George Hulme, Frank Marcus and Iris Murdoch, to name the best known. Certainly the King Street audience has played a part in encouraging new work: quietly enthusiastic, middle class and middle to upper middle-brow, schoolteacherly, loyal through some edgy experimental productions that have raised local eye-brows.

That audience had to show loyal patience while the Theatre Royal, closed for eighteen months to two years, adapted the noble Palladian-fronted Coopers' Hall next door as a new entrance area, today perhaps the finest in Britain. The Old Vic bought land near the theatre, while the City Council leased the Coopers' Hall at a nominal rent. A £500,000 appeal was launched. The successful project has given the theatre the worthy front it has lacked, as well as social space, a new adaptable studio theatre for experimental work, a circle foyer for chamber music, jazz, poetry or cabaret, and much greater work-space behind. Has it necessarily been an improvement, though? Possibly the expansion of the regular company from thirty to fifty will give King Street a long-term resident company for the first time. But one of the attractions in the pioneer days was the freshness of the productions and the visible maturing before our eyes of young actors. By 1974 financial problems were creating doubt as to whether the company could be kept at full strength and whether the Little Theatre could be kept running as well as the Theatre Royal.

Art and music have taken second place to literature and the theatre, though painting has an honourable tradition in the city. Sir Thomas Lawrence was born in Bristol in 1769, his father being for a short time the landlord of the 'White Lion' in Broad Street where the Grand Hotel now stands; but Lawrence left when he was still a boy and hardly counts as a Bristol artist. E. H. Bailey, who made the statue of Nelson for Trafalgar Square—and the delicate bust of Southey in the cathedral—was the son of a Bristol carver of ship's figure-heads. Francis Danby, the water-colour artist, born in Ireland in 1793, settled in Bristol where his sons, James Francis and Thomas, began their careers as painters. Bristol's best known painter was William James Müller, son of a German-born father who had come to Bristol after fleeing Napoleon. Müller began to exhibit at the Royal Academy at 21, was a pioneer of painting in the open air, and was one of the first English artists to visit and paint Egypt and Turkey (where he caught a disease that killed him in 1845 at the age of 33). He painted Stapleton, Hanham, Whitchurch, Pensford, the Gorge and other outlying districts; but his favourite haunt was the Brislington valley around St. Anne's. Basil Cottle has written of the "bright oily assurance" of his canvasses "caught as they were in the perpetual sunshine of nineteenth-century merchant prosperity" and they are perhaps too bland for real distinction. Müller was only one of a number of artists, some Bristol-born, who painted the local scene in the first half of the nineteenth century, among them James Baker Pyne, Samuel Jackson, the Danbys, Joseph Walter, painter of Bristol nautical scenes including the *Great Western*, and James Sharples and his talented daughter Rolinda, whose local genre scenes are rich in atmosphere and documentary value. The City Art Gallery has many of these paintings, which constitute almost a 'Bristol' School.

The development of the Arnolfini Gallery—originally near the university, then in Queen Square, then in an old wharf shed near Neptune's statue in the Centre—is one of the most encouraging episodes in Bristol's recent cultural history. (Its success contrasts with the rather sad story of the Western Theatre Ballet, which, despite warm reviews when it performed outside Bristol and abroad, never succeeded in establishing itself in its city of origin and has now moved away to Edinburgh.) Jeremy Rees, director of the gallery, thinks that an important factor in its success has been the development of a local centre where cautious Bristolians can see and get used to new art styles. The moves from Triangle West in the university area to relatively remote Queen Square in early 1970 and then to the Canon's Road shed were successes, as, it is hoped, will be its latest move to the imposing Bush's warehouse on Narrow Quay, which has now been finely restored. The Arnolfini's devotees were prepared to make the longer journey and attendance and sales went up. In 1970 the gallery began informal and sometimes experimental musical evenings. The City Art Gallery contains a good representative exhibition of the fine arts in general and of Bristol applied arts in particular: the naïvely beautiful Bristol glass with its deep butterfly-wing blues, reds and greens, the Bristol hard-paste porcelain (which ceased to be made in 1777), and the charming local delftware.

Music has been the Cinderella of Bristol arts. It is difficult to think of local composers of note, though the city fostered the talents of Clara Butt and Eva Turner. It has been suggested that music is an extrovert art not native to introvert Bristol; but such vaguely psycho-sociological judgments can hardly be sustained. The city still has no full-time civic orchestra. The Paragon Orchestra did good work in the 1950s, and today the B.B.C. Training Orchestra and Sidney Sager's prestigious chamber orchestra, the Bristol Sinfonia, help to keep professional musical life interesting. There is little tradition of training young musicians, but there has always been a lively amateur tradition, still flourishing in a number of choirs of all sizes and in several enterprising orchestral and operatic societies. Both the B.B.C. and the university act as patrons of music, though more could be done for chamber music. This has a thinnish time, possibly because no very suitable hall exists for it; even a chamber orchestra sounds rather lonely in the vast Colston Hall.

A full survey of the arts would certainly include more about the work and influence of the former West of England service of the B.B.C., with its early Victorian terrace headquarters in Whiteladies Road. This was for years the most distinctive and 'homely' of the B.B.C.'s regions, much loved for its devotion to the West

Country, for its understanding of rural life, its talks and especially for its plays which featured well-known local actors like Hedley Goodall. How much of this local feeling will survive the B.B.C.'s new regional policies remains to be seen; but the reduction in the number of locally produced plays, outside broadcasts, religious programmes and light entertainment suggests that a powerful source of local interest is being shut off. During the early years of the Second World War the B.B.C. became the centre of a lively intellectual and artistic 'renaissance' when the drama, religious and variety departments were evacuated from London to Bristol; a movement which linked at several points with the existing local activity in the literary and artistic worlds, of which the bookshop run by Douglas Cleverdon (later the distinguished radio producer) in Charlotte Street off Park Street, with its fascia lettering by Eric Gill and its handsome limited editions, was an attractive example.

For a mercantile city Bristol has been, as Southey claimed, remarkably literary and artistic in its cautious, undramatic way. If its merchants have tended to patronize the more public arts, such as the theatre and architecture, rather than risk their money on imponderables like poets, they have nevertheless rarely been the bigoted philistines pilloried by Savage and Chatterton. They created their own culture in the Georgian houses of Kingsdown, Hotwells and Clifton and in the Bristol tradition of philanthropy. If the tired word 'culture' has any meaning left, it must surely include Colston's Almshouses and Dowry Square as well as the 'Rowley' poems and the *Lyrical Ballads*.

VIII

OUTER BRISTOL—AND BEYOND

IT WOULD be surprising if a city as idiosyncratic visually as Bristol had uninteresting suburbs. Something of the varied, chaotic, jostling liveliness and unexpectedness of the inner city has spilled over into the outer districts, creating an extended Bristol rather than the waste land of Laburnum Groves that characterizes suburban Birmingham, London and Manchester. Suburban monotony and desolation can be found easily enough, of course; but they are offset by surviving rural enclaves such as Snuff Mills Park along the River Frome at Stapleton, and Henbury and Westbury between the Downs and the Channel.

From the incoming train they can look monotonous enough, rolling their grey masses over the city's hills and plateaux, punctuated increasingly by the sharp, unfriendly clusters of tall towers of flats. The endless terraces and switch-back roads carry the eye over mile after mile of Victorian proletarian and lower-middle-class faubourgs. It is a shabby, broken-down world in many places, the world of *Sketches by Boz* and of the early *Punch* cartoons of John Leech, a scratchy, steel-engraved Dickensian quarter of corner pubs, greengrocers' shops spilling their vegetable stands on to the pavements, of suburbanized cottages and farm-buildings squatting below disused railway arches, of chapels turned into warehouses and once respectable middle-class houses with cracked windows and sagging lintels or deserted and boarded up before the onward march of the Parkway. A correspondent in the *Evening Post* in the mid-1960s said that the whole of East Bristol from St. James's Barton outwards was an industrial slum and the sooner it disappeared the better. But it was once a warm human environment, however impoverished, and it could be still if the rebuilding preserves the old inter-relationship of dwellings, shops, recreation grounds, pubs and the gossipy life of the streets. If the train stops before entering Temple Meads there is a chance to observe more closely the specifically Bristolian atmosphere of these early and mid-Victorian backwaters: the quiet cul-de-sacs (pudding-bag streets, as they were once known in Bristol) with their tiny, gritty front gardens and soap-polished potted plants in the windows, the dusty-red pantile roofs; or, from the rear, the sloping glass roofs of verandahs, and the jumble of chicken-houses, garden sheds, abandoned toys and piles of broken flower-pots.

Some of the suburbs shade off almost indistinguishably from the city; it would take a keen topographical eye to mark exactly where the inner city merges into districts like Cotham and Montpelier. Others are more individual. Brislington, Bedminster and Stapleton are old villages that have been suburbanized (or, in the case of Bedminster, urbanized) to a greater or lesser degree. Kingswood and Hanham to the east (now in the new County of Avon) are old mining villages, famous in the past for the roughness of their miners and for their primitive Methodism. They are still districts with strongly individual characters, centres of the boot and shoe trade, straggles of mean, semi-rural streets and austere chapels. Knowle is an early Victorian suburb, intended for businessmen's bijou villas (Joseph Cottle retired and died there) but less socially exclusive today. Fishponds keeps a residential look about it, though there is a considerable amount of industry, particularly factories for cartons and cardboard boxes, interspersed among the residential areas. Filton, created by and dependent upon the aircraft works, and neighbouring Southmead, are uncharacteristic in their lack of character: meaninglessly long avenues, wan little groups of shops, traffic islands, bus shelters, vandalized telephone boxes and scuffed grass verges.

By contrast, the extensive semi-rural suburbia between the Downs and the coast, from Westbury through Henbury to Sea Mills (a pioneer garden suburb in the 1920s), with its posh end climbing up towards the Downs at Stoke Bishop and Sneyd Park, is a district of unrivalled charm among the outliers of large British cities. On golden autumn mornings the sunny haze hangs over Henbury Hill, transforming the banal, bow-fronted semis, with their bosomy late roses, into garden-houses in Japanese prints. This is archetypal, Betjemanesque suburb, the "blue, remembered" avenues, crescents and closes that haunt the childhood memories of middle-class Englishmen.

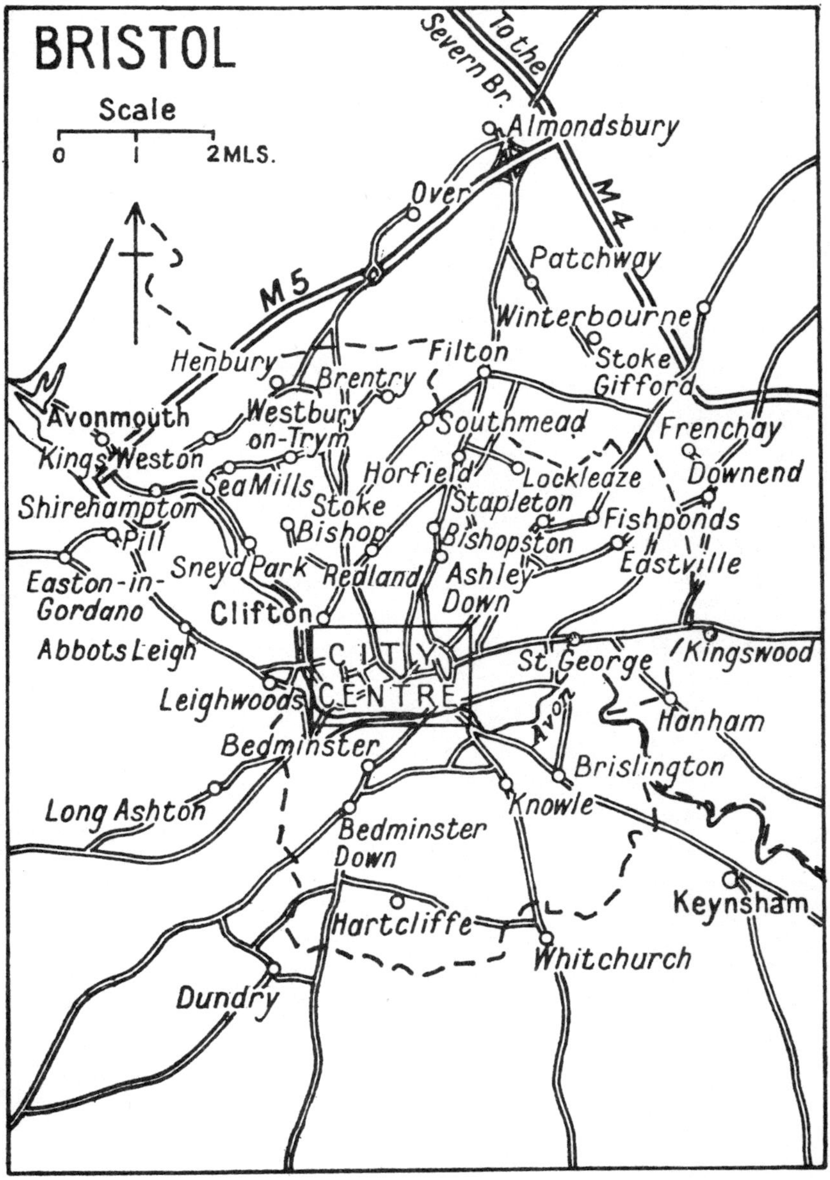

BRISTOL
Scale
0
1
2MLS.
To the Severn Br.
Almondsbury
M4
M5
Over
Patchway
Winterbourne
Henbury
Filton
Stoke Gifford
Brentry
Avonmouth
Westbury on-Trym
Southmead
Frenchay
Kings Weston
Horfield
Lockleaze
Downend
Shirehampton
Sea Mills
Stoke Bishop
Stapleton
Fishponds
Pill
Bishopston
Eastville
Easton-in-Gordano
Sneyd Park
Redland
Ashley Down
Clifton
Abbots Leigh
CITY CENTRE
St George
Kingswood
Leighwoods
Avon
Hanham
Bedminster
Brislington
Long Ashton
Knowle
Bedminster Down
Keynsham
Hartcliffe
Whitchurch
Dundry

Because Clifton and the old inner suburbs of Kingsdown and Hotwells were always agreeable to live in, the later suburbs were not the desperate refuges from urban gloom that they were in so many nineteenth-century cities. Bristolians were not particularly concerned to create their suburbs as new small towns with their own amenities, and today Bristolians have no obsessional dislike of coming back into the city centre for pleasure in the evenings or at weekends as, for example, Birmingham people have. One can wander for hours through Redland, Cotham, Ashley Down, Henleaze and Bishopston without coming across more than a handful of shops. They do not have shopping or commercial centres of their own, but rely on the amenities of the radial road centres of Whiteladies Road and Gloucester Road. Buses are occasional and there is a rare quietness. It is possible to walk to one's work in the more immediate fringes of the inner city, in the university complex, to the many small business offices and shops strung along Whiteladies Road or to the old commercial district at the city end of Gloucester Road at Stokes Croft. The city retains its social pull and the northern suburbs, apart from Clifton, remain suburbs. This situation, like much else of value in Bristol today, is at risk as the city centre loses trades and amenities in favour of ring roads and multi-storey car parks. When the city no longer exerts its gravitational pull people will stay in their suburbs and demand shopping and entertainment centres locally, to the detriment of Bristol as a balanced community.

It would be difficult to explain to an outsider, perhaps even to some Bristolians, what is so compelling about these aloof, grey-walled avenues of Redland and Cotham, Ashley Down and Bishopston, to some connoisseurs of Bristol 'atmosphere'. Perhaps the atmosphere is largely created by personal memories and associations. The pleasant bustle of the Gloucester Road shops in the car-less days just after the 1939–45 war, wandering the quiet streets around the county cricket ground or up the long artery of Cranbrook Road to Westbury Park and the Downs, or ambling on Spring mornings down Gloucester Road to Stokes Croft and so into the blitzed shambles of the old city, the willow-herb wilderness whose London counterpart was so vividly caught by Rose Macaulay in *World My Wilderness*: these are the personal associations that can glamourize a suburb that means nothing to the alien eye.

They have notable buildings in their own right, though. Redland Chapel on Redland Green is an exquisite proprietory chapel of 1741–43, built by William Halfpenny for John Cossins, who made a fortune as a grocer in London and retired to Redland in 1732. It is a beautiful building standing inside a small railed and bush-enclosed churchyard, which contains the graves of T. E. Brown, the Manx poet who was a master at Clifton College, T. R. Lysaght the architect, and a stout company of retired service officers. It has a classical Wren-ish west front in honey-coloured stone, with a handsome octagonal bell-turret above, crowned by a dome. One enters through an octagonal vestibule and a three-arched gallery screen (with busts of Mr. and Mrs. Cossins by Rysbrack in the niches) into a simple, panelled nave ending in a shallow semi-circular apse with a stucco coffered ceiling above soaring cherubs. It is a place of powerful charm; I have sat in it late on a dark winter afternoon after switching all the lights on and nobody has come to inquire why the place was suddenly lit up inside. It has a strong resemblance to the Oxford and Cambridge college chapels, and today, as Redland Parish Church, has strong links with the many students who live in the district. The Green outside is still quiet and isolated despite the busy road nearby. Children still play on the immemorially old stone, which may be pre-historic or may have had something to do with the Roman road to Aust which passed this way.

Nearby stands Cossins's house, Redland Court, now a girls' school, built in 1735 as an early essay in English Palladianism, still approached through 'Lovers' Walk', its famous avenue of tall trees. Redland has changed much since the days when it was a country suburb and gipsies camped along the unbuilt side of Cranbrook Road late in the last century. But it has kept something of its special character as a more bourgeois Clifton. Down from the Green stretch the misty, sloping avenues of middle-class houses until they reach Gloucester Road and Zetland Road, their quietness disturbed only by short-cutting cars and the occasional cruising bus. Diffident Victorian churches and deferential little groups of shops stand at avenue-corners.

An exception to the local pattern of largely residential suburbs is Bedminster, the bustling workaday district that lies immediately across the New Cut opposite Redcliffe and the peninsula of docks between the river and the Floating Harbour. Be'minster, as

Bristol tends to call it, has always been a place apart, from the days when it was linked with Redcliffe as a rival to Bristol for domination of the growing medieval city. Bristol won, but Bedminster has asserted its individuality ever since; until well into this century Bristol people talked of "going to Bedminster" to the Hippodrome music-hall as if going to another town. Nevertheless, it shared in the fortunes of the parent-city; it was involved in the sieges of the Civil War, and there were coal-pits among its streets up to the earlier part of this century.

Bedminster was still little more than a village in 1855, but grew rapidly in the later years of the century until by 1908 the parish contained a population twice that of Bath. Fields and farms disappeared giving place to houses and factories, and notably to the massive works and offices of W. D. & H. O. Wills' (or Willses, as Bristol often calls them), the famous tobacco firm, a branch of the Imperial Tobacco Company since it was formed in 1901 as a defence against the American Tobacco Company's attempts to infiltrate the British market. Bristol, in touch with the West Indies and Virginia, had been a natural port for importing tobacco since the seventeenth century. By the middle of the eighteenth century there were more than a dozen tobacco and snuff firms, largely concentrated in the Old Market Street—Castle Street area. Henry Overton Wills (1761–1826), son of a Salisbury watchmaker, joined a firm in Corn Street in 1786, and eventually took it over. It flourished during the nineteenth century, absorbing smaller firms, in its handsome Bristol Byzantine premises in Redcliff Street. New buildings in East Street, Bedminster, were opened in 1886 and, with their extensions, long dominated the district economically and socially; a considerable proportion of the local population depended upon the Wills factory and there was a strong mutual relationship between firm and employees. Successive generations of the Wills family proved themselves generous local benefactors. Early in the century Sir Frederick Wills gave £100,000 towards the new university; later Sir George Wills bought the Victoria Rooms at a cost of £30,000 for the social activities of the university, and built a men students' hall of residence at Stoke Bishop. Sir George also gave Nightingale Valley on the other side of the Avon Gorge as a pleasure-ground for the city.

Wills' were early in the field with the cigarette when it became popular in the 1870s, and the cheap, democratic Woodbine, subject of affectionate jokes, was a powerful symbol of nostalgia for 'Blighty' during the First World War. With the arrival of the cigarette the evocative old names of tobaccos began to fade: Dutch Cut, Real Latakia, Fine Bird's Eye, Bogie Roll, Real Havanah—all no doubt easily identifiable by Sherlock Holmes who wrote a monograph on tobacco ashes. The great bonded tobacco warehouses near the Cumberland Basin, pioneers in their building techniques in the early years of the century, are a prominent and dramatic part of the local industrial landscape. Each of Wills' factories was thought the last word in their day; each has had to be extended. The firm is now approaching yet another move, from Bedminster to a new 57-acre site on the southern outskirts, between Hartcliffe and Whitchurch, part of the general movement of old-established city firms to the outlying suburbs. The scheme, which is planned to be complete by 1978, will cost about £16 million. Only two thirds of the land will be occupied by buildings; the firm and the Corporation are collaborating on designing the area as a public open space and beauty spot, with trees, shrubbery and a lake to enhance the rather dull slopes of Dundry at that point. The main factory building will measure about 180,000 square feet and the roof will not be supported by pillars.

It will be a wrench for Bedminster; but Bedminster is preparing for drastic changes anyway. Much of the poorer section is scheduled for large-scale redevelopment. The crowded shopping area which developed along East Street has always been prosperous and popular due to the wide variety of goods and the competitive prices. On a recent visit I found it as democratic and busy as ever: jostling pavements, old clothes shops, street-barrows, caffs, a sheep's-head and pigs'-trotters butcher's shop. But its future as a shopping centre has been threatened by the increasing use of East Street as a major traffic route for the South as part of the A38; pedestrians find it increasingly difficult to cross. The redevelopment plan proposes "an environmental area—shops, precincts, gardens—between the proposed Bedminster by-pass and the Outer Circuit Road". East Street itself will become a pedestrian shopping area retaining some at least of the existing shops. There will also be office blocks, flats and maisonettes, an expansion of the existing trading estate and two multi-level car-parks. It looks well on paper and nobody would claim that the old Bedminster was attractive.

Brislington, another old village that has become a suburb, lies further to the south-east along the winding course of the New Cut as it becomes the Avon at Netham Weir. It is an old place. A Romano-British villa was discovered there in 1899. The vale of the Brislington brook, which falls into the Avon, was famous for its medieval shrine of St. Anne, visited by the newly crowned Henry VII in 1486. The chapel had been founded some centuries before; St. Anne was patron of harbours and the chapel had hanging models of ships given by sailors as votive offerings. The well associated with the chapel, said to be the oldest well in Somerset, is still there under a comparatively modern stone canopy inside St. Anne's Wood in its curve of the industrial Avon. An annual pilgrimage is still made there as it has been for thirty years. The Wood, a park and bird sanctuary, lies in an unexpectedly deep valley with a stream, rustic bridges and benches; green and peaceful in spring, in winter it echoes rather spookily and forlornly to the voices of boys kicking a ball in a neighbouring field and seems a long way from the neat residential suburb at its gates. The suburb itself seems oddly placed so near the old industrial valley of Crew's Hole just the other side of the Avon. This was a place of flaring brass furnaces in the eighteenth century, fired by coal brought upriver from nearby coalfields. In 1754 there were eighty-one brass furnaces at Warmley, Conham and Crew's Hole. The trade later moved to South Wales, but there are relics still in the valley, notably a dramatically placed chimney-stack on a hill above the river. Today industry is represented by the substantial St. Anne's Board Mills, an important component of Bristol's packaging manufacture. Pottery was made in St. Anne's Valley up to the middle of the eighteenth century and there is a direct link between the seventeenth-century Brislington kilns and the city's long-surviving pottery firm, Pountney's of Fishponds, now moved to Penzance.

Brislington was the setting for a remarkable experiment in the treatment of the mentally ill in the early nineteenth century, when Dr. E. L. Fox built a large house in the district to further his ideas about the humane and medical treatment of the insane in place of the barbarities of Bedlam. Taking his inspiration, as did so much philanthropic work in Bristol, from his Quaker faith, he conducted games, country drives, occupational pursuits and regular church services for the patients. Early in this century the hospital was still known in Bristol as 'Dr. Fox's', a place one schoolboy told another to go to, as Londoners referred to Colney Hatch. A block of flats preserves his name.

The original village keeps a villagy aspect around the fifteenth-nineteenth-century parish church on its hill: a Perpendicular Somerset village church with a characteristic 'Somerset' tower. The vicarage is a fine early Georgian house. When Sir Nikolaus Pevsner surveyed Brislington in the middle 1950s there were still farms in the district. Much has changed since then; factories have gone up along the Bath Road as along other radial roads out of Bristol, and a new shopping-flats development has robbed Brislington Hill of the last traces of village atmosphere. Arno's Vale cemetery under the steep hills of Knowle is a nobly melancholic graveyard of the 1830s and 40s with two Greek Doric lodges and a resident population of worthy citizens of the last century and this, all presumably with one Bristol eye open so that the Last Judgment does not catch them unprepared. But Brislington's most interesting and curious relic has fared badly; this is the group of buildings around Arno's Court House, built in the Gothick style in 1760–65 by William Reeve, a rich Bristol copper-smelter. The house itself, now a hotel, is mainly classical Georgian, with vaguely Eastern trimmings around the windows. Separated from it now by the main Bath Road stands a charming gateway and nearby the bizarre Arno's Castle, a mock-medieval fort built to house stables and estate offices and constructed out of oblong blocks of blackish-blue slag from his smelting works. Horace Walpole aptly called it the Devil's Cathedral and it still looks slightly unnerving. It is now a private club. The jewel of the group was the Bath House, with an Indian-Gothick colonnade and fine plaster-work by Thomas Stocking. This stood derelict for years among cabbage patches and tatters of flower gardens. Neglected, and despite many appeals by local conservation groups, the colonnade was finally removed to Clough Williams-Ellis's Portmeirion estate in North Wales, where no doubt it feels at home among the Italianate buildings. The whole group was that rare creation, a Bristol fantasy, a quietly smouldering outbreak of Gothick eccentricity among the classical streets and crescents and 'Grecian' public buildings of a city not given to fantasy.

Brislington was an organic community, based on local trades around a village nucleus. Knowle on its bricky heights is an early to mid-Victorian suburb with little history, apart from Wesley's visit to the French prisoners-of-war, whose harsh fate he did much to alleviate by rousing public sympathy. Its original character as an upper-middle-class businessmen's suburb has been steadily eroded by the surrounding development areas and council housing estates. There are some interesting Victorian and Edwardian buildings for the curious, notably Bodley's Chapel at the House of Charity (about 1900). Otherwise, it is one of those anonymous, slightly despairing suburbs of nineteenth-century commercial Europe. It resembles others of the kind, such as Bradford's Horton or Leeds' Horsforth. Totterdown, the tangle of impossibly steep streets (with a marvellously apt name) above the junction of the Bath and Wells Roads (with its famous early nineteenth-century finger-post) has more character, a knife-edge precipice of rooftops like a town from a fairy-tale book illustrated by Arthur Rackham. The district is now much eroded to make a new ring road.

To the south stretch the pitiless acres of newer housing estates in Hartcliffe, Withywood and Stockwood, Bishopsworth and Whitchurch, straggling out into Somerset. Here there are no sharp hills—apart from Dundry which keeps growing Hartcliffe in order—valleys, gorges or rivers to halt the spread of housing as elsewhere in the city, where the Downs, the Gorge and substantial outcrops like Purdown have kept districts apart and idiosyncratic. Like most of Bristol's suburbs, though, they have views and patches of green and rural Somerset is never far away.

The eastern suburbs have more character. They have swallowed up but not obliterated the old coal-mining areas of Kingswood ('Kangs'ud' in old Bristol speech) and Hanham, and the village of Stapleton. They have a marked geographical character deriving from their closeness to the Avon snaking in from Keynsham and Bath on one side, and to the first foothills of the Cotswolds on the other. Kingswood and Hanham were charcoal-burning districts from the Middle Ages at least—burning timber from the King's Wood—and in the eighteenth century George Whitefield and John Wesley literally risked their lives bringing evangelical religion to the miners. The combination of Primitive Methodism and rough labour produced an aggressively radical type of worker who often alarmed respectable Bristol down the hill. Kingswood

John Nash's Hamlet at Blaise Castle
Colston's Almshouses on St. Michael's Hill

miners formed trouble-making elements in the 1831 riots, and one of my grandmothers remembered the miners marching into Bristol—possibly in an organized union demonstration—and being much feared. By 1911 there were forty-two Methodist chapels flourishing and seventeen other non-conformist places of worship. Kingswood is still a centre of the boot and shoe trade—G. B. Britton's is the largest firm—though the outwork trade, which used to be considerable, has almost disappeared. Both Kingswood and Hanham keep a certain rough look of the Industrial Revolution about them, like the small hillside towns of the West Riding, complete with cracked pavements, tumbledown side streets, small shops and frequent chapels. A plan for a 'New Kingswood', with a redeveloped shopping centre, was accepted by Gloucestershire County Council in early 1970; no doubt Kingswood will look like everywhere else in time. Hanham grew rapidly in the 1960s; an impressive £28,000 Folk Centre was opened in 1964 after twenty-one years of effort and quickly began to draw 3,000 people a week to its varied activities.

The distinct character of this eastern edge, certainly in the past and to some extent still, has been created by the conflict between the dogmatic, chauvinistic, inland temperament of the Gloucestershire countryman and the more flexible, commercial, cosmopolitan temperament of the Bristolian. In addition, miners have traditionally been regarded as a race apart by their neighbours, associated with the mystery of underground, kobold-figures to be given a wide berth when angry. The aggressiveness softens the nearer East Bristol approaches the centre, but the area keeps its distinctiveness as 'deep' Bristol, throatier and more incomprehensible in speech, more parochial, more turned in on itself. There is still a claustrophobic air about the narrow streets despite handsome open spaces like St. George's Park and the open sward around the modern flats at Barton Hill, some of the first of the city's high-rise dwellings to replace slummy streets. Here until 1968 stood the Great Western cotton factory, which employed over 1,000 people when it was opened in 1837 (it was later used for making artificial fibres and then as a warehouse). It was originally a Lancashire firm and Lancashire officials—among them the father of Dame Eva Turner, the operatic singer who grew up in Bristol—and workers came with it. Elderly Bristolians remember girls at the factory wearing shawls and clogs (and with cotton

Schoolgirls run through the grounds of Blaise Castle near Henbury

fluff in their hair)—but were they Lancashire girls or Bristol girls adopting Lancashire ways?

To the north of Kingswood lies Fishponds, with its pioneer post-1918 housing estates with neo-Georgian details, its carton and cardboard factories, and its sad bronze soldier of 1914–18 keeping watch in the little memorial park in front of the Victorian parish church (clinging japonica and a fine magnolia) and Hannah More's birthplace (1745); local factory workers in their overalls eat their lunch sandwiches in his company on fine days. And to the north of Fishponds, and just outside the Bristol boundary, lies Frenchay, a relic of the eighteenth-century cult of village life close to a large city, and the sort of village survival all cities ought to be able to maintain. Georgian houses surround the extensive common on which W. G. Grace played. The Manor House (1737), with its handsome façade, is by the elder Wood of Bath; Frenchay Park (1780) is now the sisters' house in the grounds of the hospital complex for which modern Frenchay is noted. The Unitarian church of 1720 (founded 1672) is thought to be the oldest Unitarian church in the country, while William Penn, who courted his bride Hannah Callowhill in Frenchay, is associated with the Quaker Meeting House (1673, rebuilt 1809). Frenchay Grove was the home of J. S. Fry, who died in 1835 and is buried behind the Meeting House. But the surprise of Frenchay is the rather drab-looking William IV parish church (1834) on the common. This hides a ravishing Nightmare Abbey interior of forest-like, early neo-Gothic pillars and arches. Today Frenchay shares the schizophrenia of most commuter villages. To the commuters into Bristol or further afield (via the nearby motorway and Severn Bridge) it is a peaceful refuge; to the locals it is a dead end. They complained in the Bristol papers that there was no fish and chip shop, no public convenience and no entertainment.

Stapleton, further down the Frome river towards the city, also retains a semi-rural atmosphere from its days as a residential village for Bristol merchants. Snuff mills and corn mills turned in the Frome valley and there were coal mines nearby. The rural atmosphere is well kept in Snuff Mills Park, through which the Frome wanders. Up to the Second World War at least this was still very much a country valley with weirs, footbridges over the river and ruined mills. Today it is tidier, more park-like and behind the clustering trees above the river the ends of suburban streets can be glimpsed.

The secluded aspect of Stapleton has been preserved by the proximity of the Purdown slopes with its complex of hospitals, old houses and downland paths; whether that seclusion will survive the Parkway that has been driven into Bristol alongside Purdown is a question locals do not like to ask themselves. Until that time it will no doubt keep its village aspect, though the parish church is a Victorian suburban church of 1857. Colston's School is built around the nucleus of an early Georgian red-brick house. The old French prison, where 5,000 French prisoners were housed until they were sent home in 1814, is today part of Manor Park Hospital. The area is a nostalgic reminder of the days when the northern and north eastern outskirts of Bristol were a sequence of linked villages, rather as outer London and Middlesex were in the 1870s.

Between semi-rural Westbury and semi-rural Stapleton lies Horfield with hardly a trace of its own rural, farming past. More typical was its grim barracks (recently pulled down) and even grimmer prison. Horfield Common just about survives as an open space. In the 1920s there were still cottages and farms hereabouts, and even today there is a pleasant air up on the common. How rural and remote the district was in the last century is illustrated by a memorial window in Horfield Church: it commemorates a local boy who was lost with a younger one in the fields between Stokes Croft and Horfield on a winter's night. The elder one saved the younger one's life by wrapping him in his coat, but himself died of exposure. Horfield has been a classical marginal seat on the City Council; the poll has traditionally been high and the majority low, reflecting a slow-burning conflict between voters of the extensive council estates and those of the intermingled owner-occupier estates who have felt that their rates were being pushed unfairly high by the alleged preferential treatment given to council estate residents.

North of Horfield, on the main road to Gloucester—and once actually in Gloucestershire, now in Avon—lies Filton, a suburb so important to the local economy that it can hardly be called a suburb. Here are the works of the Filton branch (formerly the Bristol Aeroplane Company) of the British Aircraft Corporation, and now, together with the associated Rolls-Royce aero-engine works, the biggest employer in the area—and here the Concorde is being built. Sir George White, who created the original company and Filton, would have taken Concorde in his stride. After making a fortune out of building tramways in major cities, including Bristol, Sir George, who had been born in Bristol in 1854, turned his attention to creating an industry based on aeroplanes, still thought of generally as amusing toys when he announced his plans in 1910. A spectacular flying display arranged by White on Durdham Down in November 1910, in which pioneer French aviators took part, convinced many spectators, though not, unfortunately, the army: reconnaissance was still the job of the cavalry. The Bristol fighter planes used in 1914–18 soon proved White's point about the future of the aeroplane, and more than 5,000 planes built at Filton took part in the war. The nippy Bristol fighters followed the pioneer Bristol Boxkite and by 1914 400 Filton workmen were turning out a plane a day. The man who had made Bristol one of the first English cities with electric trams helped to ensure that Britain was not left behind in the new aeronautical age, though it was from Blériot and other French enthusiasts that White caught his own enthusiasm.

In the Second World War Filton produced more than 14,000 Blenheims, Beauforts and Beaufighters—valuable if hardly dramatic planes. The works and district took some heavy punishment from the Luftwaffe; the worst raid was the daylight attack on 25th September 1940, causing many deaths and considerable damage. though only eight planes were actually destroyed in the works. Filton had some difficulty in the post-war years in repeating its successes with war-planes. The huge Brabazon, seating 180, was to be the great civil airliner of its day, challenging American supremacy. The great Assembly Hall built for the Brabazon—and now used for the Concorde—is one of the most impressive industrial buildings of the century. The sweep of its doors away from the eye in diminishing perspective is unforgettable, though from the nearby railway line it is a visual puzzle; the passing traveller finds it difficult to grasp the shape and proportions of the building. In the late 1940s the huge plane lumbering around the Channel skies seemed the last decibel in technological brilliance. The Brabazon was a failure, though; the body was not strong enough to resist the pressures put upon it, nor the engines powerful enough. But the Bristol Britannia, developed shortly afterwards, soon filled the gap left by the non-starting Brabazon.

Concorde has brought international fame, prosperity, challenge and anxiety to Filton. It is the largest single technological project in the country and the first to be developed on a joint basis with another country. Launched in 1962, the Concorde programme had reached the flight test stage by 1970 and production versions were expected to enter commercial service in early 1976 with British Airways and Air France—were expected to by Filton, that is. Doubters and opponents of the project, who were numerous enough by 1970 to be called a lobby, thought that Concorde would never be a commercial success, and even if it were its commercial value would be outweighed by its nuisance potential as a causer of noise and pollution. The possibility that the project could be cancelled was still a source of local anxiety in late 1974. Would Concorde go the way of the Brabazon and the ill-fated TSR-2 fighter, cancelled by the Government in 1965? A substantial proportion of the city's 25,000 aircraft workers (probably about 10,000 directly) were directly or indirectly engaged on Concorde, as well as many local firms supplying components, and although the British Aircraft Corporation has other aeronautical and astrospatial schemes in hand, including the rapid expansion of the Electronic and Space System work of British Aircraft Corporation—Guided Weapon Division (which now employs about one third of the Filton work force), there was no doubt that cancellation of Concorde would be a serious shock to Bristol, both economically and psychologically. However, in 1974 the Labour Government decided with their French counterparts to continue with the first sixteen aircraft authorised by the previous government. It is now felt that once the British and French airlines are operating Concorde, other airlines would have to follow suit or lose totally their first-class traffic and a proportion of their economy-class passengers.

Filton and Bristol were more confident about Concorde in the mid-70s now that the previous 'options' from British Airways and Air France had become firm orders. But anxiety had not entirely disappeared.

The future apart, the project has brought bustle and change to Filton. Bristol teams have gone to Toulouse, the French end of the project, thus renewing Bristol's ancient links with France, and French teams of twenty to thirty specialists, some with their families, have come to Bristol on postings of two to three years. National differences do not mean much on this highly technical level, though the French apparently still like what seem to the British long, abstract conferences, whereas the laconic, empirical British approach may have struck some of the French as not entirely '*sérieux*'. There has been a great increase of interest in learning French among the Filton staff at both the corporation's own technical college and the Filton Technical College.

Whatever one may think of Concorde in economic or environmental terms it is an impressive monster that is taking shape on the Assembly Hall stocks, being put together—at £10 million a plane —like a fretwork galleon being put together in the living-room. Where our twentieth-century industrial revolution has failed is in creating the dreary, featureless suburbs outside the factory: the box-like, stuccoed houses, the false promises of the 'crescents' and 'avenues', the banal look of the B.A.C. offices themselves. Men who can build Beaufighters, Britannias and Concordes deserve better human environments than this; even if the future is assured by such developments as the new £500,000 space craft assembly centre opened in April 1970, the craftsmen will still have to live in these streets. At the bus stops and cafés opposite the main factory gates there is the tired bustle of shift-work. The neatly restored and extended church in its garden seems to have little to do with the life around it. A block of flats called Cotswold View looks across to the Cotswolds as if looking for lost roots.

Filton spreads its industry into Patchway in the flat, sour Gloucestershire (now Avon) land either side of the London–South Wales railway line, and industry begins again at Severnside where the new I.C.I. works blots the coast. Here is the nucleus of the vast industrial complex, to be linked some day perhaps with the Severnside city dreamed of by planners still caught in the toils of the Victorian nightmare of progress. But the suburbs lying between the Downs and the coast keep their charm and semi-rural atmosphere so far. The buses dip down Westbury Road from the Downs, past the Red Maids' School and Badminton Girls' School, past Sir George Oatley's spacious buildings for St. Monica's Home of Rest, past falling terraces of grey and white Victorian villas—into another world, village Westbury clustering its white-washed cottages and rural back lanes along the sluggish stream of the Trym. Westbury has a place in national history as well as in Bristol history. For a brief time in the tenth century, perhaps only ten years, it was the home of a small monastic family, settled there about A.D. 962 by Oswald, Bishop of Worcester, to found a monastic rule like that he had known at Fleury. Monks went out from Westbury to found some of the most celebrated abbeys in England. If there is a proprietory air about Westbury today it may be because it was briefly one of the three centres of spiritual life in England.

It was still an important ecclesiastical centre in the fifteenth century when John Carpenter, Bishop of Worcester (in which diocese Westbury then stood) established the church and college with fine new buildings. William Canynges, Chatterton's merchant-saint, became a priest after his wife's death, and eventually Dean of Westbury College, which surrendered to Henry VIII in 1544–45. A monumental gate-tower, two of the angle turrets and the foundations of a north east tower on the river side, together with some of the southern range of buildings, survive to form a picturesque contrast to the handsome row of Victorian houses opposite, all white paint and potted plants. In July 1643 Prince Rupert had his headquarters in the college during the siege of Bristol and set fire to it when he left to prevent Parliament using it against Royalist-occupied Bristol. In 1894 the whole site was bought by public subscription and in 1907 vested in the National Trust. Since 1965 complete renovation has been going ahead to turn the college into a vigorous parish centre.

The church in its hilly churchyard, with fine views over the village and neighbouring slopes, contains some important early thirteenth-century arcades between nave and aisles. In 1967 it celebrated its 1,250th anniversary. Westbury keeps a village feeling despite the arrival of modern shops—mostly confined to a pleasant new precinct off the main street. Locals still talk of the 'village', though the green has gone, and until recent years there were old people who remembered it as a real village, with lime kilns and a clay pipe factory—the lane near the pit was always white with lime from the carts. The two girls' schools, Red Maids', founded in 1634 behind the Lord Mayor's Chapel on College Green, and Badminton, founded in Clifton in 1858, bring a touch of Angela Brazil's world to workaday Westbury: hockey on sunny winter mornings is a boisterous affair and the Red Maids' boarders are still seen on special occasions in their poke bonnets, red dresses, white tippets and aprons. Old and new Westbury intermingle amicably, early twentieth-century streets blending neatly into the white cottages and terraces. There is a rumble of gossip from the 'White Lion' at lunchtime and altogether one wishes that Westbury could keep for ever its present balance between the old and new, commercial and residential, urban and rural. But the outgrowing tentacles of Bristol are moving in on most sides.

Henbury Hill sweeps away from Westbury to Henbury village with its church and its Norman pillars surmounted by Early English arches (all heavily restored in 1878) and its notable Georgian churchyard tomb of a Negro slave, servant to the Earl of Suffolk. The slave, Scipio Africanus, died in 1720 aged 18 and his epitaph includes the lines:

> I who was born a pagan and a slave
> Now sweetly sleep a Christian in my grave

The epitaph, merely formal as it may have been, is one of the most poignant of the memorials to Bristol's slave days. Strenuous local efforts have been made to preserve Henbury's village aspect and several proposals to demolish a fine eighteenth-century house to widen an awkward traffic junction have been fought off in recent years. A Conservation Area report of 1968 stated that "the retention of the existing village character is of prime importance".

The churchyard is closed on one side by the wall of Blaise Castle, Bristol's finest demesne, rivalled perhaps only by Temple Newsam at Leeds; the estate consists of a splendidly sober house of 1796 built by William Paty for a Quaker banker, John Harford, a sham castle of 1766 hidden away on a wooded hill like a princess's tower out of Perrault, and Blaise Hamlet, a group of estate cottages for old servants, designed in 1811 by John Nash. This is a show-piece of the picturesque; the cottages are all different in a deliberate manner, and the effect is either charming or over-sentimental according to personal taste. The many visitors love it; to some, Blaise Hamlet rather chillingly recalls another attempt to stop the village clock at ten to three, Marie Antoinette's '*hameau*' at Versailles. The house is now a most rewarding folk museum, not over-cluttered with by-gones as such museums often are, and an old woollen mill, from the area now covered by the Chew Valley lake, has been re-erected in the 400 acres of magnificently wooded grounds. These were laid out by Humphrey Repton and on the right day in the right light compose one of the most satisfying groupings of the picturesque in England, an effect not spoiled by their utilitarian use as cricket pitches, hockey pitches and children's playgrounds. The sward rises to the wooded slopes, while the lower woods run alongside the Trym through a gorge 120 feet deep to Coombe Dingle. From the woods with their perpetual carpet of dead leaves, or from the grassy plateau where the 'castle' stands, there are magnificent Turneresque views towards Avonmouth, and it is easy to understand why the tract of country from Henbury and Blaise along the wooded Kings Weston Down to Penpole Wood was a hunting-ground through the eighteenth century for amateurs of the picturesque. Their vision of the Italianate views across the smoky woods and misty coastal flats to the Severn is preserved in paintings in the City Art Gallery.

The focus of this aesthetic tract was—and to some extent still is—Kings Weston House, the most imposing Baroque building within easy reach of Bristol, designed by Vanbrugh for Sir Edward Southwell in about 1710. It is a sober house, without the bizarre splendour of Blenheim or Seaton Delavel or the more restrained, almost Austrian charm of Castle Howard. Pevsner did not care much for it: "This masculine, somewhat forbidding and certainly entirely graceless design did not—perhaps quite sensibly so—start a fashion for Bristol's town houses."

But it is noble in its heavy way and certainly deserving of more respect than it has had in recent years. It was to have been the central block of a group of buildings for the Bristol College of Science and Technology which was to move there from Müller's orphanage buildings in Ashley Down. But expansion involved extra students and more ground than Kings Weston could offer without biting into the prized amenity area nearby; planning permission was refused and the college moved to Claverton, Bath, to become the new Bath University of Technology. The university's school of architecture did move to Kings Weston, but moved out in 1970, leaving a large aesthetic question mark hanging over the house. Conservationist groups anguished about its future, especially as local vandalism was increasingly damaging the outbuildings, the dilapidated garden and the house itself. Then in late 1970 the police came to the rescue. Negotiations between the City Architect, the City Council and the Home Office resulted in a plan for the Home Office to use the house as a training college for policemen in the South-west and South Wales areas, half the cost of restoration and adaptation to be borne by the council. Everyone seems to have come well out of this admirably eighteenth-century rationalization of the situation: the conservationists, the City Architect, the council—much criticized for letting old buildings disappear—and the police, who already occupy the restored classical stables (1763) up the road. The arcaded chimney stacks of the house, a striking Vanbrugh fantasy, were restored some years ago, but much will have to be done to make the house fit for the interested visitors who will still have guided access to it. But the important point is that Kings Weston has a future.

The house kept a green retreat in the middle of the rapidly growing Lawrence Weston housing estate with its 12,000 or so people, one of the many post-1945 developments that threaten to link up with the garden suburbs of Sea Mills. The suburbs are not resumed on the farther bank of the Avon, apart from scatterings of suburbia on High Failand and around Pill and Portishead. The Westbury–Henbury–Kings Weston area has been fortunate to keep its pastoral character, though this may not last the century. The Patchway–Filton–I.C.I. complex builds up at one side, Avonmouth at the other, and along the coastal strip the M5 motorway has now crossed the river into Avon and Somerset. Possibly the new industry will build up so close to the motorway exits that the present charm of the existing suburbs will not be encroached upon. In any case, the greatest threat to the area is not the motorway but the shadow of a Severnside city, which will certainly have no room for the demesnes, pleasaunces, romantic chasms, sham castles, tea gardens and other aspects of the picturesque that made this unique rural tract so unlikely a neighbour to a great commercial city.

Bristol's hinterland is extensive and varied, though not always obviously attractive. It is flat and dull around Patchway and Filton to the north; but beyond Kingswood and Hanham the Cotswold slopes begin, and one climbs from Winterbourne on the north-east to Wotton-under-Edge and high, thundery Cotswold. Beyond the Avon lie the four Gordano villages in the shallow Gordano valley, its peace invaded by the motorway. The cars pour out across the suspension bridge in the evening to commuterdom in the High Failand country, in rapidly expanding

Nailsea, or in Flax Bourton and Brockley. Many go on to Clevedon, a grey, huddled Victorian resort of great charm to certain eyes, with a toy pier out on the muddy bay. (A large section of the pier collapsed in late 1970 and its fate was then uncertain.) Here is the old church on the low Channel cliff, where Tennyson's friend, Hallam is buried. On summer evenings the windows of Clevedon and Newport flash amiably at each other across the gleaming stretches of the Channel. There are fine houses in the area: Nailsea Court, partly medieval; Barrow Court; and Ashton Court, with its remains of fifteenth- and sixteenth-century work and its south front reputedly rebuilt by Inigo Jones. (The condition of Ashton Court, in its great park of 840 acres, opened to the public in 1960, has been worrying conservationists; in July 1970 the council offered support for the £275,000 restoration scheme, which will make the house available for public events and for conferences. The whole of the restoration of the exterior was expected to be finished by the end of 1975.)

Further out, beyond Wrington where John Locke was born and Hannah More lived, we are into the dour Mendips, with their quarried flanks, stone villages and walls, and deep caves still being explored and discovered. It is disconcertingly austere country; well into this century the people kept old customs, filled their fonts from holy wells and looked askance at corrupt Bristol. Weston-super-Mare still offers donkey-rides along the immense muddy sands with their views of the stranded whale-shapes of Flat Holm and Steep Holm and the isolated promontory of Brean Down with its bird sanctuary. Weston was Bristol's favourite seaside place through much of this century, and there cannot be many ordinary Bristol families without their albums of browning 1930s snapshots of the children digging sand speed-boats.

The relationship over the centuries between Bristol and its close neighbour Bath, has been complex. Quietly, Bristol is rather proud of having Bath so near; but Bath tends to look down on Bristol and look up to London, a fast two hours up the line. Bath has its own problems now: a university and long-haired students in the streets where the long-haired gentry strolled; a terrible traffic problem and a conflict over solutions; a constant fight to warn off developers from the city centre. Bath is more vulnerable than it looks to change and commercial vandalism. The two cities, so close and so similar in the development of their fashionable quarters, have remained distinct and aloof from one another.

To the north, beyond the dull no-man's-land around Patchway and Winterbourne, lies the Vale of Berkeley with its elm-studded meadows, solitary church spires, its hunt and its nuclear power stations, its wildfowl centre at Slimbridge, its magnificently gloomy castle at Berkeley and its deeply aggressive main road between Bristol and Gloucester (less so since the completion of the M5 to Bristol.)

Bristol's surroundings are still relatively rural and agreeable. Bristolians have gone to live outside the city boundary in such numbers that Bristol is one of the few large cities whose population has tended to decrease rather than increase; but on the whole the commuters and the retired have been quietly and inconspicuously absorbed into the villages. Leigh Woods and Failand on the other side of the Avon Gorge are largely protected by the National Trust which owns much land there, or by being parts of large estates. Dundry Hill appears to have stemmed the spread of the city in that direction. To the north, though, the nuclei of industry and housing at Patchway, Thornbury and the Severnside I.C.I. plant could link up some day. A new town is planned for Yate on the Stroud–Cirencester road, and the Gordano–Portishead–Clevedon area is likely to build up as the M5 motorway brings them closer to Bristol as commuter territory. This, together with the creation of new docks on the Somerset bank of the Avon opposite Avonmouth, and the linking of Clevedon–Gordano with the developments along the Bristol–Weston road, hints at the dark beginnings of a huge semi-suburban conurbation round large sectors of outer Bristol. If the city is consciously developed as a huge regional centre—and the creation of the new County of Avon, taking over responsibility for functions formerly exercised by the city of Bristol, seems to be a first step in that direction—and if the Severn City nightmare becomes a reality, Bristol's present favoured position as a great commercial city surrounded by pastoral greenness will quickly disappear. The charm of present-day Frenchay and Henbury, Weston-in-Gordano and Kings Weston, will go the way of the Brislington hayfields and the frozen hedgerows of Horfield.

XIX

THE THREAT OF SUPER-BRISTOL

THE future of Bristol is an exclamation mark rather than a question mark. The economic, geographic and ecological factors that relentlessly increase the size of cities in favoured positions are stronger than any human means of resisting them, and it is difficult to see how Bristol can stop itself becoming a major regional capital, a centre of commercial activity, banking, insurance, administration, education and the manufacturing and distributive industries for the South-west, and perhaps for the whole of southern England south of Birmingham and west of London.

As it grows larger it is certain to lose some of its present attractiveness as a place to live and work in. In the past its combination of physical beauty and commercial utility, together with its relative remoteness in a non-industrial region, enabled it to postpone the future. It missed the worst effects of the Industrial Revolution. Its industries and trades were clean compared with those of the North. It was a place of culture as well as commerce. Today its attractiveness may be its undoing in bringing more people and industry than its present decent proportions can contain.

If there is an elegiac air about this book it is perhaps not surprising; one does not need to be a fanatical preservationist to regret, in the company of Reece Winstone, Bryan Little and others who care about the city, the thoughtless demolition or neglect of so many fine buildings since the war. Bristol has some 2,000 scheduled buildings of historic interest, almost certainly more than any British city outside London, and it cannot afford to lose one of them if it is to keep its rank as an outstandingly visual historic city. And one is not necessarily a reactionary alarmist to be alarmed by the pressures that are driving Bristol towards massive expansion and regional capital status. These include the intersection of the M4 and M5 motorways at Almondsbury, placing Bristol at a major cross roads in the national motorway system and bringing it within easy reach of London, the Midlands and South Wales; the 14 per cent increase in employment between 1951 and 1968, including a 28 per cent increase in the 'service' industries (construction, transport, distribution, insurance, banking, administration); the growth in office accommodation, making Bristol fourth after Birmingham, Manchester and Liverpool as a provincial office centre; the population increase, of the city and surrounding area, 7·6 per cent compared with the national average of 5·3 per cent (though the city itself tends to lose population to the immediate surrounding area); the effects of the Severn Bridge; the possibility of 50,000 new jobs in the region by 1981; and the obvious development possibilities of the Avonmouth–Severnside area.

It would be easy to take an apocalyptic, doom-laden view of Bristol's future in the terms of Lewis Mumford's vision of the urban future, described in *The City in History* (1961): to see it succumbing to a consumer society's need to change the 'container' as rapidly as the contents, to become a mere background to the transient 'enterprises' of developers, and finally to become another Los Angeles, "a gigantic motor-car moving along a one-way road at an ever-increasing speed" while the "driver has quite forgotten the purpose of the journey".* Certainly the monstrous roundabout at Old Market Street and the hacking of the Parkway through the suburbs have nightmare aspects. Bristol is aware of the dangers, and guarantees given by the council that the disused city waterways will not be covered in have been backed up by the House of Lords Select Committee's emendations of the City Docks Bill. But fears of urban doom are not calmed by well-informed predictions for the year 2010: a population of more than a million; with 460,000 cars and 140,000 other vehicles; 109,000 people working in the city centre, 26 per cent more than at present.

But Lewis Mumford can be a misleading prophet when he uses the specific conditions of modern cities as evidence for his more general theories about the decadence of modern civilization. Asa Briggs in his *Victorian Cities* points out that Mumford is wrong to condemn all Victorian cities as "insensate ant-heaps". They also found a place, despite the noisome industry, for a greater independence and organization of "the lower ranks of society" than small towns could afford. Welfare work progressed and the cities,

* *The City in History*, Pelican Edition, Chapter 17, page 636.

Briggs contends, were never mere collections of individuals, some weak, some strong.

The surest way to allow a Mumfordian doom to overtake Bristol is to assume that it will and to do nothing about it. Possibly the civilized attractiveness of the city will have to be preserved in enclaves within the much larger urban area of the future, and conservers and preservers may have to work on that assumption. If Bristol's attempts to fit the new into the old have failed badly since the war, it may be because such attempts are impossible within the narrow confines of the present city centre. It is arguable that no further commercial development can take place within the existing centre without endangering the areas of "special architectural or historical interest", such as King Street and the Corn Street-flower market area. Not the least agonizing of the many choices Bristol will have to make in the next ten years is between a vandalized historic centre with a relatively open countryside, and a preserved, balanced centre and an urbanized, semi-industrialized, though still (one hopes) semi-open country belt around it. Bristol cannot afford any more environmental mistakes like the siting and dimensions of the Robinson building and of the tower-block that dwarfs and mocks the church of St. John's on its medieval gateway.

The prospect is not all apocalyptic. Considerable areas will remain relatively unchanged for some time to come. Clifton, Whiteladies Road, Gloucester Road, Redland, Cotham, the whole of the northern suburbs rising away from the Royal Fort and Kingsdown are likely to remain much as they are, though with new buildings interspersed here and there. The College Green area could be vastly improved by the long-discussed closing of Deanery Road to traffic. The Corn Street area will keep its London 'City' character for many years to come, and the arts and recreation complex in the Wine Street area, if it is ever built, can only be an improvement. Broadmead at last became a pedestrian precinct. One can only hope that the worst has by now been done to Kingsdown. The hospital complex around the Royal Infirmary presents a visual and environmental problem, but it does not dominate the sky-line as the university complex above dominates it, and some of the recent hospital buildings are lively and interesting. The tall new administrative buildings in the Rupert Street canyon are inevitable in such a limited site and are fortunately slender and un-bulky so far. The Centre needs much improvement, but the proposed overhead pedestrian walkways hardly seem the answer; they suggest an ignoble surrender to the car rather than a concern for the rights of pedestrians. St. Michael's Hill seems to have survived its gutting and filleting by the university remarkably well, and the High Kingsdown residential project, a sort of Top People's Casey's Court of staggered houses and alleys, is an attractive scheme. The restoration and redevelopment of Old Market Street may offset the horror of the roundabout and underpasses. Although the Welsh Back comes into a scheduled historic area, and amenity plans have been made for it, one wonders desperately what will happen to the towering warehouses facing it. Some are in bad condition admittedly; but their disappearance would radically alter the atmosphere of central Bristol. East of the city centre there is little one would want to preserve. A 200-acre redevelopment scheme has been started in Easton, providing accommodation for about 7,500 people, with 26 acres for new or relocated factories. Barton Hill already has its tower-flats, but the Bristol sky-line can take a certain number of tall, thin, well spaced-out buildings.

From the models in the city's permanent planning exhibition at Quakers' Friars and from the planners' rather too lyrical drawings, it is possible to be quite optimistic about the future Bristol: the Floating Harbour transformed into a 'new Amsterdam', with some picturesque ships (including the *Great Britain*, now that it seems certain that the great ship will remain in its home port) moored where the working ships used to moor; the Centre traffic thinned out; Queen Square restored to peace; College Green leafy and strollable again; the Wine Street desolation replaced by museums, galleries, restaurants, pubs, sports halls and riverside promenades; the squalid inner suburbs cleaned up and weeded out. If the Germans and East Europeans can do it, we, who taught the world the idea of the garden-city, ought to be able to attempt it.

The great 'but' in this attractive prospect is, of course, the new road system. While accepting the existence and continuance of our car-owning democracy we can still justifiably be alarmed by the image of whizzing, fume-sodden new roads cutting the city up into new ghettoes. The system includes, first, the Parkway, designed as a fast urban freeway linking the motorway intersection with the centre of the city. This has already reached

How not to do it: the tower of St. Mary le Port Church behind the Norwich Union Building in High Street

How to do it: Regency or early Victorian terraces seen through a span of the Cumberland Basin fly-over

Norwich Union House
NORWICH UNION
INSURANCE GROUP

the city centre close to Broadmead. Its admirers will not be deterred by the fate of the semi-detached residents of Eastville and Stapleton who are already looking out of their front windows at the sombre pillars supporting the overhead spans of the new road, nor by the criticism that the walk from the multi-storey car park or parks at the end of the Parkway to the Broadmead shops will be longer than from any bus stop. The new Outer Circuit Road, the first section of which is being built in conjunction with the Easton development scheme, will vary in distance from half a mile to a mile from the Inner Circuit Road, a product of the 1930s, which is being brought up to date by the improvement of its junctions. A route by-passing Bedminster and taking traffic from the city to the south-west is being improved and re-aligned in conjunction with the Bedminster redevelopment plan. The existing radial routes out of the city are to be improved. The most controversial plan is for a road across Canon's Marsh, the dockside area below the cathedral, with a road-bridge across the end of St. Augustine's Reach, sealing off the stretch of water seen from the Neptune statue. Opponents claim that such a road would be the thin end of a disastrous wedge and would be a precedent for more roads across the disused Floating Harbour. But many of Bristol's road schemes, including the Outer Circuit Road, are being re-thought and modified as roads give way to housing and environment in civic priorities.

The danger of such a road-system is that it will cut the city up into isolated social fragments. Subways and footbridges are provided, of course; but many people are not prepared to detour for up to a quarter of a mile to reach a crossing-point. They prefer to rearrange their lives so that they do not have to cross the dangerous roads and to confine themselves to the amenities and society of their segment. Already Temple Way has barred access between the city centre and the Old Market Street area and the old district known as The Dings. It is laborious to get to the subways or to the overhead footbridge.

Another great danger to a harmonious future city is the uncontrolled building of offices. The growth of Bristol as a regional capital can only increase the demand for office building; during the twelve months up to January 1970 four of the ten leading industrial estate development companies opened offices in Bristol. There is not much building space left in the city centre, and today

Roman Catholic Cathedral, Clifton

offices mean not only workers but the space occupied by their cars; by the early 1970s the number of cars bringing office workers into the centre will probably have increased to 9,000 a day. The corporation admits the need to control the density of central office buildings, but already the city skyline has thickened irreversibly and the steepled picturesqueness of the old city has largely vanished, as it has in the City of London. It is fair to recall, though, that the panorama of central Bristol today is no worse than it was in the late nineteenth century when factory chimneys and black-glass cones shared the filthy air with church steeples and towers. And it is fair to note that decent new buildings do exist: the discreet office block Spillers fitted behind a corner of Queen Square; and the seemly if not very exciting Bristol and West Building Society tower in the Centre. A recent headache for conservationists was the high tower the Post Office proposed to put on top of its new building between Baldwin Street and King Street. This, however, has been modified from a grotesque 300 feet to a more reasonable 90 feet.

In some ways Bristol has a number of natural guarantees against civic and commercial vandalism. The variety of trades means that no one trade is likely to dominate the others and thus have its own way in building. The dispersed character of the centre and the intervening areas of scheduled historic interest should prevent unsightly developments linking up too easily, and Bristol's hills and rivers are natural barriers against uninterrupted visual ugliness. A substantial cultured professional class keeps a watchful eye on planning and development and has already won some battles, such as the fight to cut the Kingsdown flats from six to four storeys. And the fight is sometimes carried on from within the City Council rather than between the council and conservationist groups.

The possibility of Bristol becoming a South-west regional capital is widely discussed in the city, though not every one accepts that an industrialized, booming South-west would look naturally to Bristol as its capital. There is some resentment of Bristol's claims and much of Devon and Cornwall would look to Exeter or Plymouth rather than to Bristol as their natural administrative centres. Bristol, on its Channel coast, looks as much to the Midlands or across to Wales as it does to the South-west, and there are many Cornishmen and Devonians who know Bristol only as a station to pass through on their way elsewhere, and who do not think of it as particularly a West Country city. There are grave risks involved in its becoming a super-regional capital. In the past its civilized qualities have depended upon the balance and intercourse between a strongly focusing city centre and loosely connected, individualistic suburbs. When the suburbs move out beyond the pull of the city centre and turn into dull little suburban towns on their own, swallowing up the ring of attractive semi-suburbanized villages, we shall start to see the disadvantages of the modern city listed by the city-planner Constantines Doxiadis: more urban space but less privacy, residential areas without sociable town centres, tearing motorways dividing communities rather than bringing them together.

The human community, as it existed in inward-looking cities like Bristol, has started to dissolve already. Bristol remained pleasantly out-of-date for many years because of its geographical remoteness from large industrial regions and because of its deep country hinterland. It preserved, like an old cylinder record, lower-class customs and ways that had died in other large cities, as outlying towns of the industrial West Riding do still. The 'Bristol' characters linger on, practising—for the dwindling few who are interested—their local stories and jokes, their memories of Bristol personalities, of vanished buildings and landmarks. Ironically, the fading of the Bristol character is due to improved living conditions. The pugnacious, whimsical Bristolian was a character developed by a kind of urban evolution to survive in an uncertain economy. It was a gesture of defiance to be apparently gay, self-confident and assertive in the face of a doubtful present and future, and it was a way of acquiring prestige and privileges in one's own society (the 'characters' were not confined to one class; they could be met among the city merchants as well as among the cabbies and dockers). The dispersal of the city residents to outlying districts has broken up the tight circles of gossip and rumour, and with them has gone something of the old unmistakable tone of Bristol conversation: a conspiratorial, muttering, oblique running commentary on people and events.

Will the elimination of the sociable, whimsical elements in the Bristol character leave exposed the less pleasant, more aggressive and domineering elements in an age of get-rich-quick pressures? In a future Bristol, with the old parish and class loyalties and humours subordinated to a wider rôle as provincial capital, the Bristol 'cheek' and independence might take an unpleasant turn, or the local character might become colourless and bureaucratic. (Cardiff is a city where the bureaucratic influence of capital status has emasculated local characteristics.) At the moment Bristol keeps its character and characters, as recorded in the local Press and particularly on local television programmes like *Points West*; whether the Greater Bristol of the future can keep that character is another matter.

The secret of Bristol's obvious success as a city in the past has been its sense of proportion and its sense of rational purpose; the means were adequate to the ends and the ends were those of a balanced, pleasant city, large enough to provide civilized amenities, small enough to allow its citizens to enjoy them in comfort. It is still something to be proud of in the context of a modern commercial city that an employee in the Council House on College Green (probably a senior official, admittedly) can live in Clifton or Redland and walk to his work down tree-lined streets and past interesting shop-windows and handsome buildings. One can only hope that the commonsense traditional in the city will not let itself be bemused by the obsession with scientific and technological 'advances' for their own sakes; that aberrations like the proposal to amalgamate Bristol and Bath are put in their place; and that any plan to develop Bristol as the centre of a vast new Severnside industrial complex should be carefully weighed against the survival of Bristol as a civilized place to live in.

These nightmare visions of a frightful Super-Bristol may, after all, be only nightmares. The future of regional devolution of administrative power is uncertain, and Whitehall will not decentralize and delegate willingly. The Severnside project, based on a barrage across the Channel, may remain a Wellsian fantasy. The increasing accessibility of our large cities to each other via the motorways may make the country more dependent on London, not less. Already some firms, which before the building of the Severn Bridge, had depots in South Wales and Bristol, now have a depot in Bristol only. With a complete, fast motorway network in operation, some firms may eventually do all their distribution from London and not bother with a depot in Bristol. Six years ago Bristol was the sixth port in the country; now it is tenth. The Labour government's still largely unexplained refusal of Bristol's request to build docks at Portbury on the Somerset bank of the Avon set the docks back; the succeeding Conservative government agreed in principle to the later proposal for West Dock to be built opposite Avonmouth, though it hesitated about a grant. The new dock has now become a reality. The development of container shipping, with the decline of the city docks and the relative inaccessibility of Avonmouth compared with ports closer to the sea, may confine Bristol to a secondary rôle as a port for the rest of the century. Future Governments may prefer to invest in more developed areas, and a long-term national recession would postpone schemes like Severnside and the damming of the Channel. Bristol may remain a medium-sized city with medium-sized development problems. Not that this will allow the watch-dogs to sleep; generally they would be wiser to assume that Bristol is emerging from the long convalescence after the war, that it is ripe for a boom of some kind and that the task of those who care for the city is to control and civilize the boom rather than to protest against it. The Bristolian will turn into a more outward-looking, less provincial character. Those of us who have known Bristol only in the uneasy 1930s, during the war and in the recuperative period since 1945, may not have seen the city at full stretch and we may find the new Bristol a stimulating place, though it will not be the city whose subtle connotations and elusive charms are still bound up in the city's name. If the new Bristol is to keep anything valuable and relevant from the old, its guardians will have to improve on the old metaphor for Bristol canniness and sleep with both eyes open.

Postlude

A CITY FOR ALL SEASONS

IT IS the resident Bristolians who will have to live with their future city and it would be understandable if they reject as unrealistic and confusing the sort of nostalgia for the past—or anticipatory nostalgia for the disappearing present—that the non-resident native can indulge in. The exile can, in irresponsible moods, select what he wants to see of Bristol on visits and ignore what displeases or disturbs him. He can also choose whichever period of the city's history he wishes to dwell upon and relive imaginatively without the daily contrast with reality that living in the city would force upon him.

When, in fact, was the best time to live in Bristol, to experience the city at a peak of civilized activity? It is an exercise in historical relativity that may add to one's understanding of a complex and subtle place. It is easy to romanticize such a city and an un-romantic rationalization of its past glamour may help to reconcile those who love it to irrevocable change. For example, the end of Chatterton's beloved fifteenth century is a period rich in Bristol mythology; but I imagine that the average citizen would not have known or seen much of the sea-faring dramas of that time, while the lingering feuds and bitternesses from the Wars of the Roses would have soured the edge of Bristol life. The seventeenth and eighteenth centuries were blighted by the slave trade, by civil wars and civic unrest, by fluctuating prosperity and by the complacency and arrogance of the merchants. Yet to be a Bristol merchant at the turn of the eighteenth and nineteenth centuries must have had its pleasures. It was the period when Coleridge and Wordsworth knew the city and Humphrey Davy was inhaling nitrous oxide and making the smart set giggle all round Hope Square. The worst economic effects of the Napoleonic wars were still to come. Bristol, about to construct its New Cut, had settled its conscience over the slave trade and was diverting attention to humanitarian enterprises, while the more arid effects of non-conformity had mellowed. Clifton was growing and was regarded as a healthy, breezy place to live in. It must have been very pleasant to have a house in Kingsdown, a seat in the Merchant Venturers' Hall, and some sturdy ships reported safe past Lundy on the way home. This halcyon time declined into the shabby recession of the 1820s and 1830s, when Mr. Winkle wandered the dirty streets, and through much of the nineteenth century central Bristol must have been a huddled, insanitary place of tottering seventeenth-century slums, foul alleys, smoking glass cones and factories, with the hard-worked Rivers Frome and Avon as open sewers. (The Frome has recently been cleaned and is now supporting fish life again.) Clifton may have been a magic place for John Addington Symonds, but Clifton was a world removed from the hellish alleys and courts depicted to such effect in some of the old photographs collected by Reece Winstone.

For personal choice, if I could return to a particular Bristol I should choose a year between 1905 and 1914. There were still slums and barefoot children and poverty-lines to live close to. But the worst of Victorian squalor had been relieved by medical and social reform. School clinics existed and the authorities cared, if in a rather regimented way. The new university was getting into its stride. The open-topped trams clanged brusquely around the Centre, but it was still possible for cloth-capped, clay-pipe smoking workmen to stroll unconcernedly in the roadway. The ships still came clustering up to St. Augustine's Bridge. The shop-blinds created cool stretches of pavement on hot summer afternoons in Park Street; or if the pavements were even then too hot there were the tall, episcopal trees of College Green to sit under. The regular floods inundated the low-lying parts of the city (as they did again in November 1970). The first picture houses opened and the oyster bars still did a good trade. The first aeroplanes were seen on Durdham Down and at Filton, and the last horse cabs began to seem old-fashioned. If wages were low and housing bad, there was nevertheless a strongly cohesive social sense. Parties of slum children were taken by wagon or bus to the country. The streets were crowded in the evenings, bright with lamps and window lights and late-evening shoppers. For a child the street life was an inexhaustible spectacle and many elderly men who were boys then can hardly remember being at school or even at home, so enthralled were they by the life of the streets.

Neighbours chatted at street doors. An elaborate credit system of borrowed lumps of sugar or twists of tea flourished among the people of shabby-respectable St. Paul's and City Road. Things were lent and borrowed, and not returned or pawned in error or despair. There were still swells to be seen, top-hatted merchants with gold fobs; but the workmen, now being organized by Ernie Bevin and others, knew their rights better than their place. Almshouses and charities bustled. The docks were berthed to capacity and the tobacco works boomed on Woodbines. The Merchant Venturers were in their Hall and all was well with the narrow, intense world of Bristol. At Weston or on the Mendips the doomed Territorials drilled and posed boyishly for the camera.

By comparison the Bristol of the last twenty-five years has always seemed to me, brought up on stories of that immensely busy pre-1914 city, curiously empty. Characteristic impressions of the city today, in contrast to the animation of the Edwardian city, are of the Welsh Back deserted on a summer evening, of the chasm of Victoria Street under the sodium lamps as one walks for a late-night train, of one's unaccompanied footsteps pacing the nave of the cathedral.

The problem for the devotee of such a city is that he knows it must change to keep its metabolism working, yet resents every change from the city he knew when his feelings about it first crystallized. Perhaps it is better not to live in a place one loves, but to live well away from it, visit it occasionally and then only the areas that revive old feelings. I think particularly of the flower market at winter dusk, with the steak bars getting up steam, the sherry drinkers getting their first schooner down, and the late chrysanthemums burning in the misty alleys behind the Exchange; or King Street, cobble-still on quiet summer dusks after the play; the drifted leaves in Queen Square and King William riding aloof above the republican traffic; the toy theatre charm of George's bookshop on winter afternoons with the lights on; the incomparable freshness of the Downs in early spring. Bristol is there even in the dingy back streets and the rotting barges of the Floating Harbour.

Above all, perhaps, 'Bristol' can be felt most strongly from the point of Narrow Quay, with its chains, cobbles and bollards, as one looks across the reach to the warehouses of Canon's Marsh and up to the Cabot Tower with its flashing light, or down to the bright lights of the Centre, or back to still, dark St. Mary Redcliffe. Late on a winter evening, with the water black and slopping, and distant church bells ringing up for practice, the busy, thrusting, secretive, infinitely romantic city flows timelessly around like a Dickensian fantasy, while Cabot and Colston, Chatterton and Hannah More, W. G. Grace and my Uncle Bert, the policeman, hover in the air like the ghosts of Christmas Past, Present and To Come. The only way to live at ease with a city so potent in its atmosphere and so unpredictable in its changes of mood and purpose is to look at it each time as if it were the last: which is what its wiser lovers have done throughout its long, memorable, and unfinished history.

INDEX